OCR Gateway
Physics for GCSE
Combined Science
Student Book

Author:
Helen Reynolds

Series Editor:
Philippa Gardom Hulme

OXFORD
UNIVERSITY PRESS

Contents

How to use this book

Welcome to your *OCR Gateway Physics for GCSE Combined Science* Student Book. This introduction shows you all the different features *OCR Gateway Physics for GCSE Combined Science* has to support you on your journey through Physics for GCSE Combined Science.

Being a scientist is great fun. As you work through this Student Book, you'll learn how to work like a scientist, and get answers to questions that science can answer.

This book is packed full of questions well as plenty of activities to help build your confidence and skills in science.

Higher Tier

If you are sitting the Higher Tier exam, you will need to learn everything on these pages. If you will be sitting Foundation Tier, you can miss out these pages. The same applies to boxed content on other pages.

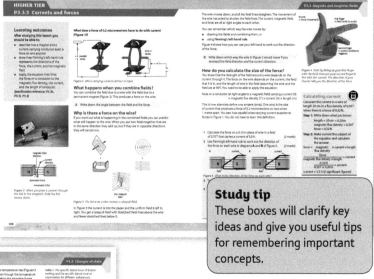

Learning outcomes

These are statements describing what you should be able to do at the end of the lesson. You can use them to help you with revision.

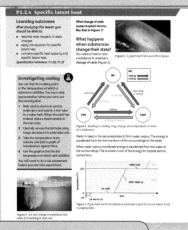

Study tip

These boxes will clarify key ideas and give you useful tips for remembering important concepts.

Key words

These are emboldened in the text, to highlight them to you as you read. You can look them up in the Glossary if you are not sure what they mean.

Literacy

Literacy boxes help you develop literacy skills so that you are able to demonstrate your knowledge clearly in the exam.

Using Maths

Together with the *Maths for GCSE Physics* chapter, you can use these feature boxes to help you to learn and practise the mathematical knowledge and skills you need.

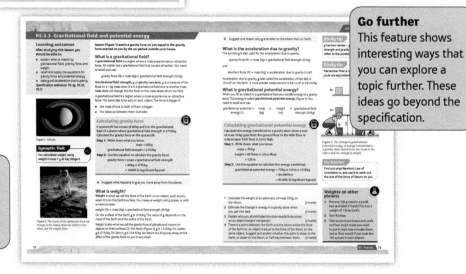

Go further

This feature shows interesting ways that you can explore a topic further. These ideas go beyond the specification.

Synoptic link

This feature shows links between the lesson and content in other parts of the course, as well as any links back to what you learned at Key Stage 3.

Practical skills

Over the course of your GCSE studies you will carry out a number of practicals. Examples of practicals you may carry out, one from each activity group, are discussed in these pages. You will also find practical boxes on other pages throughout the book.

Working Scientifically

Scientists work in particular ways to answer scientific questions. Together with the *Working Scientifically* chapter, these boxes contain activities and hints to help you to develop skills so that you can work scientifically.

Spread questions

These questions give you the chance to test whether you have understood everything in the lesson. The questions start off easier and get harder, so that you can stretch yourself.

End-of-chapter questions

These questions give you the chance to test whether you have learned and understood everything in the chapter. The Revision questions are designed to familiarise you with the style of questions you might find in your examinations.

Topic summary

This is a summary of the main ideas in the chapter. You can use it as a starting point for revision, to check that you know about the big ideas covered.

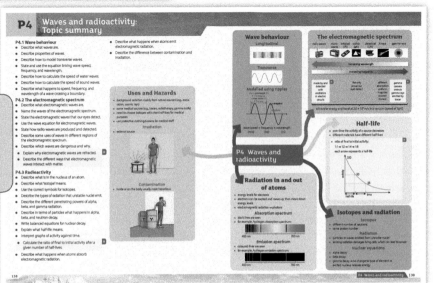

Kerboodle

This book is also supported by Kerboodle, offering unrivalled digital support for building your practical, maths, and literacy skills.

If your school subscribes to Kerboodle, you will also find a wealth of additional resources to help you with your studies and with revision:

- animations, videos, and revision podcasts
- webquests
- maths and literacy skills activities and worksheets
- on your marks activities to help you achieve your best
- practicals and follow up activities
- interactive quizzes that give question-by-question feedback
- self-assessment checklists.

Watch interesting animations on the trickiest topics, and answer questions afterward to check your understanding.

Check your own progress with the self-assessment checklists.

If you are a teacher reading this, Kerboodle also has plenty of practical support, assessment resources, answers to the questions in the book, and a digital markbook along with full teacher support for practicals and the worksheets, which include suggestions on how to support and stretch your students. All of the resources that you need are pulled together into ready-to-use lesson presentations.

OCR Gateway GCSE
Physics Student checklist   P1

Name _____ Class _____ Date _____

The particle model

Lesson	Level	Outcome	
P1.1.1 The model of the atom 1	Securing Grade 4	I can describe Dalton's and Thomson's atomic models.	☐
		I can describe Thomson's experiments with cathode rays.	☐
		I can state how Democritus developed his atomic model.	☐
	Securing Grade 6	I can compare Dalton's and Thomson's atomic models.	☐
		I can explain Thomson's evidence for electrons.	☐
	Securing Grade 8	I can explain why the atomic model did not develop between the times of Democritus and Dalton.	☐
		I can evaluate Thomson's atomic model given prior knowledge of the modern model of the atom.	☐
		I can explain how Thomson's observations led him to develop his atomic model.	☐
		I can explain how new technology helped Thomson to develop Dalton's atomic theory.	☐
P1.1.2 The model of the atom 2	Securing Grade 4	I can describe the observations of Rutherford, Geiger, and Marsden's experiment.	☐
		I can name the subatomic particles in the modern (Bohr) model of the atom.	☐
		I can state the size of a typical atom.	☐
	Securing Grade 6	I can explain how Rutherford's observations led him to reject Thomson's model.	☐
		I can describe in detail the structure of the Bohr atom.	☐
		I can estimate the size of a molecule based on the size of an atom.	☐
	Securing Grade 8	I can explain how Rutherford's observations led him to suggest that an atom has a nucleus.	☐
		I can explain why Bohr's atomic model is better than Rutherford's model.	☐
		I can calculate the relative size of atoms and nuclei in scale models.	☐

© Oxford University Press 2015

Assessment objectives and key ideas

There are three Assessment Objectives in OCR Physics for GCSE (9–1) Combined Science (Gateway Science). These are shown in the table below.

Assessment Objectives		Weighting	
		Higher	Foundation
AO1	**Demonstrate knowledge and understanding of:** • scientific ideas • scientific techniques and procedures.	40	40
AO2	**Apply knowledge and understanding of:** • scientific ideas • scientific enquiry, techniques, and procedures.	40	40
AO3	**Analyse information and ideas to:** • interpret and evaluate • make judgements and draw conclusions • develop and improve experimental procedures.	20	20

Studying science at GCSE helps us to understand the world around us. It is important to understand the essential aspects of the knowledge, methods, processes, and uses of science. There are a number of key ideas that underpin the complex and diverse phenomena of the natural world. These key ideas are shown in the table below.

OCR Gateway GCSE (9–1) Combined Science A Key Ideas
Conceptual models and theories are used to make sense of the observed diversity of natural phenomena.
It is assumed that every effect has one or more causes.
Change is driven by differences between different objects and systems when they interact.
Many interactions occur over a distance and over time without direct contact.
Science progresses through a cycle of hypothesis, practical experimentation, observation, theory development, and review.
Quantitative analysis is a central element of many theories and of scientific methods of inquiry.

Working Scientifically

WS1 The power of science

Learning outcomes

After studying this lesson you should be able to:

- describe some applications of science
- evaluate the implications of some applications of science.

Figure 1 *A solar cooker.*

In a solar cooker (Figure 1), mirrors direct heat from the Sun onto the frying pan, cooking the sausages. Could you use a solar cooker at home?

What are applications of science?

The solar cooker is an example of an application of science. Its designer used knowledge of reflection to work out the best shape for the mirror, and where to place the pan holder. **Technology** is the application of science for practical purposes.

Scientists are developing new ways of using energy transferred from the Sun to generate electricity. In a solar thermal power plant (Figure 2), mirrors focus radiation from the Sun onto boilers at the tops of high towers.

Figure 2 *The mirrors in this solar thermal power plant focus light to the top of the tower, which is so hot that it glows.*

Water in the towers boils, producing steam. The steam makes a machine called a turbine turn. The turbine is connected to another machine called a generator, which generates an electrical potential difference, which makes a current flow.

A Write down an application of science that has improved human health.

How can you evaluate science applications?

Any application of science brings drawbacks as well as benefits. When you evaluate an application of science, think about its personal, social, economic, and environmental implications. You will also need to consider **ethical issues**. An ethical issue is a problem for which a choice has to be made concerning what is right and what is wrong.

Consider, for example, the Ivanpah solar thermal power plant in the USA. Its construction and operation has created jobs, so it has personal and social benefits. Building the power plant was expensive, but selling its electricity will make money. These are examples of **economic impacts**.

The power plant was built on the habitat of the desert tortoise (Figure 3). Its glowing towers attract insects, which in turn attract birds, but few birds survive close to the hot towers (Figure 4). Is it morally acceptable to kill birds in order to generate electricity?

The power plant generates electricity without producing carbon dioxide, which is a greenhouse gas. This is an **environmental** benefit. However, carbon dioxide was produced in making and transporting the mirrors and towers.

B Describe an ethical issue arising from the Ivanpah solar thermal plant.

People are concerned about hazards linked to the power plant, such as aeroplane pilots being dazzled by glare from the mirrors. A **hazard** is anything that threatens life, health, or the environment. Managers at the power plant work hard to reduce the **risks** linked to these hazards. They do this by reducing the probability of a hazard occurring, as well as by trying to reduce the consequences if it does occur.

C Suggest how to reduce the risk caused by dazzling.

How can you make decisions about applications of science?

Government officials had to decide whether or not to allow the Ivanpah power plant to be built. It is often difficult to make decisions about the applications of science, as most have both benefits and drawbacks. The government had to weigh up these benefits and drawbacks before making its decision.

Other applications of science

There are many other applications of science (Figure 5). Scientists use their knowledge of viruses and antibodies to create new vaccines. They use knowledge of microwaves to improve mobile phone technology, and an understanding of properties of materials to develop scratch-free cars and chip-free nail varnish.

Figure 3 *The Ivanpah solar thermal power plant was built on the habitat of the desert tortoise.*

Figure 4 *This scientist is looking for birds flying close to the solar towers.*

Key words

As you read this chapter, make a glossary by writing down all the key words and their meanings.

1 Write down what the word *technology* means. (*1 mark*)

2 Suggest two hazards of using a solar cooker. (*1 mark*)

3 Write down one impact of mobile phones in each of these four categories: personal, social, environmental, and economic. State whether each impact is a benefit or a drawback. (*5 marks*)

4 Evaluate the impacts of building a solar thermal power plant. (*6 marks*)

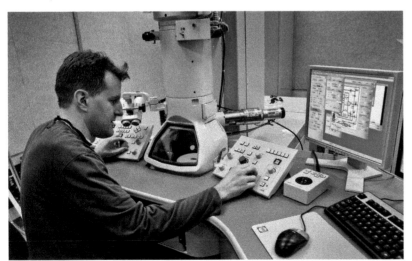

Figure 5 *This scientist is using an advanced electron microscope to research and control the structure and behaviour of new nanomaterials. Nanomaterials have many potential uses, including in medical treatments.*

WS2 Methods, models, and communication

Learning outcomes

After studying this lesson you should be able to:

- explain why scientific ideas change
- describe different types of scientific models
- explain why scientists communicate.

The MRI scan in Figure 1 shows the brain of a person with alcoholic dementia. The enlarged gap between the brain and skull shows that his brain has shrunk.

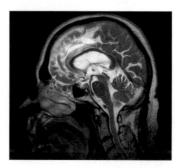

Figure 1 *The brain of a person with alcoholic dementia.*

Figure 2 *Drinking too many alcoholic drinks can cause alcoholic dementia.*

How do scientific methods and theories develop over time?

For centuries, people have known that drinking too much alcohol causes memory loss, poor judgement, and personality changes. It is only recently that a new technology – magnetic resonance imaging (MRI) – has allowed scientists to observe directly the effect of alcoholism on the brain (Figure 1).

The robot spacecraft Cassini recently sent photographs of Saturn's moon, Enceladus, back to Earth (Figure 3). Its on-board instruments identified materials ejected by the moon's geysers. Scientists analysed this evidence and suggested a new explanation, that Enceladus has liquid water beneath its icy surface.

These examples show that developing technologies allow scientists to collect new evidence and develop new explanations.

> **A** Suggest how the invention of the telescope helped scientists to collect new evidence.

Figure 3 *An image of Enceladus from Cassini.*

Figure 4 *This is a model car, but you cannot see and hold all models in science.*

Synoptic link

You will find out how new technology led to improved models of atoms in P1.1.1 *The model of the atom 1*, and P1.1.2 *The model of the atom 2*.

What are scientific models?

Models are central to science. They make scientific ideas easier to understand. They also help in making predictions and developing explanations. Scientists spend hours creating, testing, comparing, and improving models. Models are simplified versions of reality, so no model is perfect.

There are different types of models:

- Representational models use familiar objects to describe and explain observations. An example is using marbles to model water particles.

- Spatial models often represent things that are tiny, or enormous. An example is the metal model of DNA shown in Figure 5.
- Descriptive models use words and ideas to help you imagine something, or to describe something simply. An example is using chemical equations to represent reactions.
- Mathematical models use maths to describe systems and make predictions. Scientists have developed mathematical models to describe and predict the movements of planets and stars.
- Computational models are a type of mathematical model. At the Met Office in Exeter supercomputers process millions of pieces of data to predict the weather (Figure 6).

Figure 6 *A supercomputer.*

Figure 5 *Watson and Crick with the first model of DNA.*

B Give an example of a spatial model, other than the one shown here.

Why do scientists communicate?

Scientists describe their methods, share their results, and explain their conclusions in scientific papers. Before a paper is published other expert scientists check it carefully and suggest improvements. This is called **peer review**. Scientists also tell other scientists about their work at conferences (Figure 7).

Scientists use internationally accepted names, symbols, definitions, and units so that scientists everywhere understand their work. The international system of units (SI units) is a system built on seven base units, including the metre, kilogram, and second. The International Union of Pure and Applied Chemistry (IUPAC) publishes rules for naming substances. You will use SI units and IUPAC names when communicating your investigations.

Scientists may also tell doctors and journalists about their work. For example, when researchers found that paracetamol may reduce testosterone levels in male fetuses they asked journalists to warn pregnant women about this possible hazard.

Figure 7 *This scientist is studying scientific posters at a conference in York.*

C Suggest two reasons for peer review.

1 Explain why it is important to use internationally accepted units, symbols, and definitions in science. *(1 mark)*

2 Suggest why, before the invention of the microscope, scientists did not know that cells make up living organisms. *(1 mark)*

3 A teacher uses marbles to model water particles. Use your knowledge of particles to evaluate this model. *(6 marks)*

Maths link

To find out more about SI units, look at *Maths for GCSE Physics: 11 Quantities and units.*

Learning outcomes

After studying this lesson you should be able to:

- describe how to develop an idea into a question to investigate
- explain what a hypothesis is.

Figure 1 shows an early microwave oven. In the 1950s, engineer Percy Spencer accidentally discovered that microwaves cook food when he was experimenting with microwaves. He was standing in front of the microwave source and noticed the bar of chocolate in his pocket had melted.

Figure 1 *A 1961 microwave oven.*   Figure 2 *A modern microwave oven.*

What are scientific questions?

Scientists ask questions. They ask about unexpected observations, for example, *What made my chocolate melt?* They also ask questions to solve problems, such as: *Which malaria treatment is most effective?* Some questions arise from simple curiosity, for example, *What makes rocks move on Mars?* (Figure 3).

All these questions are **scientific questions**. You can answer them by collecting and considering evidence. Of course, scientists and other people also ask questions that science cannot answer, such as: *Who should pay for vaccines?* or *Why did the Big Bang happen?*

Figure 3 *The surface of Mars, taken by a camera on the Curiosity rover.*

A Write down a scientific question that you have investigated at school.

What is a hypothesis?

Imagine you have warm water in one container, and the same volume of cold water in another container. You put both containers of water in the freezer (Figure 4). Which freezes first? Surprisingly, the warm water freezes more quickly. This is called the Mpemba effect, after the Tanzanian school student who described and investigated this unexpected observation.

You could make a hypothesis for the Mpemba effect. A **hypothesis** is based on observations and is backed up by scientific knowledge and creative thinking. A hypothesis must be testable. Here are some examples:

Figure 4 *Warm water freezes more quickly than cold water.*

- Hot water freezes faster because more of the warm water evaporates, so reducing the mass of water to be frozen.
- Hot water freezes faster because cooler water freezes from the top, forming a layer of ice that insulates the water below.
- Hot water freezes faster because faster-moving convection currents in warmer water transfer energy to the surroundings more quickly.

There is still no accepted explanation for the Mpemba effect. In 2012 the Royal Society of Chemistry ran a competition to find the best explanation. More than 20 000 people entered.

Go further

Find out which organisations pay for scientific research and how they allocate their money. Suggest why different areas of scientific research receive different amounts of funding.

> **B** Use the paragraphs above to help you write down two possible hypotheses to explain the Mpemba effect.

How do scientists answer questions?

Answering a scientific question involves making observations to collect data, and using creative thought to explain the data. Science moves forward through cycles or stages like those shown below (Figure 5), building on what is already known. Of course, scientists do not always follow these stages exactly.

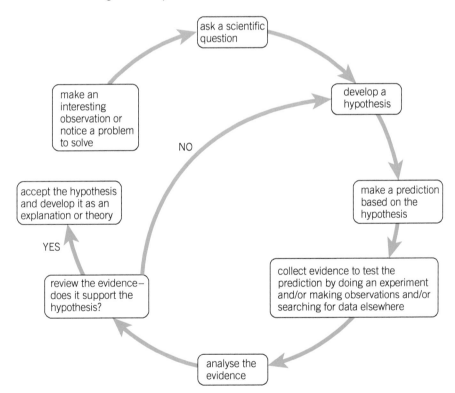

Figure 5 *Scientists may answer a scientific question by following these stages. Of course scientific advances do not always follow this route.*

> **C** Write down these stages in the order shown by the cycle above, starting with *ask a scientific question*: make a prediction, ask a scientific question, collect evidence, develop a hypothesis.

1 State which of the following are scientific questions, giving reasons.
  a Which material is harder, glass or diamond? *(1 mark)*
  b Which type of car travels fastest? *(1 mark)*
  c Which type of car is best? *(1 mark)*
  d How many years can you expect a robin to live? *(1 mark)*

2 A student asks a scientific question, *Which has a higher boiling point, water or ethanol?* He knows that the forces holding the particles together in water in the liquid state are stronger than those in ethanol.
  a Use your scientific knowledge to suggest a hypothesis. *(1 mark)*
  b 🖊 Outline how the student could investigate his question, referring to the steps in Figure 5. *(4 marks)*

3 🖊 Suggest how you could test the hypothesis that the Mpemba effect happens because cooler water freezes from the top, forming a layer of ice that insulates the water below. *(4 marks)*

Learning outcomes

After studying this lesson you should be able to:

- identify different types of variable
- describe how to plan an investigation.

Figure 1 *Young people using a mobile phone.*

Figure 2 *In this investigation the dependent variable is the battery life.*

Synoptic link

You will find out how to present continuous, discrete, and categoric variables in charts and graphs in WS6 *Presenting data.*

Do you ever wish your phone battery lasted longer?

How can you start an investigation?

Some students noticed that using social media seemed to make their phone battery run down quickly (Figure 1). They made up a scientific question to investigate:

How does the time spent on social media affect mobile phone battery life?

They used their observations, and scientific knowledge, to make a hypothesis:

Using social media involves downloading significant amounts of data. This means that extra energy is transferred as electricity from its chemical store in the battery to the thermal store of the surroundings. This shortens the battery life.

A Suggest a prediction based on this hypothesis.

How do you choose variables?

The students considered factors that might affect the outcome of their investigation. These are **variables**. There are three types of variable:

- The **independent variable** is the one you deliberately change.
- The **dependent variable** is the one you measure for each change of the independent variable.
- **Control variables** are ones that may affect the outcome, as well as the independent variable. Keep these variables the same for a **fair test**.

In the mobile phone investigation, the independent variable is the time spent on social media. The dependent variable is the battery life (Figure 2). Control variables include the model of the phone, as well as the number of texts sent.

You can collect data as words or numbers:

- A **continuous variable** can have any value, and can be measured. In this investigation, the time spent on social media is a continuous variable.
- A **discrete variable** has whole number values. The number of texts is a discrete variable.
- Values for a **categoric variable** are described by labels. The make and model of phone are categoric variables.

B Explain whether battery life is a continuous, discrete, or categoric variable.

How do you plan an investigation?

The students used their hypothesis to say what they thought would happen. This is their **prediction**:

The more time spent on social media, the shorter the battery life.

The students planned how to test their prediction. They thought about the apparatus, and what to do with it. This is their plan:

1   People with the same model of phone fully charge their batteries and record the time.

2   People write down when, and for how long, they use social media.

3   Apart from social media, people can use the phone for texting only.

4   People record when the battery has run down.

> **C**   Write down two pieces of equipment needed for this investigation.

The students also considered hazards. They discovered that using a phone exerts high forces on the neck (Figure 3). They took precautions to reduce the risks from this hazard, including taking breaks.

What other types of investigation are there?

There are many other sorts of investigation. Scientists work out how to make new substances, and check that substances are what they should be. A scientist might check that data are correct, or use different types of trials to investigate the effects of a medicinal drug (Figures 4–6).

Figure 3 *Bending to use a phone exerts high forces on the neck.*

Figure 4 *This scientist is using gas chromatography to check food samples for contamination.*

Figure 5 *This scientist is inspecting sorghum plants being grown as part of a crop trial. Sorghum is used for grain and as an animal feed.*

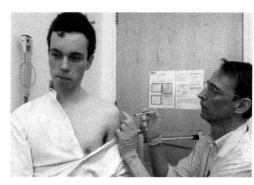

Figure 6 *This scientist is injecting an experimental Ebola vaccine into the arm of a volunteer who is testing the vaccine.*

> **1**   Compare continuous, discrete, and categoric variables.   (*3 marks*)
>
> **2**   A student investigates the effect of the number of hours of sunlight on the number of units (kWh) of electricity generated by the solar panels on the school roof.
>   **a**   Write down the independent and dependent variables.   (*2 marks*)
>   **b**   Suggest a control variable and explain whether it is possible to keep this variable the same.   (*2 marks*)
>
> **3**   A student investigates whether shoe size affects speed of swimming. Identify the variables in the investigation, and use two labels such as *independent* and *discrete* to describe each one.   (*6 marks*)

WS5 Obtaining high-quality data

Learning outcomes

After studying this lesson you should be able to:

● describe how to obtain data that is accurate and precise

● compare the meanings of the terms repeatable and reproducible.

Figure 1 *Ethiopian coffee.*

Go further

Find out why water boils at a lower temperature in Addis Ababa than in London.

Figure 2 *The resolution of this thermometer is 1.0 °C because this is the smallest change in reading that you can see.*

A cup of coffee in Addis Ababa, Ethiopia (Figure 1), might taste delicious. But it is not as hot as a cup of coffee made in London.

How can you obtain accurate data?

In Addis Ababa or London, you can use a thermometer to measure the boiling point of water. In a scientific investigation, you need measurements that are close to the true value. These data are **accurate**.

You can collect accurate data by:

● using your thermometer carefully

● repeating measurements and calculating the mean

● repeating measurements with a different instrument, for example a temperature probe, and checking that the readings are the same.

> **A** A student measures the boiling point of water three times, and obtains these values: 101.0 °C, 99.0 °C, and 100.0 °C. Calculate the mean.

How can you obtain precise data?

Precise measurements give similar results if you repeat the measurement. If repeated measurements are precise, the **spread** of the data set is small. You can calculate the spread by subtracting the smallest measurement from the largest measurement for a set of repeats.

To get precise data you need a measuring instrument with a high **resolution**. The resolution of a measuring instrument is the smallest change in the quantity that gives a change in the reading that you can see (Figure 2).

When you are using a measuring instrument, it is important to record all the readings you make with this instrument in a particular experiment to the same number of decimal places. For example, two students working together on the same experiment record the following series of masses from a balance:

| Student A: | 11 g | 9.8 g | 8.65 g |
| Student B: | 11.00 g | 9.80 g | 8.65 g |

Student B has recorded each reading to two decimal places, so his set of readings is recorded correctly.

Precision

Students in Addis Ababa and London measured the boiling point of water (Table 1). Which data set is more precise?

Table 1 *Temperature at which water boils in Addis Ababa and London.*

Place	Temperature at which water boils (°C)		
	First reading	Second reading	Third reading
Addis Ababa	94.0	93.0	94.0
London	97.0	100.0	99.0

Step 1: Calculate the spread of each data set by subtracting the smallest measurement from the largest measurement.

Addis Ababa   94.0 °C – 93.0 °C = 1.0 °C

London   100.0 °C – 97.0 °C = 3.0 °C

Step 2: Compare the spread of each data set to see which is smaller. The spread for Addis Ababa is smaller, so their data set is more precise.

You can have data that are precise but not accurate. Precise data might not be close to the true value.

Two students used a burning fuel in a spirit burner (Figure 3) to heat water for two minutes. They measured the highest temperature the water reached. They repeated the experiment four times each. Their results are marked on the temperature scales in Figure 4.

The set of measurements on the left is precise but not accurate.

> **B** Explain why the set of measurements on the right of Figure 4 is accurate but not precise.

What are repeatable and reproducible data?

If you repeat an investigation several times using the same method and equipment, and if you get similar results each time, your results are **repeatable**.

If someone else repeats your investigation, or if you do the same investigation with different equipment, and the results are similar, the investigation is **reproducible**.

> **C** You do an investigation twice, with different equipment each time. Explain whether you expect your results to be repeatable or reproducible.

1 Compare the meanings of the terms *repeatable* and *reproducible*. *(2 marks)*

2 🚫 A student is investigating how the mass of salt added to water affects boiling temperature. Describe in detail how she can make accurate measurements of mass and temperature. *(4 marks)*

3 Two students make measurements of the time for an egg attached to a parachute to fall from a window. Their data are in Table 2.
  a Explain which data set is more precise. *(3 marks)*
  b Explain why you cannot tell which data set is more accurate. *(2 marks)*

Table 2 *Time taken for an egg to fall from a window to the ground.*

| Student | Time for egg and parachute to reach the ground (s) | | | |
	First measurement	Second measurement	Third measurement	Mean
A	3.0	2.8	3.2	3.0
B	3.2	3.4	3.3	3.3

Figure 3 *A spirit burner.*

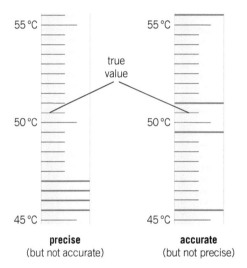

Figure 4 *Two sets of temperature data obtained when heating water with a burning fuel. Each piece of data is represented by a pink line.*

WS6 Presenting data

Learning outcomes

After studying this lesson you should be able to:

- describe how to present data in a table
- compare bar charts and line graphs
- explain what an outlier is.

Figure 1 *A pet tortoise can live for 60 years.*

Table 1 *The lifespans of different pets.*

Pet species	Mean age at death (years)
cat	12
dog	10
guinea pig	5
mouse	2
tortoise	55

Maths link

Maths for GCSE Physics: 7 Mean average shows how to calculate the mean value from a set of data.

Tortoises are not easy to look after, but with proper care they can live for 60 years (Figure 1). A pet mouse has a much shorter lifespan.

How do you design a table to display data?

A group of students asked, *What is the lifespan of different pets?* They collected data by asking pet owners to complete a survey about the age of death of their pets.

The students calculated the mean lifespan for each pet. Table 1 summarises their results. In any table:

- Write the independent variable in the left column
- Write the dependent variable in the right column
- Write units in the column headings, not next to each piece of data.

A State which variable in the table is categoric.

When do you draw a bar chart?

If either variable is categoric, draw a **bar chart**. In the example the independent variable (pet species) is categoric, so the students draw a bar chart (Figure 2). In any bar chart:

- Write the independent variable on the *x*-axis and the dependent variable on the *y*-axis.
- Label the axes with the variable name and units (if there are any).
- Choose a scale for the *y*-axis so that the chart is as big as possible, and make sure the scale is even.

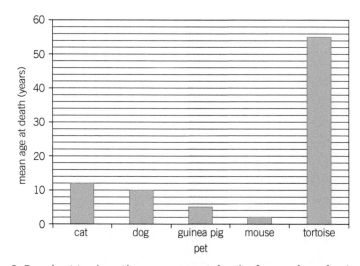

Figure 2 *Bar chart to show the mean age at death of a number of animals.*

B State whether the mean age at death is a continuous, discrete, or categoric variable. Explain your answer.

When do you draw a line graph?

Some engineers asked a scientific question, *How does car speed affect carbon dioxide emissions?* They collected data for one test car (Table 2).

As both variables are continuous, the engineers drew a **line graph** (Figure 3).

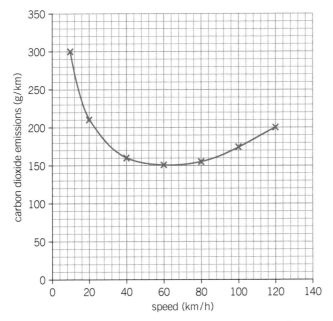

Figure 3 *Line graph to show the carbon dioxide emissions of cars travelling at different speeds.*

C Use the graph to predict the carbon dioxide emissions at 50 km/h.

What is an outlier?

Some students collected data about the lifespan of different dog breeds (Table 3). They asked five owners of each dog breed how long their pets had lived.

Table 3 *The lifespans of different dog breeds.*

Dog breed	Age at death (years)					
	Dog 1	Dog 2	Dog 3	Dog 4	Dog 5	Mean
bulldog	5	6	7	1	6	6
Doberman	10	11	8	12	9	
Toy poodle	16	14	17	13	25	15

One bulldog had a much shorter life than the others, of just 1 year (Figure 4). This value is an **outlier**. An outlier is any value in a set of results that you judge is not part of the natural variation you expect. You should consider outliers carefully, and decide whether or not to include them when calculating the mean.

D The owner of the bulldog that died aged 1 year told the students that a car ran over the dog. Suggest why the students decided not to include this value when calculating the mean.

Table 2 *How does car speed affect carbon dioxide emissions?*

Speed (km/h)	Carbon dioxide emissions (g/km)
10	300
20	210
40	160
60	150
80	155
100	175
120	200

Figure 4 *The mean lifespan of a bulldog is around 6 years.*

1 Use the data from Table 3 to calculate the mean age at death for Doberman dogs. *(2 marks)*

2 Draw a bar chart to display the data about dogs given in Table 3. *(4 marks)*

3 On a car journey, a student collected the data in Table 4. Draw a bar chart or line graph to display the data. Explain your choice. *(5 marks)*

Table 4 *Change in engine temperature over time.*

Time after start of journey (minutes)	Engine temperature (°C)
4	50
5	57
6	66
7	78
8	90
9	90
10	90

WS7 Interpreting data

Learning outcomes

After studying this lesson you should be able to:

- explain how to interpret graphs
- explain how to make a conclusion
- evaluate an investigation.

Figure 1 *An elephant.*

An elephant relieves itself of around 200 litres of urine at a time (Figure 1). How long does this take to flow out?

How do you interpret graphs?

A group of scientists collected data about mammal urination. The graphs show some of their data.

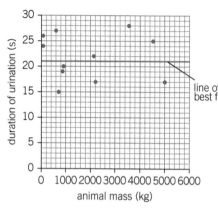

Figure 2 *Graph of urination duration versus animal mass.*

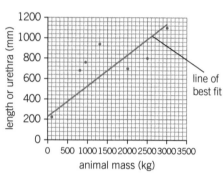

Figure 3 *Graph of urethra length versus animal mass. Urine flows from the bladder, through the urethra, to the outside.*

> **A** Describe the relationships shown on the graphs.

The graph of urination duration versus animal mass (Figure 2) shows a surprising finding. Whatever their mass, most mammals urinate for about the same time, 21 seconds.

The graph of urethra length against animal mass (Figure 3) shows a pattern – the greater the mass, the longer the urethra.

On each graph, the line does not go through all the points. Instead, there is a **line of best fit**. To draw a line of best fit, look at the points you have plotted. Then follow these steps:

1 Circle any outliers.

2 Decide whether the line of best fit is a straight line or a curve.

3 Draw a line through the middle of the points, ignoring outliers. There should be roughly the same number of points above and below the line.

How do you draw conclusions?

A scientific conclusion has two parts:

- a description of a pattern
- a scientific explanation of the pattern, linked to the hypothesis.

If you have drawn a graph and seen a pattern, there is a **relationship** between the two variables. The relationships can be:

- positive – as one variable increases so does the other
- negative – as one variable increases the other variable decreases.

Alternatively, when one variable changes the other variable might remain the same.

You can now write the first part of your conclusion. In the urine investigation, the first part of the conclusion from the second graph is:

The greater the mass of a mammal, the longer its urethra.

The scientists made a hypothesis to explain this relationship. They suggested that a longer urethra increases the gravitational force acting on the urine, so increasing the rate that urine leaves the body. The scientists used mathematical models to show that their hypothesis was correct.

B Complete the conclusion by adding a scientific explanation.

In this example, the longer urethra *causes* faster urination. However, the fact that there is a relationship does not necessarily mean that a change in one variable *caused* the change in the other. There could be some other reason for the change.

How do you evaluate an investigation?

When you evaluate an investigation, think about these two questions:

● How could you improve the method?

● What is the quality of the data?

In this investigation the scientists collected data by filming animals urinating. They also viewed videos online.

You can evaluate the quality of data by considering its accuracy, precision, repeatability, and reproducibility.

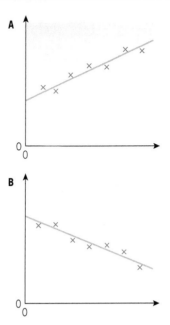

Figure 4 *These graphs show linear relationships. The lines of best fit are linear. The relationship in A is positive – as one variable increases, so does the other. The relationship in B is negative – as one variable increases, the other variable decreases.*

News report

Write the text for a news report to tell young people about the urination investigation.

1 Sketch graphs showing **a** a positive relationship and **b** a negative relationship. *(2 marks)*

2 Suggest how to collect accurate data for the duration of urination. *(3 marks)*

3 Table 1 shows data about urine flow rate and animal mass.
   a Plot the data on a graph, and draw a line of best fit. *(6 marks)*
   b Describe what the graph shows. *(2 marks)*

Table 1 *Data about the mass of an animal against urine flow rate.*

Animal	Mass of animal (kg)	Urine flow rate (cm³/s)
rat	0.3	2.0
small dog	3.5	1.0
goat	71	6.0
human	70	20
cow	640	450

WS8 Errors and uncertainties

After studying this lesson you should be able to:

- compare random and systematic errors
- explain the meaning of uncertainty
- explain the meaning of distribution.

Figure 1 *A herd of cows in a field.*

How long does it take for a cow (Figure 1) to empty its bladder?

What are random errors?

A student watched videos of three animals urinating. He timed the duration of urination for each animal. Table 1 shows his measurements.

Table 1 *The duration of urination for different animals*

Animal	Duration of urination (s)			
	First measurement	**Second measurement**	**Third measurement**	**Mean**
cow	21.4	21.6	21.5	21.5
horse	22.4	22.0	22.8	22.4
sheep	20.8	21.0	20.9	20.9

Look at the times for the cow; the measurements are not the same. You cannot predict whether a fourth measurement would be higher or lower than the third measurement. The measurements are showing a **random error**.

Random errors are caused by known and unpredictable changes in the investigation, including changes to the environmental conditions. They are also caused by changes that occur in measuring instruments, or difficulties in being sure what values show. You cannot control the cause of random errors. However, you can reduce their effect by repeating measurements and calculating a mean.

> **A** Suggest a cause of random error in this investigation.

What are systematic errors?

An error might also be a **systematic error**. This means that your measurements are spread about some value other than the true value. Each of your measurements differs from the true value by a similar amount; so all your values are too high, or too low. For example, a systematic error might be caused by an ammeter that does not read zero when there is no current.

Figure 2 *You can use different pieces of equipment to measure time.*

If you think that you have a systematic error, repeat the measurements with a different piece of equipment (Figure 2). Then compare the two sets of measurements.

> **B** Suggest a cause of systematic error when measuring the boiling point of water.

What is uncertainty?

Your readings are only as good as your measuring instrument (Figure 3). On a thermometer it might be hard to tell if a reading is 65.5 °C, or 65.0 °C, or 66.0 °C. There is **uncertainty** in your measurement because of the thermometer you are using.

If the smallest scale division is 1.0 °C then you can estimate the uncertainty as ± 0.5 °C, which is half the smallest scale division.

A better definition of uncertainty is that it is the interval within which the true value can be expected to lie, with a given level of confidence. For example you could say that the temperature is 65.5 °C ± 0.5 °C with a confidence of 95%.

> **C** A stopwatch has scale divisions of 0.2 seconds. Estimate the uncertainty of readings with this stopwatch.

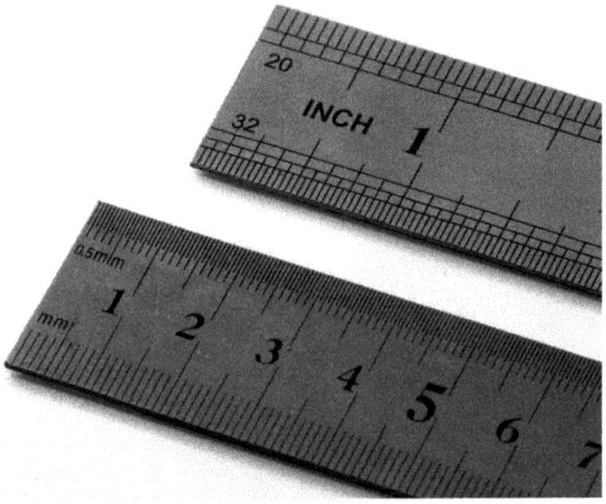

Figure 3 *There would be a greater uncertainty in a measurement taken using a ruler marked in inches than one taken with a metric ruler.*

Go further

As you know, the spread of a set of repeated measurements is the difference between the highest and lowest values. The way the measurements are distributed between the highest and lowest values can take different forms. Often, the values are more likely to fall nearer the mean than further away. This may mean that the measurements have a **normal distribution** (Figures 4 and 5).

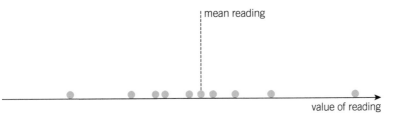

Figure 4 *Each blob on this diagram represents one measurement. There are more measurements close to the mean.*

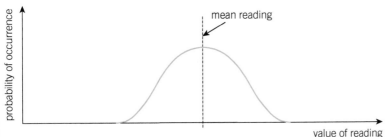

Figure 5 *This normal distribution shows that you are more likely to make measurements close to the mean.*

1 Explain the meaning of *uncertainty*.
   (1 mark)

2 Compare the meaning of *random error* and *systematic error*. *(2 marks)*

3 🔢 ✏️ Plot a blob diagram for these measurements of the duration of urination of a cow:
   21.5, 21.4, 21.6, 21.3, 21.7, 21.4, 21.8, 21.2, 22.0, 20.5
   Show the mean reading on your blob diagram, and explain what your plot shows about the distribution of the measurements. *(4 marks)*

P1 Matter

P1.1 The particle model
P1.1.1 The model of the atom 1

Learning outcome

After studying this lesson you should be able to:

- describe how and why the model of the atom has changed.

Specification reference: P1.1a

Figure 1 *The Sun, sea, sand, and clouds are all made of atoms.*

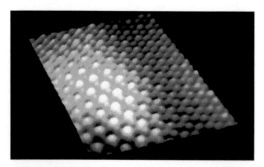

Figure 2 *Special microscopes make images of atoms.*

Figure 3 *J. J. Thomson experimented with rays which turned out to be made of electrons.*

Imagine that you could look inside a grain of sand. What would you see?

Everything, including all you can see in Figure 1, is made of atoms. Scientists use ideas about atoms (Figure 2) to explain things we see, such as clouds forming or salt dissolving. If you know about atoms you can make new materials, such as the plastic for shock-proof mobile phone cases.

What are things made of?

Over 2000 years ago, people asked questions about what everything is made of. They asked questions such as, 'Can I keep cutting up paper forever?' Some people thought that you could. Two Greek philosophers, Democritus and Leucippus, thought that eventually you could not cut any more, and you would have an atom. The word 'atomos' means 'indivisible' in Greek. Atoms, they said, were too small to see.

A Suggest why some people did not believe Democritus' and Leucippus' idea about atoms.

What was Dalton's model?

For many years, ideas about atoms did not develop. There were no instruments to measure atoms. Then, in the 1870s, John Dalton did experiments to measure how elements combined. He thought that he could explain the results of his experiments if everything was made of atoms. His **model** of an atom was a very small indestructible sphere. He thought that:

- all the atoms in an element are the same
- the atoms in one element are different from the atoms in all other elements.

It took many years for other scientists to accept Dalton's ideas.

B Suggest why, before Dalton, the model of the atom did not develop for nearly 2000 years.

What was Thomson's model?

In 1897, J. J. Thomson was investigating rays given out by hot metals, called cathode rays (Figure 3). He was not investigating atoms.

Thomson discovered that cathode rays are made of particles that have less than one-thousandth of the mass of a hydrogen atom. He had found a particle which he called an **electron** that must have come from *inside* an atom. He also worked out that the charge on an electron is *negative*.

Thomson had to make sense of two ideas:

- An atom contains negative electrons.

- Overall, atoms have no electrical charge. They are *neutral*.

C Explain why Thomson thought that part of an atom must be positive.

In 1904, Thomson suggested a new model. He said that atoms are like plum puddings (Figure 4), which are like blueberry muffins. This is called the **plum-pudding model of the atom**. In this model, the atom is thought to consist of *positive* mass with negative electrons embedded in it. He did not know what the positive mass was made of, or the structure of the atom. He thought that the positive mass might be solid, or like a cloud.

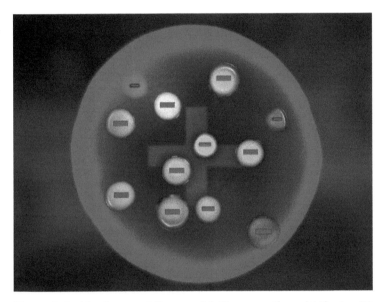

Figure 4 *In his plum-pudding model, Thomson thought the positive mass was like a cloud.*

Evidence and idea change

The history of the model of the atom shows that ideas change when there is new evidence that cannot be explained using old ideas.

What is science?

Doing 'science' is quite a new activity. The word 'science' wasn't used until the 1850s.

Before that people studied 'natural philosophy'.

1 Democritus and Dalton both believed that all matter was made of tiny particles which they called atoms. Explain the difference between their theories. *(2 marks)*

2 Compare Dalton's model of the atom with J. J. Thomson's model of the atom. *(2 marks)*

3 State the evidence that Thomson used to produce his plum-pudding model. *(4 marks)*

4 A student suggests that atoms should no longer be called atoms. Suggest how she might justify her suggestion. *(1 mark)*

Go further

The image of atoms in Figure 2 was made with a scanning electron microscope. Find out how this instrument makes images.

Learning outcomes

After studying this lesson you should be able to:

- describe how and why the model of the atom has changed
- describe the structure of the atom
- recall the typical size (order of magnitude) of the atom and of small molecules.

Specification reference: P1.1a, P1.1b, P1.1c

Figure 1 *The Moon is about 384 400 km away from the Earth.*

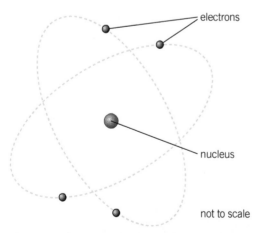

Figure 3 *The Rutherford model – if an atom was the size of Wembley stadium then the nucleus would be the size of a pea on the centre spot.*

Atoms are very, very small. If all the atoms in your body were the size of apples your height would be greater than the distance to the Moon (Figure 1).

What is the Rutherford model?

In 1899, Ernest Rutherford discovered that some materials emit particles. He called them alpha particles. They have a positive charge. He decided to fire alpha particles at a piece of gold foil (Figure 2).

Two younger scientists, Hans Geiger and Ernest Marsden, helped him with his work. What happened in the experiment was amazing. Rutherford said:

"It was quite the most incredible event that has ever happened to me in my life. It was almost as incredible as if you fired a huge shell at a piece of tissue paper and it came back and hit you."

It was not possible to explain this result using the plum-pudding model.

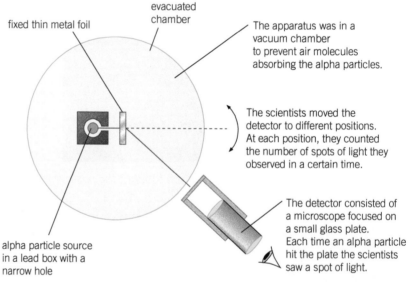

Figure 2 *Most of the alpha particles went through, but a few bounced back.*

To explain his results, Rutherford suggested that an atom is made of a tiny, positively charged **nucleus** with electrons around the outside (Figure 3). This is called the **Rutherford model of the atom**. Almost all the mass of an atom is in its nucleus. When alpha particles hit a nucleus, they bounce back. Later, scientists discovered the nucleus is made of two different types of particle, which they called **protons** and **neutrons**.

A Suggest what Geiger and Marsden might have seen if the plum-pudding model was correct.

What is the Bohr model?

The problem with Thomson's model was that you would expect the electrons to spiral in until they hit the nucleus. In 1913, Niels Bohr suggested that electrons can only move in fixed orbits, called **electron shells**, around the nucleus (Figure 4). The **Bohr model of the atom** has been improved over the past century, but it still provides a good basis for imagining how protons, neutrons, and electrons in atoms are arranged.

B Explain how Bohr knew that Thomson's model was not correct.

How big are atoms and molecules?

Order of magnitude

An atom is about 0.000 000 0001 m in diameter. You can write this number as 10^{-10} m, or as 1×10^{-10} m. This is an **order of magnitude** estimation because it just involves a power of ten.

Molecules are collections of atoms, strongly joined together, or bonded. You can work out roughly how big they are if you know the size of an atom.

Think of a molecule with 100 atoms in a long line.

The length of the molecule = 100 atoms $\times 10^{-10}$ m / atom

$$= 10^{-8}\,m$$

We now have machines that can make images of atoms, and move them around one by one.

Tiny, massive nucleus?

Sometimes the words that we use every day have a special meaning in science.

- In everyday language 'massive' means 'very large', like an elephant.
- In scientific language 'massive' means 'has lots of mass'.

1 Describe the model of the atom that we use now. (1 mark)
2 Describe evidence to show that the plum-pudding model is no longer an acceptable model of the atom. (2 marks)
3 **a** Estimate the number of atoms in a molecule that is 2×10^{-9} m long. (2 marks)
   b Explain why the number that you have calculated is a maximum. (1 mark)
4 The radius of a nucleus is about 10^{-15} m. Calculate the size of the nucleus or atom in each of the models in Table 1. (6 marks)

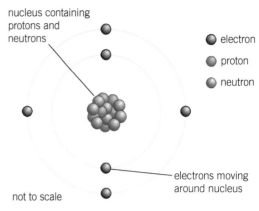

Figure 4 *Scientists now use the Bohr model of the atom.*

Figure 5 *Fabiola Gianotti is a physicist in charge of the Large Hadron Collider, which smashes atoms together.*

Go further

In this course you assume that electrons behave as tiny particles. Find out about the experiment that shows electrons can also behave like waves.

Table 1 *Modelling the atom.*

	Diameter of 'atom'	Diameter of 'nucleus'	Example of an object with the diameter you have calculated
modelling the atom as the Earth	12.7×10^6 m		
modelling the atom as your classroom	10 m		
modelling the nucleus as an apple		10 cm	

Matter

P1.1 The particle model

Summary questions

1 **a** Match the name of the model of the atom to the correct description. Write the matched letters and numbers to show your answer.

Model	Description
A Thomson model	**1** very small positive nucleus with electrons in orbit around it
B Rutherford model	**2** positive mass with negative electrons embedded in it
C Bohr model	**3** very small positive nucleus with electrons in shells around it

   b Choose the order of magnitude of the diameter of an atom:

   10 m   0.1 m 10^{-3} m 10^{-10} m 10^{-15} m

2 **a** Describe Geiger and Marsden's experiment with alpha particles.

   b Explain why the results of the experiment were surprising.

3 Suggest one reason why scientists took many years to accept Dalton's ideas about atoms.

4 **a** Copy and label the diagram of a model of the atom in Figure 1.

   b State the name of this model.

   c i The atom shown has no overall charge. Explain why.

   ii State the name of another model that shows that an atom has no overall charge.

5 **a** State and explain the minimum number of atoms in a molecule.

   b i A molecule contains 50 atoms. Estimate the length of the molecule.

   ii Explain why your answer to **i** is only an estimate.

6 You pick up a grain of sand from a beach. Assuming that the grain of sand is a cube:

   a Estimate the volume of the grain of sand.

   b Use your answer to **a** to estimate the number of atoms in the grain of sand.

7 Describe and explain how and why the model of the atom has changed over time.

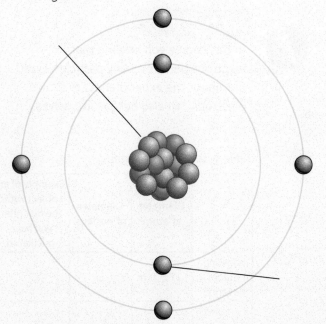

Figure 1 *Model of the atom.*

Revision questions

1 In 1899, Ernest Rutherford discovered that some materials emit particles. He called them alpha particles. They have a positive charge. He decided to fire alpha particles at a piece of gold foil.

Hans Geiger and Ernest Marsden, both students of Rutherford, observed that most of the alpha particles passed through the gold foil. Some went straight on and many were deflected through different angles. A small fraction (1 in 8000) of these particles were deflected backwards from the foil. Their impacts were observed as spots of light in the dark, using a microscope detector.

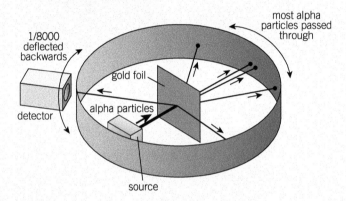

Rutherford and his team developed scientific explanations for their observations. This led to a new model of the atom.

How did Rutherford and his team explain their observations?   *(6 marks)*

2 In 1879, Sir William Crookes was investigating cathode rays. He subjected air, at very low pressure, to a very high voltage.

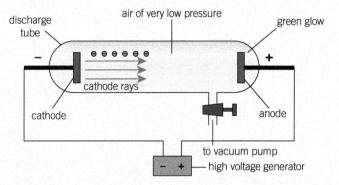

He observed:

● a green glow at the anode

● a pinwheel in the path of the cathode rays began to spin

● the rays deflected towards the positive when placed in an electric field

● the rays deflected towards the north when placed in a magnetic field

● the rays were easily deflected by electric and magnetic fields

● metal objects in the path of the rays became hot

● the rays could pass through thin metal sheets

● objects struck by the rays gained a negative charge.

a J. J. Thomson later identified cathode rays by another name.
  State the name that Thomson gave to cathode rays.   *(1 mark)*

b State the charge of the cathode rays and give one observation that supports this conclusion.   *(2 marks)*

c Give two observations which, when put together, show that the cathode rays have a very small mass.   *(2 marks)*

d Give one observation which shows that cathode rays are much smaller than atoms.   *(1 mark)*

Learning outcomes

After studying this lesson you should be able to:

- define density
- recall and apply the equation for density where mass is conserved
- explain why substances in different states have different densities.

Specification reference: P1.1d, P1.1e, P1.1f

Figure 2 *The density of a block depends on its mass and its volume.*

Figure 3 *Mercury is the densest liquid at room temperature and pressure.*

Which has more mass – a kilogram of popcorn or a kilogram of metal (Figure 1)? You might think that the metal has more mass. In fact, they both have the *same* mass, but the metal is denser.

Figure 1 *Steel has a higher density than popcorn.*

What is density?

Density tells you how much **mass** there is in a certain **volume**.

The blocks in Figure 2 have the same volume but different masses. This is because they have different densities.

If you have two different sized blocks made of the *same* material the density of the blocks is the *same*. Density is a property of a material (Figure 3), not of an object. The mass of each block depends on its volume.

How do you calculate density?

To calculate density in situations where mass is conserved (there is no loss of mass), you need to recall and apply this equation:

$$\text{density (kg/m}^3) = \frac{\text{mass (kg)}}{\text{volume (m}^3)}$$

Calculating the density of air

A classroom has a volume of 300 m³. The mass of air in the room is 3.6 kg. Calculate the density of the air.

Step 1: Write down what you know.

mass = 3.6 kg

volume = 300 m³

Step 2: Calculate the answer and give the unit.

$$\text{density} = \frac{\text{mass}}{\text{volume}}$$

$$= \frac{3.6\,\text{kg}}{300\,\text{m}^3}$$

$$= 0.012 \text{ kg/m}^3 \text{ (2 significant figures)}$$

A Suggest the equipment you would need and the data you would need to collect to find the density of steel.

Why is a substance denser as a solid than as a liquid or gas?

You can use particle theory to explain density differences (Figure 4).

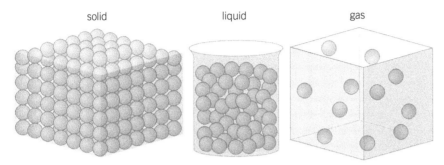

Figure 4 *Particles are arranged differently in the solid, liquid, and gas states.*

In 1 cm³ of a substance in the solid state there are many more particles than in 1 cm³ of the same substance as a gas. The mass of 1 cm³ of the solid is greater, so its density is also greater.

The densities of a substance in the liquid and solid states are more similar to each other than they are to the density of the same substance as a gas.

B State whether oxygen has a lower density in the solid state or the gas state.

Density does not depend *only* on the particle arrangement, but also on the mass of the particles.

What is conservation of mass?

You have to add or remove material for the mass of a system to change. Particles do not appear or disappear. This is the Law of Conservation of Mass. It applies when substances change state by melting, freezing, evaporating, condensing, or sublimating. If 1 g of ice melts, then you have 1 g of water. Water molecules do not disappear.

1 Explain why the density of a substance in the solid state is greater than the density of the same substance in the liquid state. (*2 marks*)

2 Calculate the density of a block of material with a mass of 160 g and a volume of 200 cm³. Show your working. (*2 marks*)

3 Calculate the volume of water that has the same mass as 2 cm³ of gold using the data in Table 1. (*2 marks*)

4 **a** Estimate the mass of one teaspoonful of the material in the black hole in Figure 5. (*3 marks*)

  b Compare the mass of one teaspoonful of black hole material with the mass of all the people in the UK. You will need this data: mass of typical person = 70 kg; UK population = 65 million. (*4 marks*)

Figure 5 *The density of the material at the centre of this black hole is 1.4×10^{14} kg/m³. This is much greater than the density of any material on Earth. Outer space has the lowest density of all.*

Go further

We can only estimate the density of outer space (Figure 5). Find out how to estimate the density of the Universe.

Figure 6 *This scientist has used an extra-low-density material called aerogel to catch dust from a comet.*

Table 1 *The densities of different substances in different states at room temperature.*

Substance	State	Density (kg/m³)
gold	solid	19 300
water	liquid	1000
oxygen	gas	1.33

Learning outcomes

After studying this lesson you should be able to:

● describe how heating a system affects the energy stored within the system in terms of its temperature or its state

● describe the differences between physical and chemical changes.

Specification reference: P1.2b, P1.2c

Can you guess what the person in Figure 1 is holding?

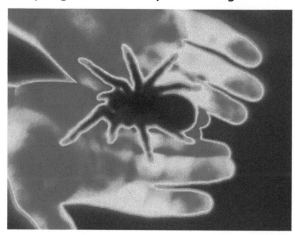

Figure 1 *A thermal imaging camera shows temperature. In this image the spider is cold compared with the person holding it.*

Table 1 *Comparing the units of temperature.*

Temperature (°C)	Temperature (K)
−273	0
0	273

Study tip

It is easy to confuse energy in a thermal store and temperature. You increase the temperature by heating, which is a process that involves the motion of particles, or emission or absorption of radiation.

What is temperature?

Temperature tells you how hot or cold something is. You can measure temperature with a thermometer (Figure 2) or temperature sensor. One unit of temperature is the **degree Celsius (°C)**. Another unit of temperature is the **kelvin (K)**. A difference in temperature of 1 °C is the same as a difference of 1 K. Table 1 compares the units of temperature.

Table 2 *Temperature and energy for two volumes of water.*

Container of water	Temperature (°C)	Energy in the thermal store (kJ)
cup	30	10
swimming pool	30	5 million

What is the difference between energy and temperature?

When you heat up water, you transfer energy from the chemical store of a fuel to the thermal store of the water. The water particles move faster or vibrate more. You cannot say that the individual particles get hotter.

The energy in a thermal store and temperature are *not* the same:

● The energy in a thermal store is measured in **joules (J)**. It depends on the arrangement of the particles and how fast they are moving or vibrating.

● Temperature tells you about the average kinetic energy of the particles.

Figure 2 *The person is using a thermometer to check the meat has reached a high enough temperature.*

A **a** State the units of temperature. **b** State the unit of energy.

Figure 3 *There is more energy in the store of a heated swimming pool than in a cup of water at the same temperature.*

Figure 4 *Sparks from a sparkler can reach a temperature of 2000 °C. If a spark lands on you it does not burn. This is because there is not enough energy in a spark to damage your skin.*

What happens when you heat things up?

Heating can:

- change the energy stored within the system to increase the temperature (ready for your hot shower)
- produce a change of state (such as ice melting in your drink)
- make chemical reactions happen (such as wood burning in a bonfire).

Changes of state are examples of **physical changes**. Dissolving is also a physical change. You do not make new substances in a physical change. Many physical changes are easy to reverse. This is because the particles are simply rearranged.

> **B** Describe two physical changes that might happen in a bathroom.

A physical change is different from a **chemical reaction**. Chemical reactions, such as burning (Figure 4), involve joining atoms together in different ways. You cannot easily reverse a chemical change.

1 State the object with the least energy in a thermal store: a cup of hot water; a saucepan of hot water; a cup of cold water. *(1 mark)*
2 Explain why cooking an egg is not reversible, but melting butter is. *(1 mark)*
3 The coldest temperature is called absolute zero, or zero kelvin (0 K), but you cannot reach it. Suggest and explain what happens to the particles in a piece of metal that is cooled close to absolute zero. *(3 marks)*
4 a Estimate the volume of water in a cup. *(1 mark)*
   b Use your estimate and the data in Table 2 to estimate the volume of water in a swimming pool (Figure 3). *(4 marks)*
   c State the assumptions you made in **b**. *(1 mark)*

Units of temperature

By the 1700s there were over 30 types of ways of writing down a temperature. There are now three main scales: Farenheit (used in the USA), Celsius, and kelvin. Scientists use Celsius and kelvin.

The hottest temperature ever recorded on Earth is 56.7 °C (Figure 5).

Figure 5 *The hottest temperature ever recorded on Earth is 56.7 °C in Death Valley, USA.*

Learning outcomes

After studying this lesson you should be able to:

- define the term specific heat capacity
- apply the equation for specific heat capacity.

Specification reference: P1.2d, P1.2e

Figure 2 *Portable radiators are filled with oil, but the radiators in your house are full of water.*

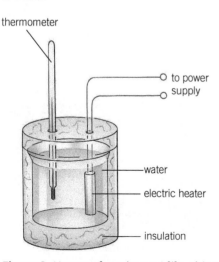

Figure 3 *You need equipment like this to measure the specific heat capacity of water.*

It is great to cool off in a swimming pool. Why does the water feel so cool when the air temperature is high?

What is specific heat capacity?

You need to transfer a great deal of energy to water to raise its temperature. The concrete around a swimming pool (Figure 1) is much hotter than the water. It takes about one fifth of the energy to raise the temperature of concrete by 1 °C (or 1 K) compared with raising the temperature of water by 1 °C.

Figure 1 *After a short time, the concrete feels much warmer than the water.*

The amount of energy needed to raise the temperature of an object depends on:

- the type of material (Figure 2)
- the mass of the material
- the temperature rise.

The energy needed to raise the temperature of 1 kg of a material by 1 K is its **specific heat capacity (J/kg °C)**. Heating increases the **internal energy** of the material. The internal energy is the energy that relates to the motion, vibration, rotation, and arrangement of the particles.

Figure 3 shows the equipment used to measure the specific heat capacity of water.

> **A** Explain how the specific heat capacity affects the rate at which concrete heats up compared with water.

How do you calculate with specific heat capacity?

You need to apply this equation to calculate with specific heat capacity:

$$\text{change in thermal energy (J)} = \text{mass (kg)} \times \text{specific heat capacity (J/kg °C)} \times \text{change in temperature (°C)}$$

Table 1 *Some specific heat capacities.*

Material	Specific heat capacity (J/kg °C)
aluminium	913
copper	330
concrete	880
water	4200
oil	1500

Energy to heat aluminium

Calculate the energy you need to transfer to raise the temperature of a 500 g block of aluminium by 10 °C. The specific heat capacity of aluminium is 913 J/kg °C.

Step 1: Write down what you know and convert quantities to standard units.

mass = 500 g = 0.5 kg

specific heat capacity = 913 J/kg °C

change in temperature = 10 °C

Step 2: Put the numbers in the equation and calculate the answer and unit.

$$\text{change in thermal energy} = \text{mass} \times \text{specific heat capacity} \times \text{change in temperature}$$

$$= 0.5\,\text{kg} \times 913\,\text{J/kg °C} \times 10\,\text{°C}$$

$$= 4565\,\text{J}$$

$$= 4600\,\text{J (2 significant figures)}$$

Figure 4 *Luckily you are mainly water, so your temperature rises only a few degrees when you are ill.*

B Copper has a specific heat capacity of 330 J/kg °C. Calculate the energy needed to raise the temperature of 0.5 kg of copper by 10 °C.

Where does specific heat capacity make a difference?

Table 1 shows some specific heat capacities for different materials.

Specific heat capacity tells you how resistant a material is to a change in temperature.

Water is especially resistant to temperature change (Figure 4). This makes it a good material to use in a central heating system. It also means that oceans are less likely to freeze.

Saucepans are made of materials with low specific heat capacities because they need to heat up quickly. However, there are other considerations when choosing a metal to make a saucepan. Gold and platinum have very low specific heat capacities, but are very expensive, and some metals are poisonous.

Figure 5 *Cooking oil reaches a high temperature so you can cook food.*

Units in equations

You can make sure that you have changed the subject of an equation correctly by checking that the units on each side of the equation are the same.

1 Describe the difference between a material with a low specific heat capacity and a material with a high specific heat capacity. *(1 mark)*

2 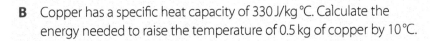 Calculate the energy needed to raise the temperature of 250 g of oil (Figure 5) by 200 °C. *(2 marks)*

3 Copy and complete Table 2. *(3 marks)*

4 Compare the time needed to heat 1 kg of water and 3 kg of oil to the same temperature using the same heater. Explain your answer. *(5 marks)*

Table 2 *Calculating specific heat capacity.*

Energy	Specific heat capacity (J/kg °C)	Mass (kg)	Change in temperature (°C)
1 MJ	4200	70	
3.78 kJ		10	3
44 kJ	880		10

Learning outcomes

After studying this lesson you should be able to:

- describe what happens in state changes
- apply the equation for specific latent heat
- compare specific heat capacity and specific latent heat.

Specification reference: P1.2d, P1.2f

Investigating cooling

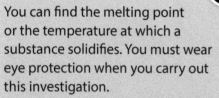

You can find the melting point or the temperature at which a substance solidifies. You must wear eye protection when you carry out this investigation.

1   Melt salol (a chemical used to make glue and wax) in a test tube in a water bath. When the salol has melted, place a thermometer in the test tube.

2   Carefully remove the test tube using tongs, and place it in a test tube rack.

3   Take the temperature every minute, and plot a graph of temperature against time.

4   Use the graph to find the the temperature at which salol solidifies.

You will need to do a risk assessment before you start this experiment.

Figure 3 *Ice can change temperature but when it is melting it does not.*

What change of state causes tropical storms, like that in Figure 1?

What happens when substances change their state?

You need to heat or cool a substance to produce a **change of state** (Figure 2).

Figure 1 *A giant hurricane seen from space.*

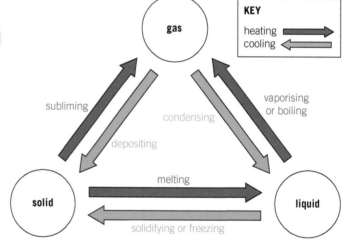

Figure 2 *Heating or cooling may change the temperature or state of a substance.*

Water in lakes or the sea evaporates to form water vapour. The energy is transferred from the thermal store of the surroundings to the water.

When water vapour condenses energy is transferred from the water to the surroundings. This is where much of the energy for tropical storms comes from.

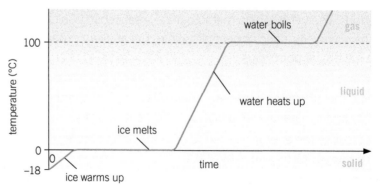

Figure 4 *If you heat ice the temperature increases only if the ice (or water) is not changing state.*

When you melt ice or boil water there is no temperature rise (Figures 3 and 4). The internal energy is increasing even though the temperature is not. The energy that is transferred is breaking the attractive forces between the water molecules.

A Explain why there is no temperature increase when water is boiling.

What is latent heat?
The **specific latent heat of fusion (or melting)** is the energy transferred when 1 kg of a substance changes from the solid state to the liquid state, or from the liquid state to the solid state.

The **specific latent heat of vaporisation** is the energy transferred when 1 kg of a substance changes from liquid to gas.

B Use the data in Table 1 to explain why a drop of ethanol evaporates from your hand more quickly than a drop of water of the same volume.

How do you calculate with specific latent heat?
You need to apply this equation to calculate with specific latent heat:

$$\text{thermal energy for a change in state (J)} = \text{mass (kg)} \times \text{specific latent heat (J/kg)}$$

Energy to melt an ice cube
Calculate the energy that you need to transfer to melt an ice cube at 0 °C with a mass of 25.0 g. The latent heat of fusion of water is 334 kJ/kg.

Step 1: Write down what you know, and convert quantities to standard units.

mass = 25.0 g = 0.025 kg

specific latent heat of fusion = 334 kJ/kg = 334 000 J/kg

Step 2: Put the numbers in the equation and calculate the answer and unit.

thermal energy for a change in state = mass × specific latent heat of fusion
= 0.025 kg × 334 000 J/kg
= 8350 J (3 significant figures)

How is specific latent heat different from specific heat capacity?
Both specific latent heat and specific heat capacity involve energy changes for 1 kg of a substance.

Latent heat is about change of state, and heat capacity is about change of temperature.

Table 1 *The specific latent heat of fusion/ melting and the specific latent heat of vaporisation for different substances.*

Substance	Specific latent heat of fusion/ melting (J/kg)	Specific latent heat of vaporisation (J/kg)
water	334 000	2 260 000
lead	24 500	871 000
ethanol	108 000	855 000

Study tip

Remember that melting point (a temperature) is not the same as latent heat of fusion (an amount of energy).

'Specific' and 'latent'

In science, the word 'specific' usually means 'per kg'. The word 'latent' means 'hidden'. It seems as if the energy is 'hidden' because the temperature does not change when the state changes.

1 Describe the changes of state in taking ice from a freezer, putting it in a saucepan, and heating until the pan is empty. *(2 marks)*

2 Calculate the energy required to:
  a melt 1.2 kg of ethanol *(2 marks)*
  b evaporate 500 g of lead. *(2 marks)*

3 Calculate the mass of ice that you could melt with the energy needed to melt 250 g of lead. *(4 marks)*

4 **a** Suggest how you could use a 2 kW kettle full of water, some digital scales, and a stopwatch to measure the specific latent heat of vaporisation of water. Include the equations you would need. *(6 marks)*
  b Explain why the number that you calculate is probably larger than the actual value. *(2 marks)*

Learning outcomes

After studying this lesson you should be able to:

- explain how the motion of the molecules in a gas is related to both its temperature and its pressure
- explain the relationship between the temperature of a gas and its pressure at constant volume.

Specification reference: P1.2g, P1.2h

Figure 1 *What will happen to the lid of the tin when you heat the air inside?*

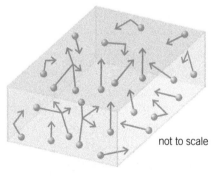

not to scale

Figure 2 *When particles in a gas collide with the container they exert a pressure.*

When you heat the air inside an empty tin as in Figure 1, what will happen to the lid?

Why do gases exert pressure?

When you blow up a balloon it gets bigger. You are increasing the number of air particles in the balloon. The particles collide with the inside surface of the balloon, like the container in Figure 2.

Each collision produces a very small force. There are many collisions, each producing an outward force over a certain area. This produces a **gas pressure**. The force on the rubber makes the balloon get bigger.

If you add more air particles to a container that *cannot* expand, the pressure increases.

> **A** State and explain what happens to the pressure inside a bicycle tyre when you get a puncture.

How does temperature affect gas pressure?

If the temperature of a gas increases, the gas particles have a higher average speed. They collide more frequently with the sides of the container. The collisions produce a bigger force over a certain area. This produces a bigger pressure (Figure 3).

You can use a pressure gauge to measure the pressure of air that is trapped in a bottle. The pressure of a gas is measured in **pascals (Pa)**. One pascal equals one newton per square metre ($1\,N/m^2$). You will sometimes see the unit kilopascals (kPa): $1\,kPa = 1000\,Pa$.

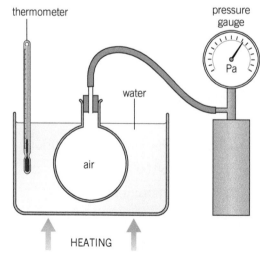

Figure 3 *The glass bottle does not expand, so the pressure increases as you heat the gas.*

> **B** Convert $100\,000\,N/m^2$ to kPa.

If you measure the pressure or volume of a gas as its temperature increases, you can draw a graph like the ones in Figure 4.

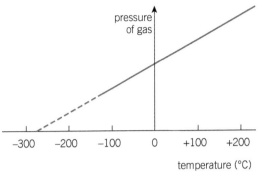
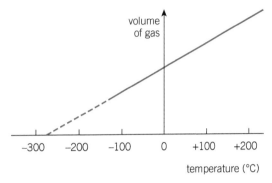

Figure 4 *Graphs showing how the pressure or volume of a gas varies with temperature. You can extrapolate to find absolute zero.*

Figure 4 shows that as you *decrease* the temperature the pressure also decreases. The dotted line shows what *would* happen if you carried on cooling the gas. The pressure would reach 0 Pa at −273.14 °C. This is 0 K, or **absolute zero**. We cannot reach absolute zero, but we can work out the value of absolute zero by extrapolating.

Extrapolating a graph

The dotted line on the graph in Figure 4 is an *extrapolation*. It shows what you estimate would happen if you continue to change the independent variable.

Sketch a copy of the graph. Extrapolate the graph so that you can predict pressure values at higher temperatures.

Assumptions in models

When you use the idea that the particles in a gas produce pressure you are using a model called *kinetic theory*. Scientists use this model to explain and predict the behaviour of gases. All models are based on assumptions. An assumption is something that you accept to be true, without proof.

You can measure the pressure of a gas using a manometer, as shown in Figure 5.

1. Describe and explain the relationship between the temperature of a gas and its pressure. *(5 marks)*

2. Explain why it is dangerous to throw a canister full of pressurised gas into a fire. *(3 marks)*

3. Describe and explain what would happen to the shape of the graph shown in Figure 4 if the tube was not connected tightly to the pressure gauge. *(2 marks)*

4. Explain the extent to which pressure is, or is not, proportional to the temperature of a gas. *(3 marks)*

Study tip

Make sure that you use the correct unit for pressure, Pa or N/m².

Synoptic link

At Key Stage 3 you learned about the link between force, area, and pressure.

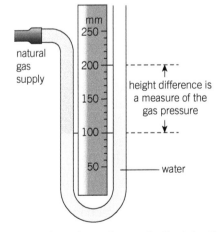

Figure 5 *If you heat the gas in the tube the height difference will increase.*

Go further

Find out the assumptions of kinetic theory.

Matter

P1.2 Changes of state

Summary questions

1 Copy and complete the sentences below.
 a Energy is measured in _____. It depends on the arrangement of particles and their _____.
 b Temperature is measured in _____ or _____. It is a measure of how _____ or _____ something is.

2 a State the type of change of state that happens when ice turns to water.
 b Explain what happens to the arrangement of the water molecules as the ice melts.
 c Describe the difference between the motion of particles in a hot solid and a cold solid.

3 a Calculate the change in energy needed to raise the temperature of 0.5 kg of oil with a specific heat capacity of 2100 J/kg°C by 50°C. Use the equation:

$$\text{change in energy in thermal store} = \text{mass} \times \text{specific heat capacity} \times \text{change in temperature}$$

 b Calculate the energy needed to melt 0.03 kg of ice with a specific latent heat of melting of 334 000 J/kg. Use the equation:

$$\text{energy for a change in state} = \text{mass} \times \text{specific latent heat}$$

4 You put the same mass of two different liquids in two identical saucepans on the same type of cooker.
 a Describe how you could find out which one has the larger specific heat capacity.
 b It takes 80 kJ to raise the temperature of 500 g of one of the liquids by 50°C. Calculate the specific heat capacity of the liquid.
 c Explain why it is difficult to measure specific heat capacity accurately in the laboratory.

5 Table 1 shows what happens to some ethanol over a 30 minute period. The mass of the ethanol is 20 g.

Table 1 Results from observation of ethanol over 30 minutes.

Time (min)	Energy transferred (kJ)	Arrangement/movement of particles
0–10	20.00	slowing down, moving closer together
10–20	18.00	close together and moving, not changing speed
20–30	0.05	slowing down

 a Describe what is happening to the ethanol in terms of change of state.
 b Describe what is happening to the ethanol in terms of density.
 c Calculate the specific latent heat of the ethanol.
 d The density of the ethanol in the first 10 minutes is 1.4×10^{-3} g/cm³. Suggest and explain what the density would be in the last 10 minutes.

6 a Copy and complete the sentences below. A gas exerts a _____ because the molecules in a gas collide with the walls of the container. If the temperature of the gas increases the molecules move _____ and collide _____ often with the container walls.
 b You have a glass bottle full of air that has been sealed. You put the bottle in a large bowl of hot water. Copy and complete Table 2 by ticking the correct column.

Table 2 Changes observed when you put a sealed bottle of air in hot water.

	Increases	Stays the same	Decreases
The mass of the gas …			
The density of the gas …			
The speed of the molecules of the gas …			
The pressure exerted by the gas …			
The volume of the gas …			

7 a Explain why the densities of a material in the liquid state and the solid state are similar, but the densities of a material in the liquid state and the gas state are not.
 b Choose the correct equation for density:

$$\text{density} = \text{mass} \times \text{volume}$$

$$\text{density} = \frac{\text{mass}}{\text{volume}}$$

$$\text{density} = \frac{\text{volume}}{\text{mass}}$$

 c Estimate the density of a person. (Hint: assume that a human is a rectangular box, so estimate height, width, and depth.)
 d Gold has a density of 19.3×10^3 kg/m³. Estimate the volume of gold that has the same mass as a person.
 e Describe how to measure the density of a silver ring.

Revision questions

1 Students investigate substances X and Y.
The density of X is 0.85 g/cm³.
The density of Y is 1.11 g/cm³.

  a i Write down the mass of X that has a
     volume of 100 cm³.   *(1 mark)*

    ii Calculate the volume of Y that has the
     same mass as 100 cm³ of X.   *(2 marks)*

  b The students heat the substances. They combine
    their results as shown in the graph.

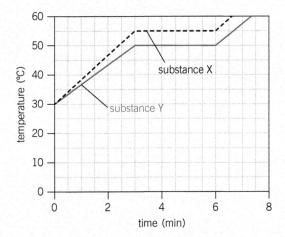

  Use the graph to determine

  i the melting temperature of X   *(1 mark)*

  ii the time taken by both X and Y to change
    from fully solid to fully liquid.   *(1 mark)*

  c Substance X has a specific heat capacity
    of 2.3 J/kg °C. Use your answer to **a i** and the graph
    to calculate the energy supplied to X in the
    first 3 minutes.   *(3 marks)*

2 Gallium is a metallic element that has a melting point of
29.8 °C.
The figure shows a piece of gallium shaped into a key. It
is melting in the palm of a hand.

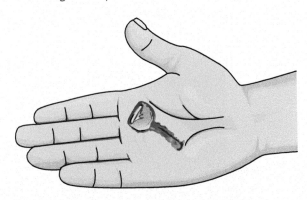

  a Explain why the gallium key is melting.
    Use ideas about particles in your answer.   *(2 marks)*

  b Describe a method for finding the volume
    of the gallium key.   *(2 marks)*

  c i The volume of the gallium key is 2.2 cm³.
     It has a mass of 13 g.
     Calculate the density of gallium.   *(2 marks)*

    ii The latent heat of fusion of gallium is 80.1 J/g.
     Use $Q = mL$ to calculate the energy needed
     to melt the gallium key.
     (Q is the thermal energy needed to melt the key,
     m is the mass of the key, and L is the latent
     heat of fusion.)   *(2 marks)*

P1.1 The particle model

- Describe how and why the model of the atom has changed.
- Describe the structure of the atom.
- State the order of magnitude sizes of the atom and of small molecules.
- Explain what density means.
- State and use the equation linking density, mass, and volume.
- Explain why substances in different states have different densities.

P1.2 Changes of state

- Describe the difference between energy and temperature.
- Describe the differences between physical and chemical changes.
- Describe what specific heat capacity is.
- Use the equation for specific heat capacity.
- Describe what happens in state changes.
- Use the equation for specific latent heat.
- Compare specific heat capacity and specific latent heat.
- Explain how a gas exerts a pressure.
- Describe the relationship between the temperature of a gas and its pressure.
- Explain the relationship between pressure and volume for a gas at constant temperature.

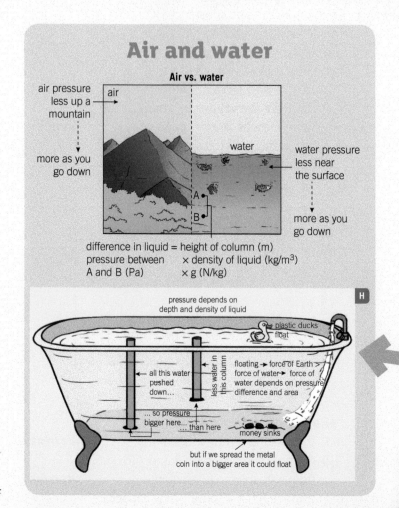

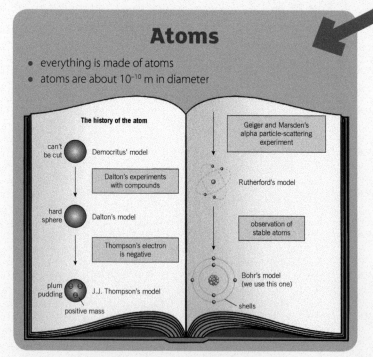

- everything is made of atoms
- atoms are about 10^{-10} m in diameter

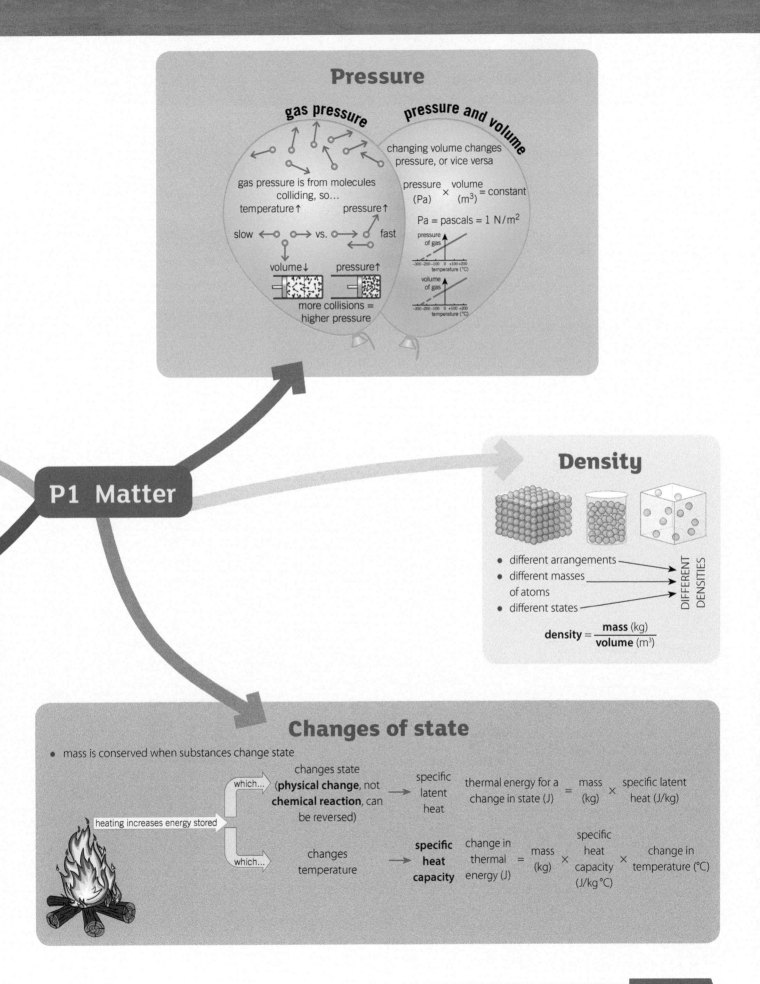

Pressure

gas pressure

gas pressure is from molecules colliding, so...

temperature↑   pressure↑

slow ←○→ vs. ○→ fast

volume↓   pressure↑

more collisions = higher pressure

pressure and volume

changing volume changes pressure, or vice versa

$$\text{pressure (Pa)} \times \text{volume (m}^3\text{)} = \text{constant}$$

Pa = pascals = 1 N/m²

pressure of gas

-300 -200 -100 0 +100 +200
temperature (°C)

volume of gas

-300 -200 -100 0 +100 +200
temperature (°C)

P1 Matter

Density

- different arrangements
- different masses of atoms
- different states

DIFFERENT DENSITIES

$$\text{density} = \frac{\text{mass (kg)}}{\text{volume (m}^3\text{)}}$$

Changes of state

- mass is conserved when substances change state

heating increases energy stored

which... → changes state (**physical change**, not **chemical reaction**, can be reversed) → specific latent heat

thermal energy for a change in state (J) = mass (kg) × specific latent heat (J/kg)

which... → changes temperature → **specific heat capacity**

change in thermal energy (J) = mass (kg) × specific heat capacity (J/kg °C) × change in temperature (°C)

P2 | Forces

P2.1 Motion

P2.1.1 Distance, time, and speed

Learning outcomes

After studying this lesson you should be able to:

- describe how to measure distance and time in a range of scenarios
- use measurements of distance and time to calculate speed
- make calculations using ratios and proportional reasoning to convert units and compute rates
- apply formulae relating distance, time, and speed for uniform motion
- calculate average speed for non-uniform motion.

Specification reference: P2.1a, P2.1b, P2.1c, P2.1g, P2.1h

The motion of a sprinter is 'non-uniform'. What does this mean? What do we mean by the 'speed of a sprinter'?

Figure 1 *Being able to measure distance and time accurately is very important in athletics.*

How do you measure distance and time in the laboratory?

Table 1 shows how to make suitably accurate and precise measurements of different moving objects in the laboratory.

Table 1 *How to measure distance and time for different objects.*

Moving object	How to measure the distance	How to measure the time
trolley moving down a ramp	use a ruler	use a stopwatch or light gates
falling object	use a ruler	use light gates

In a science lesson you usually use a ruler to measure distance, and a stop clock or stopwatch to measure time. It is difficult to measure very large or very small distances. When you use a stopwatch there is a reaction time that affects the accuracy and precision of your measurement. You can measure very short periods of time using light gates (Figures 2 and 4) – a timer starts and stops when an object interrupts a light beam.

You can also use **ultrasound** (high-frequency sound waves) to measure distance (Figure 3). The device measures the time taken for a pulse to travel there and back. It uses this value, and the speed of the pulse, to work out the distance.

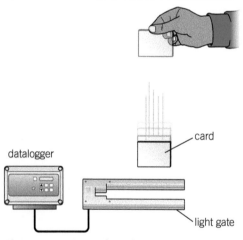

Figure 2 *A piece of card passes a beam of light and a datalogger works out the time.*

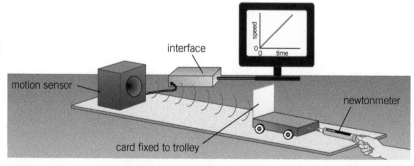

Figure 3 *You can connect some motion sensors to a computer to show a graph of distance or speed against time.*

Investigating speed and surface

Plan an investigation to find out how the average speed of a trolley down a ramp depends on the surface on the ramp.

You need to find the time it takes a trolley to travel a set distance down a ramp, and use the formula to calculate average speed. Then change the surface and repeat.

A Suggest the best device to obtain a precise measurement of the length of an aeroplane.

How do you calculate using the equation for speed?

In uniform motion speed does not change. You need to be able to recall and apply this equation linking distance, speed, and time for uniform motion:

distance travelled (m) = speed (m/s) × time (s)

Motion where speed changes is called non-uniform motion. If you run 100 metres in 10 seconds your average speed is 10 m/s, but you do not travel at 10 m/s for the entire race. 10 m/s is an *average* speed.

$$\text{average speed (m/s)} = \frac{\text{total distance (m)}}{\text{total time (s)}}$$

B   Change the subject of the equation to 'total time'. Show your working.

How do you convert between units?

The **SI unit** of distance is the metre, and the SI unit of time is the second, but you usually use miles and hours when you measure speed in a car (Figure 5).

There are 1000 m/km – this means there are 1000 metres in one kilometre. There are 1609 m/mile. There are 3600 s/hour – this means there are 3600 seconds in one hour.

Converting from mph to m/s

Convert 30 mph to m/s.

Step 1: Convert the miles to metres:

30 miles = 30 miles × 1609 m/mile

= 48 270 m

Step 2: Convert hours to seconds.

1 hour = 1 hour × 3600 s/hour

= 3600 s

Step 3: Use the equation for speed to find the answer.

$$\text{speed} = \frac{\text{distance}}{\text{time}}$$

$$= \frac{48\,270\,\text{m}}{3600\,\text{s}}$$

= 13 m/s (2 significant figures)

1   Describe in detail how to measure your walking speed.   (*3 marks*)

2   Convert 50 mph to m/s.   (*3 marks*)

3   A 5 cm piece of card moves past a light gate. The time on the datalogger is 0.01 seconds.
   a Explain why you need to use light gates.   (*1 mark*)
   b Calculate the average speed of the card.   (*2 marks*)
   c State and explain the number of significant figures in your answer.   (*2 marks*)

4   **a** You can bounce a pulse of light off the Moon. It takes 2.8 seconds to get back. The speed of light is 3.0×10^8 m/s. Calculate the distance to the Moon.   (*2 marks*)
   b Calculate the ratio of the speed of light to the motorway speed limit of 70 mph to the nearest order of magnitude.   (*4 marks*)

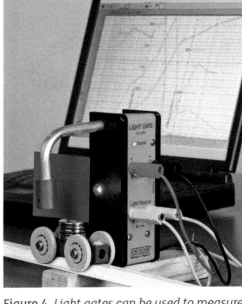

Figure 4 *Light gates can be used to measure the time when a trolley passes a certain point on a ramp.*

Figure 5 *A car's speedometer shows that 30 mph is about 45 km/h, which is 13 m/s.*

Showing uncertainties

When you make measurements there are always uncertainties. You can represent these uncertainties on a graph with 'error bars'.

Study tip

Notice that when you convert between mph and m/s the answer is about half. You can use this to check that your calculation is correct.

Learning outcomes

After studying this lesson you should be able to:

- explain the difference between a scalar and a vector
- explain the difference between distance and displacement
- explain the difference between speed and velocity.

Specification reference: P2.1d

Figure 1 *Whether you collide with the other car depends on your velocity, not your speed.*

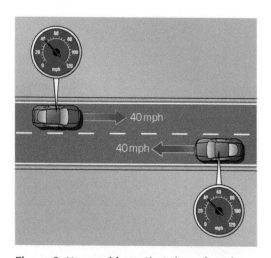

Figure 3 *You could say that the red car has a velocity of +40 mph, and the blue car has a velocity of -40 mph.*

You are travelling in a car on a single track road at 50 mph (Figure 1). There is another car on the road travelling at 50 mph. Will you collide?

What is the difference between a vector and a scalar?

Some quantities, such as force, have a magnitude (size) *and* a direction. Force is a **vector**. You represent a vector with an arrow. The length of the arrow shows the magnitude, and the direction of the arrow shows the direction.

The measurement that you make with a stop clock is a **scalar**. It has a magnitude (e.g., 10 s) but no direction.

What is the difference between displacement and distance?

Imagine that you are visiting some friends, Amy and Sunita (Figure 2).

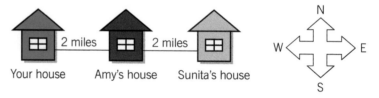

Figure 2 *Amy lives 2 miles east of your house and Sunita lives 2 miles east of Amy.*

When you get home you have travelled a total distance of 8 miles. The distance *from the place that you start* is 0 miles. This is called the **displacement**. Displacement is a vector, so it has direction as well.

When you were at Amy's house your displacement was 2 miles east. Alternatively, we could say east is positive, so the displacement is +2 miles.

> **A** State your displacement when you are at Sunita's house.

What is the difference between speed and velocity?

To a physicist, speed and **velocity** are not the same thing.

- Speed is a *scalar* quantity, so 15 m/s is a measurement of speed.
- Velocity is a *vector* quantity. It has a direction as well as magnitude (Figure 3), so 15 m/s south is a velocity.

You can decide that the velocity in a certain direction, for example, left to right, is positive. Velocities in the opposite direction are negative.

Will you collide on a single track road with a car travelling at the same speed? It depends on your direction. If your velocity has the same sign then you will not collide because you are both travelling in the same direction.

How do you add vector quantities?

You can add vectors, but you must take into account the + sign or the − sign (Figure 4).

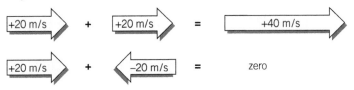

Figure 4 *How to add vector quantities.*

B Show two velocities in opposite directions that, when added, produce a velocity of −10 m/s.

Figure 6 *A sat nav device will tell you if your velocity, not your speed, is wrong.*

Calculating displacement and distance

You walk 200 m east, 400 m north, then 200 m west. Calculate the distance you travelled and your displacement.

Step 1: Add the distances to find the total distance.

distance travelled = 200 m + 400 m + 300 m
= 900 m

Step 2: Use vectors to work out the displacement.

200 m east + 200 m west = zero
displacement = 400 m north

1 Explain why temperature is a scalar. *(1 mark)*

2 You can use a pedometer to measure the distance you walk. Explain why it would read zero if you went for a walk and then returned home, if it measured displacement instead of distance. *(1 mark)*

3 **a** In Figure 2 you have a displacement of −2 miles when you are at David's house. Describe where to draw David's house on the diagram. *(2 marks)*
  b If it takes you 30 minutes to walk to David's house, calculate your velocity in mph. *(2 marks)*

4 You are cycling at 15 mph behind a lorry travelling at 30 mph in the same positive direction.
  a Calculate the velocity, in mph, of the lorry relative to you. *(2 marks)*
  b Explain how your motion appears to the lorry driver. *(2 marks)*

Learning outcomes

After studying this lesson you should be able to:

- apply formulae relating distance, time, and speed for motion with uniform acceleration.

Specification reference: P2.1h

Table 1 *Time taken to reach 60 mph for different vehicles.*

Vehicle	Time to get from 0 to 60 mph (s)
motorcycle (Suzuki)	2.4
car (Porsche)	5.0
aeroplane (777)	5.9

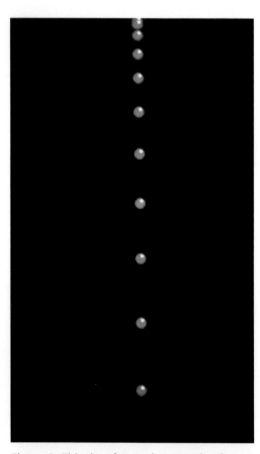

Figure 2 *This time-lapse photograph taken with a flashing light shows a ball accelerating because of the gravitational force on it.*

Imagine a race between a car, a motorcycle, and an aeroplane (Figure 1). Which vehicle will reach 60 mph first?

What is acceleration?

When you want to describe how fast a car is, you might talk about the time that it takes to get from 0 mph to 60 mph (27 m/s), as shown in Table 1.

But what is changing? The values in Table 1 were measured for vehicles travelling in straight lines, so the same figures show how quickly the vehicles change their speed or their velocity. You usually use + or − signs with velocities to show the direction of motion. The change in velocity per second is called **acceleration**. Uniform acceleration means that the acceleration does not change.

Figure 1 *Which vehicle wins depends on their acceleration.*

A Describe what you would see in the first few seconds of a race between the car, the motorcycle, and the aeroplane.

How do you calculate acceleration if you know the change in velocity?

You need to be able to recall and apply this equation for uniform acceleration:

$$\text{acceleration (m/s}^2) = \frac{\text{change in velocity (m/s)}}{\text{time (s)}}$$

An acceleration of 5 m/s² means that the speed increases by 5 m/s each second. The unit m/s² means m/s per second.

Calculating acceleration 1

Use the data in Table 1 to calculate the acceleration of the motorcycle. Assume all velocities are positive.

Step 1: Write down what you know.

change in velocity = +60 mph = +27 m/s

time = 2.4 s

Step 2: Use this equation to calculate the acceleration.

$$\text{acceleration} = \frac{\text{change in velocity}}{\text{time}}$$

$$= \frac{+27 \text{ m/s}}{2.4 \text{ s}}$$

$$= +11 \text{ m/s}^2 \text{ (2 significant figures)}$$

Do you use speed or velocity to calculate acceleration?

What is the difference between the two situations in Figure 3?

In both situations the *change in speed* is 5 m/s. However, the blue car is speeding up, and the red car is slowing down.

Table 2 *Calculating acceleration.*

	Initial velocity (m/s)	Final velocity (m/s)	Change	Change in velocity after 2 seconds (m/s)	Acceleration (m/s²)
Blue car	+10	+15	speeding up	+5	+2.5
Red car	+10	+5	slowing down	−5	−2.5

It is better to say 'negative acceleration' rather than 'deceleration'.

B Show how the acceleration values in Table 2 were calculated.

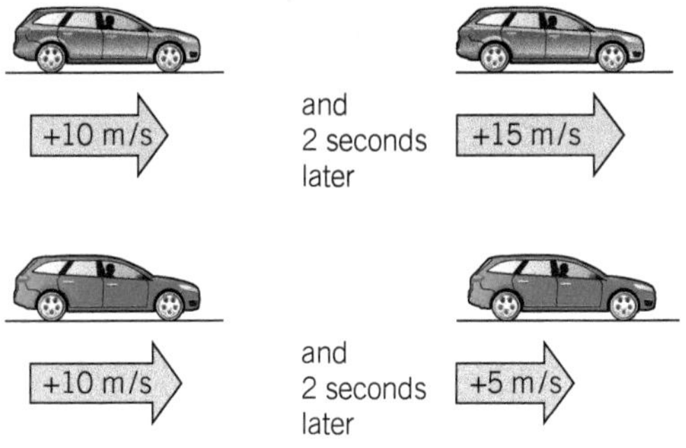

How do you calculate acceleration if you know the final and initial velocity?

You can calculate the change in velocity using:

change in velocity (m/s) = final velocity (m/s) − initial velocity (m/s)

So the equation for acceleration becomes:

$$\text{acceleration (m/s}^2) = \frac{\text{final velocity (m/s)} - \text{initial velocity (m/s)}}{\text{time (s)}}$$

Calculating acceleration 2

Calculate the acceleration of a car that changes from a velocity of +20 m/s to −5.0 m/s in 10 seconds.

Step 1: Identify the initial velocity, the final velocity, and the time.

initial velocity = +20 m/s

final velocity = −5.0 m/s

time = 10 seconds

Step 2: Use the equation for acceleration to find the answer.

$$\text{acceleration} = \frac{\text{final velocity} - \text{initial velocity}}{\text{time}}$$
$$= \frac{(-5.0 \text{ m/s}) - (+20 \text{ m/s})}{10 \text{ s}}$$
$$= -2.5 \text{ m/s}^2 \text{ (2 significant figures)}$$

The acceleration due to gravity is 9.81 m/s², or about 10 m/s². Another way of thinking about this acceleration is that when something is falling vertically (Figure 2), during each second its downwards velocity increases by about 10 m/s.

  and 2 seconds later

+10 m/s   +15 m/s

  and 2 seconds later

+10 m/s   +5 m/s

Figure 3 *Two cars changing speed.*

1 Calculate the acceleration of the car and the aeroplane in Table 1.   *(4 marks)*

2 The motorcycle is travelling at 35 m/s. Ten seconds later it is travelling at 15 m/s in the same direction.
   a Calculate the acceleration. *(2 marks)*
   b State and explain the sign of the acceleration.   *(2 marks)*

3 **a** Describe in words what is happening in Calculating acceleration 2.   *(2 marks)*
   b Explain why this scenario is unlikely for a bicycle.   *(1 mark)*

4 **a** A lorry has an acceleration of −6 m/s². It is now travelling at +20 m/s. Calculate the initial velocity if the acceleration happened over 4 seconds. *(4 marks)*
   b Explain how you can tell that the initial velocity is bigger than the final velocity.   *(1 mark)*

Learning outcomes

After studying this lesson you should be able to:

- relate the motion of an object to the line on a distance–time graph
- describe what the slope of a distance–time graph tells you
- use a distance–time graph to calculate speed

Specification reference: P2.1e

Figure 1 *Crossing a ravine using a rope bridge is not easy.*

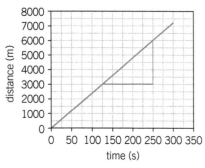

Figure 2 *A distance–time graph for a car.*

A
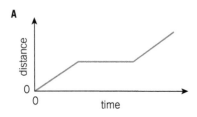

B
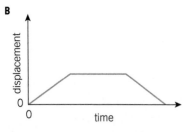

Figure 3 *These two graphs show the same journey.*

You can use graphs to represent journeys ... and some journeys are trickier than others (Figure 1). What does a distance–time graph tell you?

What does a graph of distance against time mean?

A graph of distance against time tells you about the speed of an object on its journey. The speed is equal to the **gradient** (or **slope**) of the graph.

- A straight line means the object's speed is constant because the gradient does not change.
- A horizontal line means that the object is not moving.
- The steeper the line, the faster the object is travelling.

Calculating speed from a graph

Calculate the speed from the distance–time graph in Figure 2.

Step 1: Draw a right-angled triangle under the line.

Step 2: From the triangle, find the change in distance and the change in time.

$$\text{change in distance} = 6000\,\text{m} - 3000\,\text{m}$$
$$= 3000\,\text{m}$$
$$\text{change in time} = 250\,\text{s} - 125\,\text{s}$$
$$= 125\,\text{s}$$

Step 3: Use the equation for speed to find the answer.

$$\text{speed} = \frac{\text{change in distance}}{\text{time}}$$
$$= \frac{3000\,\text{m}}{125\,\text{s}}$$
$$= 24\,\text{m/s (2 significant figures)}$$

A Draw a second triangle on the graph, and use it to show that the speed is 24 m/s.

How is a distance–time graph different from a displacement–time graph?

A distance–time graph (Figure 3**A**) shows the total distance travelled.

If you plot a displacement–time graph (Figure 3**B**), then the gradient can be positive, zero, or negative. The gradient of the graph is the velocity, so it has a direction as well as a magnitude.

Synoptic link

You were introduced to distance–time graphs at Key Stage 3.

B Explain why the gradient of a distance–time graph is always zero or positive.

Calculating velocity from a graph

Calculate the velocity at a time of 650 seconds on the graph of Figure 4.

Step 1: Draw a right-angled triangle under the line, e.g., between 350 s and 900 s.

Step 2: Find the change in displacement and the change in time from the triangle.

change in displacement = final displacement (at 900 s) – initial displacement (at 350 s)

= 50 m – 400 m

= –350 m

change in time = 900 s – 350 s

= 550 s

Step 3: Use the equation for velocity to find the answer.

$$velocity = \frac{change\ in\ displacement}{time}$$

$$= \frac{-350\ m}{550\ s}$$

= –0.64 m/s (2 significant figures)

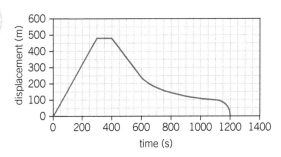

Figure 4 *Displacement–time graph showing a journey from your house to the shop and back again.*

Study tip

Sometimes axes will be shown in units that include prefixes (e.g., mm, km). Make sure that you convert to standard units.

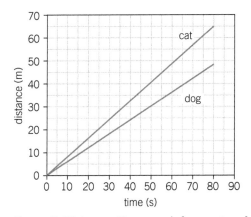

Figure 5 *Distance–time graph for a cat and a dog.*

1 Figure 5 shows a distance–time graph for a cat and a dog. Both animals are running.
   a State how you know that the cat is running faster than the dog. *(1 mark)*
   b Calculate the speed of each animal. *(4 marks)*

2 Describe the journey shown in the distance–time and displacement–time graphs in Figure 3. *(3 marks)*

3 Sketch a displacement–time graph for a ball that you throw up in the air. *(3 marks)*

4 Look at the graph in Figure 6.
   a Suggest a more appropriate label for the *y*-axis. *(1 mark)*
   b Calculate the speed in all three sections of the graph. *(5 marks)*

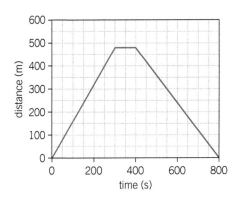

Figure 6 *A graph to represent a journey.*

Learning outcomes

After studying this lesson you should be able to:

- interpret velocity–time graphs
- use a velocity–time graph to calculate acceleration
- use a velocity–time graph to calculate the displacement.

Specification reference: P2.1e, P2.1f

Figure 1 *The bobsleigh race is all about speed.*

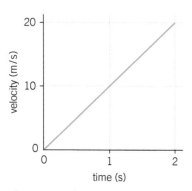

Figure 2 *Velocity–time graph for a falling mobile phone. Downwards is positive.*

Figure 3 *The velocity–time graph of a ball that goes up and then down shows positive and negative values.*

A bobsleigh team trains hard to maximise their rate of change of velocity (Figure 1). How do you work out acceleration from a graph?

What can you deduce from the gradient of a graph?

H The gradient of any graph with time on the *x*-axis tells you about a *rate of change with time*. The rate of change of speed or velocity with time tells you the acceleration.

Table 1 *Which graphs you can plot using which measurements.*

If you measure…	you can plot a…	… and the gradient is equal to…	…so then you can plot…	… and the gradient is equal to…
distance travelled and time	distance–time graph	speed	speed–time graph	acceleration (magnitude only)
distance from a starting point and time	displacement–time graph	velocity (speed + direction)	velocity–time graph	acceleration (magnitude + direction)

A State which of the quantities in Table 1 are vectors.

How do you calculate acceleration from a velocity–time graph?

Calculating acceleration from a graph

Figure 2 shows the velocity–time graph for a falling mobile phone. Calculate the acceleration of a mobile phone when it is dropped from a cliff.

Step 1: Take readings from the graph to find the change in speed and change in time.

$$\text{change in speed} = +20\,\text{m/s} - 0\,\text{m/s}$$
$$= +20\,\text{m/s}$$
$$\text{change in time} = 2\,\text{s} - 0\,\text{s} = 2\,\text{s}$$

Step 2: Use the equation for acceleration to find the answer.

$$\text{acceleration} = \frac{\text{change in velocity}}{\text{change in time}}$$
$$= \frac{+20\,\text{m/s}}{2\,\text{s}} = +10\,\text{m/s}^2 \text{ (1 significant figure)}$$

This is the acceleration due to gravity.

The acceleration is positive, so it is in the same direction as the velocity. The phone speeds up.

You can take readings from the graph in Figure 4 to find the acceleration between points C and D. The initial velocity is *bigger* than the final velocity. The acceleration is negative. Its value is −0.35 m/s². The cyclist is slowing down.

B Show that the acceleration between points A and B is 0.7 m/s².

In the examples of the falling phone and the cyclist, the object or person is moving in the *same* direction all the time. The velocity is positive.

If you roll a ball up a hill it first rolls up, and then rolls down, so the direction changes. The velocity is positive first, then negative (Figure 5).

H How do you calculate distance travelled?

The distance travelled is the area under a speed–time graph. The displacement is the area under a velocity–time graph. You can find the area by using triangles, rectangles, or by counting squares. You multiply speed and time to get distance.

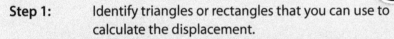

Calculating displacement from graphs

Calculate the cyclist's total displacement in Figure 4.

Step 1: Identify triangles or rectangles that you can use to calculate the displacement.

There are triangles from 0 s to 10 s and from 30 s to 50 s.

There is a rectangle from 10 s to 30 s.

Step 2: Read the lengths from the graphs and use them to calculate the area.

$$\text{area from 0 s to 10 s} = \frac{1}{2}\text{base} \times \text{height}$$
$$= \frac{1}{2} \times 10\,\text{s} \times 7\,\text{m/s} = 35\,\text{m}$$

$$\text{area from 10 s to 30 s} = \text{base} \times \text{height}$$
$$= 20\,\text{s} \times 7\,\text{m/s} = 140\,\text{m}$$

$$\text{area from 30 s to 50 s} = \frac{1}{2}\text{base} \times \text{height}$$
$$= \frac{1}{2} \times 20\,\text{s} \times 7\,\text{m/s} = 70\,\text{m}$$

Step 3: Calculate the total displacement.

total displacement = 35 m + 140 m + 70 m = 245 m

Alternatively you can find the displacement by counting squares.

Step 1: Work out the distance represented by each square.

Each square represents a distance of 0.5 m/s × 2.5 s = 1.25 m

Step 2: Count the number of squares and multiply the distance per square by the number of squares to find the displacement.

Add together parts of squares to make whole squares.

Number of squares = 196

Total displacement = 196 squares × 1.25 m/square
= 245 m = 250 m (2 significant figures)

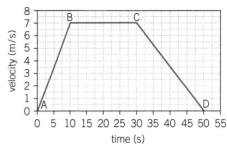

Figure 4 *Velocity–time graph for a cyclist.*

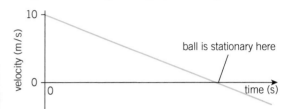

Figure 5 *Velocity–time graph for a rolling ball.*

If you are reading off scales rather than using triangles make sure the graph starts at (0, 0).

1 Look at the graph in Figure 6.

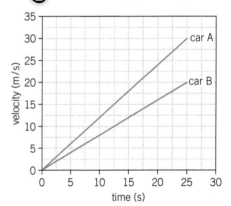

Figure 6 *Velocity–time graph.*

a State how you know that car A has the bigger acceleration. (*1 mark*)

b Calculate the acceleration of each car. (*4 marks*)

2 Describe in words the motion of the cyclist in Figure 4. (*3 marks*)

3 Explain why you can calculate the distance travelled from either a speed–time graph or a velocity–time graph. (*1 mark*) **H**

4 Sketch a velocity–time graph for a ball you drop from the time when you drop it until it reaches the top of its first bounce. (*4 marks*)

Learning outcomes

After studying this lesson you should be able to:

- apply the equation for kinetic energy
- apply the equation that links initial velocity, final velocity, acceleration, and distance travelled.

Specification reference: P2.1g

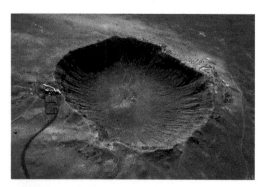

Figure 1 *This crater in Arizona is over 1 km in diameter. It was produced by a massive meteor moving very fast.*

Figure 2 *Mass and speed affect the kinetic energy of an object.*

You have to transfer a lot of energy to make a big hole (Figure 1). How do you calculate the energy of moving objects?

What is an equation of motion, and how do you use it?

There are equations that link velocities, acceleration, distance, and time for objects that have constant acceleration. You need to be able to apply this equation of motion to calculate a final velocity, initial velocity, acceleration, or displacement:

(final velocity (m/s))² − (initial velocity (m/s))²

$$= 2 \times \text{acceleration (m/s}^2) \times \text{distance (m)}$$

Physicists refer to displacement in the equation, not distance. However, here we use distance in the equation because, in the examples you will see, distance is measured in one direction only. This means that distance and displacement have the same value.

A Change the subject of this equation to 'distance'.

Calculating velocity

When dropped, a tennis ball falls a distance of 1.5 m with an acceleration of 9.8 m/s² (ignoring air resistance). Calculate the final velocity.

Step 1: Write down what you know.

initial velocity = 0 m/s

acceleration = 10 m/s²

distance = 1.5 m

Step 2: Make the final velocity the subject of the equation.

(final velocity)² = (2 × acceleration × distance) + (initial velocity)²

Step 3: Calculate the final velocity.

(final velocity)² = (2 × 10 m/s² × 1.5 m) + (0 m/s)²

= 30 m²/s²

final velocity = √30 m²/s²

= 5.5 m/s (2 significant figures)

How do you calculate kinetic energy?

You have learned that energy can be transferred to and from a **kinetic store**. A store is a system for which we can do an energy calculation – energy is a quantity (a number with joules as the unit).

You need to be able to recall and apply this equation to calculate **kinetic energy** (energy in a kinetic store):

kinetic energy (J) = 0.5 × mass (kg) × (speed (m/s))²

B State what happens to the kinetic energy if you double the mass and the speed does not change.

Calculating kinetic energy

Calculate the kinetic energy of a tennis ball (Figure 2) moving at 80 mph, which is 36 m/s.

The ball has a mass of 50 g.

Step 1: Write down what you know. Choose the values with standard units.

mass = 50 g = 50×10^{-3} kg

speed = 36 m/s

Step 2: Use the equation for kinetic energy to find the answer.

kinetic energy = $0.5 \times$ mass $\times$ (speed)^2

$= 0.5 \times 50 \times 10^{-3}$ kg $\times$ (36 m/s)^2

$= 32$ J (2 significant figures)

same mass

slow
lower kinetic energy

fast
higher kinetic energy

same speed

small mass
lower kinetic energy

large mass
higher kinetic energy

Figure 3 *Fast-moving objects with a big mass have very large amounts of kinetic energy.*

Go further

The equation of motion in the example *Calculating velocity* is just one of four equations of motion. Find out what the other equations are, and how they are derived.

Study tips

Remember that you have to square quantities *first* before you multiply, divide, add, or subtract.

If the question says 'at rest' then it means that the initial velocity is zero.

1 Calculate the kinetic energy in kJ of a car of mass 600 kg travelling with a speed of 10 m/s. *(2 marks)*

2 A train has an initial velocity of 50 m/s, and a constant acceleration of −2 m/s². Calculate the distance over which its speed changes to 30 m/s. *(2 marks)*

3 **a** Calculate the acceleration of a car initially travelling at 50 mph that comes to a stop in a distance of 100 m. Start by calculating the initial velocity in m/s. *(5 marks)*
  b Explain why doubling the speed multiplies the kinetic energy by a factor of four. *(2 marks)*
  c Copy and complete Table 1 *without using a calculator.* Explain how you got your answers. *(6 marks)*

Table 1 *Mass, speed, and kinetic energy.*

Object	Mass (kg)	Speed (m/s)	Kinetic energy (J)
football A	0.40	20	80
football B	0.40	60	
tennis ball A	0.04	20	
tennis ball B	0.04		2

Calculating speed from kinetic energy

Calculate the speed of a tennis player (Figure 2) with the same kinetic energy as the tennis ball in the example *Calculating kinetic energy*.

Step 1: Write down what you know and estimate the mass.

mass = 70 kg

energy = 32 J

Step 2: Make speed the subject of the equation.

$$speed = \sqrt{\frac{(kinetic\ energy)}{(0.5 \times mass)}}$$

Step 3: Calculate the speed.

$$speed = \sqrt{\frac{32\,J}{0.5 \times 70\,kg}}$$

$= 0.95$ m/s (2 significant figures)

Synoptic link

You learnt about energy transfer between stores at Key Stage 3.

Forces

P2.1 Motion

Summary questions

1 a Select the two measurements that you need in order to calculate speed:

distance   acceleration   temperature   time

b Select all the units of speed:

m   km/h   km/s   mph   h

c Write down an appropriate measuring instrument for measuring distance and time in the following situations:

- distance across the classroom
- time to walk across the classroom
- time for a tennis ball to fall to the ground.

2 a A dog runs across a park, a distance of 40 m, in a time of 5 seconds. Calculate its speed.

b Explain why the speed that you calculated is the average speed.

c A flea jumps off the dog and changes its speed by 1.2 m/s in a time of 0.8 milliseconds. Calculate its acceleration. (1 ms = 10^{-3} s)

d Compare the kinetic energy of the dog and the flea.

3 a Explain the difference between a vector and a scalar.

b i Explain how you know that a graph is showing speed against time and not velocity against time.

ii Runners in a beep test run between two markers at a steady speed of 4 m/s in each direction. Sketch a velocity–time graph for the beep test.

c i A runner travelling at a speed of 6 m/s is passed by a car travelling at 15 m/s. Calculate the velocity of the car relative to the runner.

ii A bus travelling in the opposite direction passes the runner with a speed of 10 m/s. Calculate the velocity of the bus relative to the runner.

4 a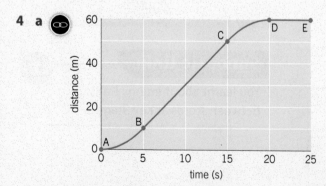

Figure 1 *Distance–time graph for a motorcycle.*

i Look at Figure 1. Describe the motion of the motorcycle shown in the graph.

ii Calculate the speed between B and C.

iii Describe how to calculate the speed on the curved sections of the graph.

b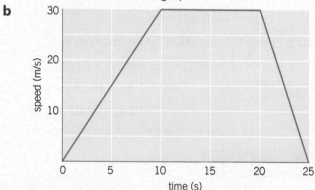

Figure 2 *Speed–time graph for a car.*

i Look at Figure 2. Describe the motion of the car shown in the graph.

ii Calculate the acceleration between 20 s and 25 s.

c i Calculate the distance travelled between 20 s and 25 s. **H**

ii Use the equation of motion:

(final velocity (m/s))^2 − (initial velocity (m/s))^2 = 2 × acceleration (m/s^2) × distance (m)

to show that the distance travelled is the same as you have calculated in part **i**.

5 A student decides to get off a London Underground train at one station and race it overland to the next station. The train travels a distance of 0.24 miles. They both arrive at the station 1 minute 20 seconds later.

a Calculate the average speed of the train in m/s and mph. (There are 1609 m in a mile.)

b Suggest and explain how it might be possible for the student and the train to have the same acceleration.

c i The mass of the train is 60 000 kg. Use the average speed of the train to estimate how fast the runner would need to travel to have the same kinetic energy.

ii Comment on your answer.

Revision questions

1 The product description of a measuring wheel is shown on a web page.

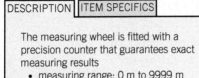

DESCRIPTION | ITEM SPECIFICS

The measuring wheel is fitted with a precision counter that guarantees exact measuring results
- measuring range: 0 m to 9999 m
- resolution: 0.1 m
- mass approx.: 1.2 kg
- wheel circumference: 0.5 m

 ADD TO BASKET

a State the measuring range to the nearest kilometre. *(1 mark)*

b Suggest what is meant by the term 'resolution 0.1 m'. *(1 mark)*

c Describe how the measuring wheel should be used to measure a distance of 50 m. *(2 marks)*

d A student uses the measuring wheel to measure the circumference of an indoor athletics track. She walks at a steady speed and she measures 200 m. It takes her 2 minutes and 15 seconds to complete her measurement.

  i Explain why the student's velocity changes, **H** even though she is walking at a steady speed. *(2 marks)*

  ii Calculate the speed of the student. *(3 marks)*

  iii State the displacement of the student when she has completed her measurement. *(1 mark)*

2 A teacher demonstrates how to use a datalogger and a light gate to find the speed of a falling object. She drops a piece of card through the light gate sensors.

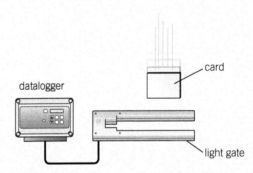

a Explain, in detail, how the datalogger and the light gate are used to find the speed of the falling piece of card. *(4 marks)*

b The acceleration of the falling piece of card is found by using two light gates, one placed above the other and both connected to the datalogger.
Explain how the measurements taken by the datalogger are used to find the acceleration of the falling piece of card. *(3 marks)*

Learning outcomes

After studying this lesson you should be able to:

- recall examples of ways in which objects interact
- describe how such examples involve interactions between pairs of objects
- recall Newton's Third Law.

Specification reference: P2.2a, P2.2b, P2.2c, P2.2o

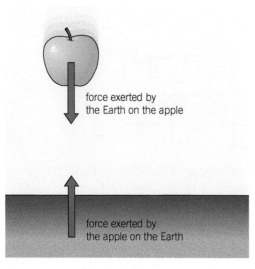

force exerted by the Earth on the apple

force exerted by the apple on the Earth

Figure 2 Gravitational forces act in pairs. In this chapter non-contact forces are shown by red arrows, and contact forces by blue or green arrows.

Synoptic link

You learned about gravitational, magnetic, and electric fields at Key Stage 3.

The diver on the diving board in Figure 1 feels a contact force, but there is also a non-contact force on him. How are these forces the same? How are they different?

How do forces arise?

You have mass and so does the Earth. The gravitational interaction between you and the Earth produces the same magnitude (size) force on both you *and* the Earth. Pairs of forces arise when objects interact. In an interaction pair:

Figure 1 Divers experience contact and non-contact forces when they dive off a board.

- Each force acts on a *different* object.
- The forces are the *same* size, and type (e.g., gravitational).
- The forces act in *opposite* directions.

This is **Newton's Third Law**. Sometimes this law is written as:

"For every action there is an equal and opposite reaction."

It is more useful to think of the law as:

"Forces always come in pairs."

A Compare the two forces in an interaction pair (e.g., Figure 2).

What are non-contact forces?

Some objects interact without being in contact with each other. You have learned about these **non-contact forces**:

- electrostatics
- magnetism
- gravity.

These forces arise because charges, magnets, and masses interact at a distance. Electric charges and magnets both repel and attract, but gravity only attracts. These forces are the result of fields. A field is a region where an electrical charge, a magnetic material, or a mass experiences a force. Forces are vectors so you represent a force with a **force arrow**. You usually draw force arrows for non-contact forces from the centre of the object.

B State one way in which the force of gravity is different from electrostatic and magnetic forces.

If you are on a diving board, the gravitational force of the Earth pulls you towards the centre of the Earth. You are exerting a force on the Earth, but the mass of the Earth is so large that the Earth does not move towards you by an amount we can measure.

What are contact forces?

When you stand on a diving board the board pushes up on you. Solid surfaces can exert a force on objects that exert a force on them. You draw contact force arrows from the point of contact.

The bonds between the atoms behave like springs (Figure 3).

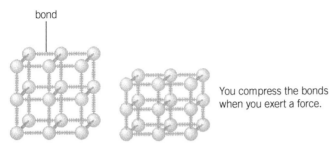

bond

You compress the bonds when you exert a force.

Figure 3 *An object will deform a surface until the normal contact force balances the weight.*

Figure 4 *When a tennis ball hits a racket it is deformed.*

Table 1 *Some examples of contact forces.*

Example of contact force	The interaction pair	The mechanism that produces it
friction on a sliding box	• the force of the box on the surface • the force of the surface on the box	The atoms that make up the surfaces interact when rough surfaces slide over each other.
drag on a falling leaf (drag is air resistance or water resistance)	• the force of the falling leaf on the air • the force of the air on the leaf	The particles of the liquid or gas collide with the object, and the object pushes them away.
normal contact force acting on an elephant	• the force of the elephant on the ground • the force of the ground on the elephant	Solid objects deform slightly when you exert a force on them (Figure 3). The bonds between the particles are compressed.
upthrust on a floating boat	• the force of the boat on the water • the force of the water on the boat	Gravity produces pressure differences in a fluid. The pressure produces a net upwards force.
tension in the cord of a bungee jumper	• the force of the bungee jumper on the bungee cord • the force of the bungee cord on the bungee jumper	Solid objects deform slightly when you exert a force on them (Figure 4). The bonds between the particles are stretched.

Remember that **weight** is shorthand for the gravitational force of one object on another.

Forces are vectors, so we represent them by an arrow. The length of the arrow shows the magnitude, and the direction of the arrow shows the direction of the force.

1   Explain why tension and compression are similar.   (*1 mark*)
2   Compare the physical interactions that occur when you are sitting in a chair and when you are floating in a swimming pool.   (*2 marks*)
3   Explain why the force of water resistance is larger than air resistance.   (*2 marks*)
4   **a**   Use what you know about the structure of the atom to suggest why the normal force is produced by a non-contact force.   (*2 marks*)
    b   Explain why the normal force is still a 'contact' force.   (*1 mark*)

What is 'normal'?

In physics, the word 'normal' does not mean regular or ordinary. It means that the force acts at *right angles* (90°) to the surface. Write down where you learned about 'the normal' at Key Stage 3. (Hint: you were drawing rays!)

Learning outcomes

After studying this lesson you should be able to:

- describe examples of the forces acting on an object or system
- use free body diagrams to describe how two or more forces lead to a resultant force on an object
- use vector diagrams to show resolution of forces, a net force (resultant force), and equilibrium situations.

Specification reference: P2.2e, P2.2f, P2.2g, P2.2h

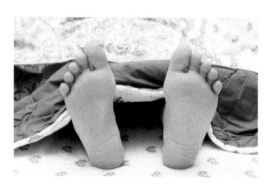

Figure 1 *When you are lying in bed there are two downwards forces due to your interaction with the duvet and Earth. The resultant of these forces is balanced by the force of the bed on you.*

How many forces are acting on you when you are lying in bed (Figure 1)?

What is a free body diagram?

A **free body diagram** is a diagram that shows the forces acting on a *single* object, such as you in bed, or a skier doing a ski jump.

You usually represent the object as a simple dot or box and the forces acting on the object by force arrows. You can use your diagram to predict or explain the motion of the object or to do calculations.

How do you draw a free body diagram?

You know that the force or forces acting on an object can be from several different interaction pairs.

- Step 1: Identify all the non-contact pairs.
- Step 2: Identify all the contact pairs.
- Step 3: Focus on a *single* object. Draw that object with arrows showing all the forces acting on the object.

When you are identifying the pairs it is helpful to think of the pairs of forces as: *"The force of X on Y, and the force of Y on X"*.

Drawing free body diagrams

Draw a free body diagram for a book on a table.

Step 1: There is the force of the Earth on the book and the force of the book on the Earth (Figure 2A).

Step 2: There is the force of the table on the book and the force of the book on the table (Figure 2B).

Step 3: Draw a diagram of *just* the forces on the book (Figure 2C).

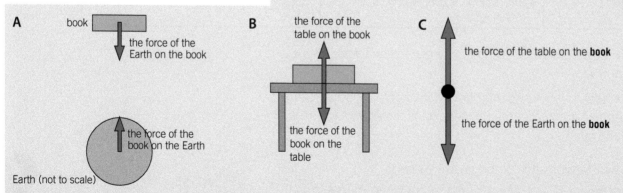

Figure 2 *Drawing a free body diagram for a book on a table. Many free body diagrams look like the diagram in C.*

A Explain why it is helpful to draw the arrows on the book in two different colours.

How do you find the resultant force?

When you have drawn your free body diagram, you can work out the **resultant force**, or **net force**. Forces are vectors so you need to take account of their direction when you add them (Figure 3).

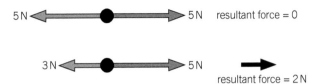

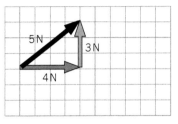

Figure 3 *Calculating resultant forces for forces acting in the same direction.*

B Explain how two forces of 10 N can add up to zero.

Sometimes forces act at different angles to each other. You can use Pythagoras' Theorem to calculate the resultant force of two forces acting at 90° to each other (Figure 4).

Figure 4 *Calculating resultant forces for forces acting at right angles. Grid scale: the length of the side of one square is 1 N.*

Calculating resultant forces

Calculate the resultant force of a 2.0 N force and a 5.0 N force acting at 90° to each other.

Step 1: Draw a diagram showing the forces, adding them in a triangle (Figure 5).

Step 2: Use Pythagoras' Theorem to work out the hypotenuse of the triangle:

$$c^2 = a^2 + b^2$$
$$= (2.0\,N)^2 + (5.0\,N)^2$$
$$= 4.0\,N^2 + 25\,N^2$$
$$= 29\,N^2$$

So, $c = \sqrt{29\,N^2}$
$$= 5.4\,N \text{ (2 significant figures)}$$

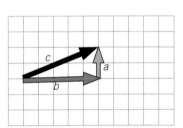

Figure 5 *Grid scale: the length of the side of one square is 1 N.*

How do you resolve forces?

You can work out which two forces at right angles add up to a particular force by resolving the force in two directions (Figure 6). If you draw the force and angle on graph paper you can use a ruler to work out the **components**.

1 Draw a free body diagram for a falling apple. *(2 marks)*

2 Explain why there will be a downwards arrow in every free body diagram that you draw for objects on Earth. *(2 marks)*

3 Draw a free body diagram for the table instead of the book in Figure 2. *(3 marks)*

4 a A force of 30 N is acting at 40° to the horizontal. Use a scale drawing to find the horizontal and vertical components. *(3 marks)*

b Use Pythagoras' Theorem to check the accuracy of your drawing. *(3 marks)*

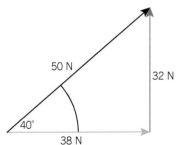

Figure 6 *You can resolve a force of 50 N acting at an angle of 40 degrees into two components.*

Study tip

The force arrow that you draw should be in contact with the object because forces act *on* objects.

Learning outcomes

After studying this lesson you should be able to:

● apply Newton's First Law to explain the motion of an object moving with uniform velocity

● apply Newton's First Law to explain the motion of an object when the speed and/or direction change

● explain that inertia is a measure of how difficult it is to change the velocity of an object.

Specification reference: P2.2d, P2.2f, P2.2h, P2.2j

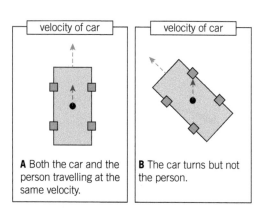

A Both the car and the person travelling at the same velocity.

B The car turns but not the person.

Figure 2 *You travel with a constant velocity (the purple arrow) until a force acts on you (usually the normal contact force of the side of the car).*

Figure 3 *A magician flicks the card and the coin drops in the bottle – there is no horizontal force acting on the coin so its horizontal velocity does not change. The coin falls.*

Astronauts on the International Space Station (ISS) are finding out how objects behave in space. An astronaut on the ISS once 'lost' a toolkit he was using (Figure 1). What would happen to the toolkit if the Earth was not there?

Figure 1 *If there are no forces acting on the toolkit its motion will not change.*

ⓗ What is Newton's First Law?

When you are in the back of a car, going round a roundabout, or on a ride going in a circle at a fair or theme park, it sometimes feels as if you are being flung sideways.

What is actually happening is that you continue travelling in a straight line while the car turns. You do not change direction until the side of the car (or another passenger) pushes on you (Figure 2).

This is an example of **Newton's First Law of Motion** which states:

"An object will continue to stay at rest or move with uniform velocity unless a force acts on it."

It takes a resultant force to change the motion (the speed or direction) of an object.

That means that if the resultant force is zero then the speed or direction of an object will *not* change (Figure 3). This law is really about the principle of **inertia**. The inertia of an object is a measure of how difficult it is to change its velocity. Moving objects keep moving, and objects that are stationary do not move. ⓗ

A Describe and explain what happens to you when you are standing on a bus that suddenly brakes.

Why do objects continue to move at a steady speed?

It can be difficult to believe that something can continue to move without a force acting on it. We often forget about friction which tends to stop things moving (Figure 4).

If the speed or direction of an object does not change then the resultant force is zero. A steady speed means that there is a zero resultant force. The toolkit lost by the astronaut will continue to move with a steady velocity if no force acts on it.

A smooth floor

stops after
a short distance

B ice

goes further
before stopping

C 'perfect' ice

never stops!

Figure 4 *If there is no friction you do not need to exert a force for something to continue to move at a uniform velocity.*

B Explain why it is difficult to demonstrate Newton's First Law in the laboratory.

What is equilibrium?

Suppose that you draw a free body diagram for a car parked in a car park. It would look like Figure 6.

A free body diagram of a feather falling at a steady speed looks like Figure 7.

In both cases, the resultant force is zero so the motion does not change. Both objects are in **equilibrium**.

1 Write down and explain the resultant force of an ice skater moving at a steady speed. *(2 marks)*

2 Draw a free body diagram of you travelling in a car in a straight line at a steady speed. *(2 marks)*

3 Explain in terms of Newton's Third Law why a stationary pen on your desk is in equilibrium but a pen that falls off the desk is not. *(3 marks)*

4 If you put a toy car on a ramp then you can raise the ramp so that the car travels at a steady speed. Suggest why this slope is called a 'friction-compensated slope'. *(3 marks)*

Figure 5 *If there was no friction or air resistance a skater would never stop.*

the force of the ground on the car

the force of the Earth on the car

Figure 6 *The forces on a parked car.*

the force of the air on the feather

the force of the Earth on the feather

Figure 7 *The forces on a falling feather.*

Go further

Galileo's thought experiment shows what happens when you remove friction. Find out what he said about it.

Study tip

Remember that a uniform velocity does *not* need a resultant force.

Learning outcomes

After studying this lesson you should be able to:

- apply Newton's Second Law in calculations relating forces, masses, and accelerations
- explain how force, mass, and acceleration are related
- describe, using free body diagrams, examples in which two or more forces lead to a resultant force on an object
- explain why an object moving in a circle with a constant speed has a changing velocity.

Specification reference: P2.2g, P2.2i, P2.2l, P2.2p

Figure 2 *The International Space Station is continually accelerating.*

small acceleration

resultant force

mass of lorry = 8000 kg

resultant force

mass of car = 1200 kg

large acceleration

resultant force

mass of motorcycle = 600 kg

Figure 4 *The acceleration depends on the force and the mass (inertia) of the object.*

Tiny tree frogs (Figure 1) accelerate by exerting forces on themselves that are bigger than their weight.

What happens when the resultant force is *not* zero?

Figure 1 *Small frogs can exert comparatively large forces.*

H A leaping animal uses its back legs to exert a force on itself. Its motion changes because there is a resultant force. A resultant force can:

- change the speed of an object
- change the direction of motion of an object
- change both the speed and direction of motion of an object.

You have learned that if the speed or direction of motion of an object changes then it is accelerating (Figure 2).

Why are there resultant forces on some objects? **H**

For objects on which a resultant force is acting, you can use free body diagrams like the ones in Figure 3.

A tennis ball accelerates towards the ground.	The ISS orbits the Earth.
the force of the air on the tennis ball / the force of the Earth on the tennis ball	the force of the Earth on the ISS *(arrow not to scale)*
Result: the ball will accelerate towards the ground.	Result: the ISS will move in a circle.

Figure 3 *Free body diagrams for a tennis ball and the ISS.*

The International Space Station (ISS) orbits the Earth roughly every 90 minutes. This means that it is moving at a steady speed. However, its direction of motion is constantly changing.

A Predict what would happen to the ISS moving in orbit if there was suddenly no gravity.

How do you calculate with Newton's Second Law?

Newton's Second Law (Figure 4) states that the acceleration that the resultant force produces on an object depends on:

- the size of the resultant force
- the mass (**inertia**) of the object.

You need to recall and apply: force (N) = mass (kg) × acceleration (m/s²)

B Change the subject of the equation to show how you calculate mass.

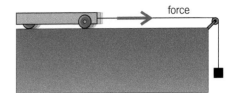
force

Figure 5 *Using a trolley and a weight to show how acceleration relates to force and mass. In this experiment, you need to compensate for the frictional forces.*

Calculating force

A lorry has a mass of 8000 kg. What resultant force is needed to produce an acceleration of 2.0 m/s²?

Step 1: Write down what you know:

acceleration = 2.0 m/s²

mass = 8000 kg

Step 2: Use the equation to calculate force.

force = mass × acceleration

= 8000 kg × 2.0 m/s²

= 16 000 kg m/s²

= 16 000 N (2 significant figures)

A newton (N) is a *derived* unit. 1 N = 1 kg m/s². The units of mass (kg), length (m), and time (s) are *SI units.*

Sometimes you need to work out the *resultant* force before you can calculate the acceleration.

Calculating acceleration

Calculate the acceleration of a car if the force due to the engine is 1000 N and drag force and friction equal 600 N. The mass of the car is 800 kg.

Step 1: Calculate the resultant force.

resultant force = force due to engine – frictional forces

= 1000 N – 600 N

= 400 N

Step 2: Use the equation for acceleration to find the answer.

$$\text{acceleration} = \frac{\text{force}}{\text{mass}}$$

$$= \frac{400 \text{ kg m/s}^2}{800 \text{ kg}} \text{ (2 significant figures)}$$

$$= 0.5 \text{ m/s}^2$$

You can show that acceleration is proportional to force and mass by doing the experiment shown in Figure 5.

Why do objects move in a circle?

An object moving in a circle at a constant speed is still accelerating even though its speed does not change. It is constantly changing direction, so its velocity is constantly changing. To do this a force directed towards the centre of the circle acts on the object.

Experimenting with force, mass, and acceleration

Set up the experiment as shown in Figure 5. Compensate the slope for friction.

Put four masses on the end of the string and use light gates to measure the acceleration. Remove two masses from the end of the string, fix them on top of the trolley and use the light gates to measure the new acceleration.

Explain why you cannot just change the force by adding masses on the end of the string.

1 On a roller coaster you loop-the-loop at a steady speed. Explain why you are continuing to accelerate. (*1 mark*)

2 A frog of mass 20 g has an acceleration of 10 m/s². Calculate the force exerted by its legs. (*2 marks*)

3 Most people can tolerate an upwards (head first) acceleration of 5 *g*, where *g* is the acceleration due to gravity. Estimate the force required to produce this acceleration. (*4 marks*)

4 Use a free body diagram to explain why astronauts in the ISS appear to be weightless. (*3 marks*) **H**

P2.2.5 Everyday forces and their effects

Learning outcomes

After studying this lesson you should be able to:

- apply Newton's First Law
- apply Newton's Second Law
- apply Newton's Third Law
- use vector diagrams to illustrate resolution of forces, a net force (resultant force), and equilibrium situations.

Specification reference: P2.2d, P2.2e, P2.2i, P2.2o

Figure 1 *A base jumper needs air resistance.*

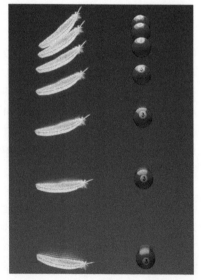

Figure 4 *In a vacuum, the velocity of a feather increases at the same rate as the velocity of the ball.*

If it wasn't for air resistance how long would a base jumper (Figure 1) take to reach the speed of sound?

How do you explain the motion of falling objects?

Skydiving can be great fun. When you jump out of a plane you accelerate. Your motion changes because there is a resultant force on you (Figure 2). The air exerts a force on you, but the Earth exerts a larger force.

As you accelerate the force of the air increases. Eventually the force of the air on you equals the force of the Earth on you, and your motion no longer changes. You have reached **terminal velocity** (Figures 3 and 4). A parachute increases the force of the air to reduce your velocity. Without air resistance you would reach the speed of sound in about 30 seconds.

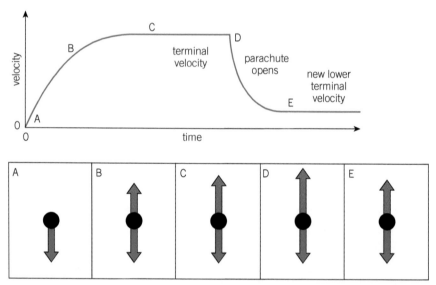

Figure 2 *You can reach a lower terminal velocity using a parachute. The free body diagrams show the forces on the parachutist at the points labelled on the graph. Red arrow: weight; blue arrow: air resistance.*

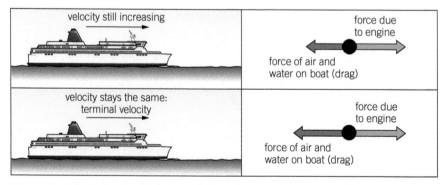

Figure 3 *Objects such as boats and cars also reach terminal velocity.*

A Sketch a velocity–time graph for an object falling in a vacuum.

How do you explain the motion of objects when the forces are at an angle?

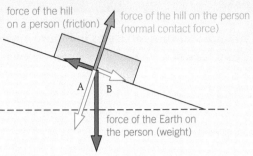

Figure 5 *The forces acting on a person sitting on a hill.*

force of the hill on a person (friction)

force of the hill on the person (normal contact force)

A B

force of the Earth on the person (weight)

Sometimes the forces acting on an object are not all in a straight line. For example, if you are sitting on a hill there is a force of friction acting on you that is along the line of the hill, and a normal contact force.

You can analyse these situations by resolving the forces so that you are only dealing with forces that act in *two* directions at right angles.

In Figure 5, the weight needs to be resolved into a force *along the slope* and a force *at right angles to the slope*.

Here, the normal contact force balances component A, and friction balances component B.

B Explain how you know that the normal contact force is smaller than the weight in Figure 5.

How do you explain the motion of rockets?

When a rocket (Figure 7) takes off there is a resultant force on it that produces a large acceleration.

The burning fuel pushes exhaust gases out of the bottom of the rocket. The gases pushing on the rocket and the rocket pushing on the gases are another example of Newton's Third Law.

When the force of the gases on the rocket is bigger than the force of the Earth on the rocket then the rocket will accelerate.

1 Explain why terminal velocity is a constant speed. *(1 mark)*
2 When someone fires a gun the gun pushes back on their shoulder. Explain why. *(1 mark)*
3 Explain the shape of the graph at points A to E in Figure 2. *(5 marks)*
4 **a** Calculate the size of the normal contact force of a block on a ramp if the weight of the block is 2 N, and the angle between the weight and the component of weight that balances it is 30°. *(2 marks)*
  b Calculate the frictional force acting on the block. *(1 mark)* (Hint: you need to find the components of weight using a scale diagram.)

H **Calculating a component**

In Figure 5 the angle between the weight and A is 20° and the weight is 500 N. Calculate A.

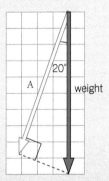

20°

A weight

Figure 6 *Scale diagram.*

Step 1: Draw a scale diagram. In Figure 6 1 square = 50 N.

Step 2: Measure the line that represents A and use the scale to calculate the force A.

force A = 470 N

H Figure 7 *Rocket engineers inspect the engines of rockets designed to send a spacecraft to Pluto.*

Study tip

Practise explaining motion that includes terminal velocity.

Learning outcomes

After studying this lesson you should be able to:

- define momentum
- describe examples of momentum in collisions
- recall and apply the equation for momentum.

Specification reference: P2.2k

Figure 1 *The skaters move apart when they push.*

Figure 2 *A charging rhino has a large amount of momentum.*

Figure 3 *When snooker balls collide, energy is transferred to a thermal store.*

If you are standing on ice as in Figure 1, why does pushing your partner forwards make you move backwards?

What is momentum?

You may have heard about **momentum** in sport. Teams with more momentum often win. In science momentum is a quantity that depends on:

- mass
- velocity.

Momentum is a vector so when you do calculations involving momentum you need to take account of direction.

How do you calculate momentum?

You need to be able to recall and apply this equation:

$$\text{momentum (kg m/s)} = \text{mass (kg)} \times \text{velocity (m/s)}$$

Calculating momentum

A rhinoceros (Figure 2) has a mass of 1500 kg. What is its momentum when it is travelling at 8.0 m/s in a positive direction?

$$\text{momentum} = \text{mass} \times \text{velocity}$$
$$= 1500 \, \text{kg} \times +8.0 \, \text{m/s}$$
$$= +12\,000 \, \text{kg m/s}$$

A Explain why you need to include a + or − sign when you calculate momentum.

What is the conservation of momentum?

In any collision momentum is conserved, so the momentum before is equal to the momentum afterwards. This is the **Law of Conservation of Momentum**.

In Figure 1 the momentum before the skaters push apart is zero. If they move away from each other with a momentum that is equal in size but opposite in direction, the momentum afterwards is also zero.

What happens when objects collide?

In an **elastic collision** no energy is transferred to other stores. The energy in the kinetic store stays the same. For example, a moving red ball that has an elastic collision with a stationary blue ball will stop, and the blue ball will move off at the same velocity as the red ball. In reality, such as in snooker (Figure 3), some energy is transferred to a thermal store, so the collision is not perfectly elastic.

B Explain how you could take measurements to show that momentum is conserved in a collision between two trolleys.

What happens when objects collide and join together?

In an **inelastic collision** some energy is transferred to other stores. One example is when snooker balls collide, and energy is transferred to a thermal store.

Another example is a collision after which the velocity of the combined objects is less than that of the original objects.

Using the momentum equation

Trolley A of mass 200 g travelling at +0.25 m/s collides with and sticks to trolley B of mass 300 g which is stationary. Calculate the velocity of the two trolleys after the collision.

Step 1: Calculate the momentum before the collision.

total momentum before

= momentum of trolley A + momentum of trolley B
= (0.2 kg × +0.25 m/s) + (0.3 kg × 0 m/s)
= +0.05 kg m/s + 0 kg m/s
= +0.05 kg m/s

Step 2: Let the velocity of the two trolleys after the collision be v.

total momentum after

= total mass of trolleys A and B × velocity

+0.05 kg m/s = (0.2 kg + 0.3 kg) × v

So, $v = \dfrac{+0.05\,kg\,m/s}{0.5\,kg}$

= +0.01 m/s

If you have spring-loaded trolleys then you can investigate what happens during collisions as shown in Figure 4. Notice that as the mass of the trolley on the right increases, its velocity after the explosion *decreases*, so that momentum is conserved.

Go further

There is a connection between the conservation of momentum and Newton's Third Law. Find out what it is.

1 Calculate the momentum of a cat of mass 5 kg travelling at 10 cm/s. *(2 marks)*
2 Two skaters push apart. One has twice the mass of the other. Compare their velocities after they have moved apart. *(1 mark)*
3 Explain why the speed of two objects that stick together on impact *cannot* be larger than the velocity of either trolley before the collision. *(2 marks)*
4 Calculate the speed of the red ball after the collision shown in Figure 5. *(6 marks)*

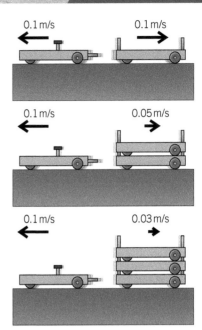

Figure 4 *The trolleys move off explosively in opposite directions with speeds that depend on their masses.*

Conservation of momentum

1 Set up two air track vehicles on an air track.
2 Set up light gates to measure the speed of each vehicle.
3 Confirm that if you collide one vehicle moving at a certain speed with a second stationary vehicle then the second vehicle moves with the same velocity as the first.
4 Put a piece of plasticine on a stationary vehicle and repeat the experiment. You can find the mass of the plasticine if you know the velocities of the vehicles, and the mass of each trolley.
5 Weigh the plasticine to check.

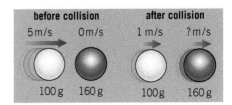

Figure 5 *Find the speed.*

P2.2.7 Work and power

Learning outcomes

After studying this lesson you should be able to:

- use the relationship between work done, force, and distance moved along the line of action of the force
- describe the energy transfer involved
- recall and apply the equation for work done
- convert between newton-metres and joules
- explain what power is, and recall and apply the equation for power.

Specification reference: P2.2l, P2.2m, P2.2n

Figure 1 *Is this girl doing work?*

Synoptic link

You learnt about work and power at Key Stage 3.

Figure 2 *A weight lifter does work when she lifts the bar.*

Why are you not doing any 'work' in a scientific sense when you sit at your desk reading (Figure 1)?

What is work?

Doing **work** in science is about using forces to transfer energy between stores (Figure 2). You use a force to lift your suitcase into a car, and you do work against gravity. You have shifted energy to a gravitational store.

When you pull your suitcase along you are doing work against friction. Energy is shifted to a thermal store. You need to recall and apply this equation:

$$\text{work done (J)} = \text{force (N)} \times \text{distance (m)}$$

You must measure the distance *along the line of the force* (Figure 3).

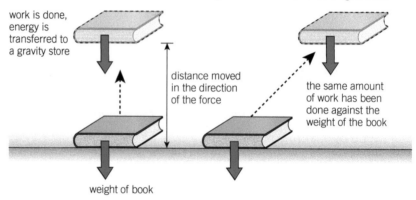

Figure 3 *The work done lifting a book.*

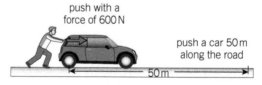

Figure 4 *Pushing a car along a road.*

> **A** Look at Figure 4 and calculate the work done pushing the car.

Why are joules equal to newton-metres?

You know that a newton is a derived unit and $1\,\text{N} = 1\,\text{kg m/s}^2$. The joule is also a derived unit.

If you multiply force and distance the unit of the quantity you calculate is the **newton-metre (N m)**.

$$1\,\text{N m} = 1\,\text{kg m/s}^2 \times \text{m}$$
$$= 1\,\text{kg m}^2/\text{s}^2$$

This is the same as the unit of kinetic energy. One newton-metre is the same as one joule.

What is power?

You have learned that **power** tells you the *rate* at which energy is transferred. A powerful person can run upstairs in a short time (Figure 5).

If both people are the same weight then they do the same amount of work. Each person transfers the same amount of energy to a gravity store. The more powerful person transfers the energy in a shorter time.

How do you calculate power?

You need to recall and apply this equation:

$$\text{power (W)} = \frac{\text{work done (J)}}{\text{time (s)}}$$

B   Explain why power is a *rate* of transfer of energy.

Figure 5   *You do work against gravity as you run up steps, and do it quickly if you are powerful.*

Calculating power

You run upstairs in a time of 1.2 seconds. Your weight is 500 N, and the vertical height of the stairs is 3 m.
Calculate your power.

Step 1: Calculate the work done:

$$\text{work done} = \text{force} \times \text{distance}$$
$$= 500\,\text{N} \times 3\,\text{m}$$
$$= 1500\,\text{N m}$$
$$= 1500\,\text{J}$$

Step 2: Calculate the power:

$$\text{power} = \frac{\text{work done}}{\text{time}}$$
$$= \frac{1500\,\text{J}}{1.2\,\text{s}}$$
$$= 1300\,\text{W (2 significant figures)}$$

1   You slide a book 30 cm across your desk using a force of 5 N. It takes 0.5 seconds.
    a Calculate the work done.   *(2 marks)*
    b Calculate your power.   *(2 marks)*

2   Explain why lifting a book is doing work, but holding a book is not.   *(2 marks)*

3   Calculate the time it would take a motor with a power of 0.6 kW to lift a suitcase of 20 kg a distance of 50 cm. *(4 marks)*

4   A ride at a theme park lifts a train of 50 people up a distance of 50 m in 30 seconds.
    a Estimate its power using the information in the example *Calculating power*.   *(4 marks)*
    b State two assumptions that you have made when doing this calculation.   *(2 marks)*
    c Explain why the motor needs even more power than you have calculated.   *(1 mark)*

Power of a motor

Set up a motor with a piece of string with a mass attached.

Put the mass on the floor and time how long it takes the motor to lift the mass a certain distance.

Calculate the work done and the power.

Compare the power you have calculated with the value of power given for the motor.

Study tip

Make sure you use the distance in line with the force, which is not necessarily the total distance moved by the force.

Converting between units

You should be able to convert between units using equations.

Forces

P2.2 Newton's laws

Summary questions

1 Copy Table 1 and match the quantity and its unit by ticking the correct box.

Table 1 *Forces and units.*

Quantity	Newtons	Joules	Watts	kg m/s
force				
momentum				
power				
work				

2 **a i** Calculate the force needed to produce an acceleration of 2 m/s² for a skateboarder of mass 40 kg.
   ii Write down which of Newton's laws you used to calculate the force.
   b i One of the forces acting on the skateboarder is the force of the Earth on the skateboarder. Write down the other force in that interaction pair.
   ii Write down which of Newton's laws relates to the answer to **b i**.
   c i There is one of Newton's Laws that you have not used in this question so far. Write it down.
   ii Write a question based on that law.

3 **a** Explain the difference between work and power.
   b Calculate the work done if a jet ski moves a distance of 20 m using a force of 10 kN.
   c It takes the jet skier 3 seconds to travel 20 m. Use your answer to **b** to calculate the power.

Figure 1 *A jet skier.*

4 **a** Draw a free body diagram for a balloon floating in a bucket of water.
   b i You push the balloon down into the water and hold it there. Draw the free body diagram for the balloon now.
   ii Use the free body diagram to explain the motion of the balloon at this moment.
   c Use a free body diagram to describe and explain the motion of the balloon when you let go.
   d Explain how Newton's laws apply to the three situations described.

5 **a** Explain how the International Space Station can be moving with a constant speed while a force acts on it, and still obey Newton's laws of motion.
   b Describe another situation in which a force acts on an object without changing its speed.

6 **a** Define momentum.
   b A father, with a mass of 70 kg, skates across an ice rink at a speed of 3 m/s. He picks up his stationary daughter, who has a mass of 30 kg, and continues in the same direction. Calculate the speed of both father and daughter after he picks her up.
   c They stop, stand opposite each other then push each other apart. If the father moves off with a speed of 0.5 m/s, calculate the speed of the daughter.
   d Explain the difference in the speeds.

7 ⬭ The fireworks for a firework display are set up on an island in the middle of a lake.
   a A person sets off for the island on a boat with an engine that exerts a force of 100 N. The wind blows the boat at right angles to the direction of travel with a force of 60 N. Calculate the magnitude of the resultant force on the boat.
   b A spark from the firework falls at a steady speed as it burns. Explain why.
   c A child watches the display sitting on a hill. Explain how you can resolve the force of the Earth on the child to explain why his motion does not change.

Revision questions

1 An eye bolt has three cables attached. The cables are 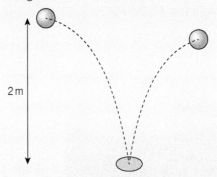 under tension as shown in the diagram.

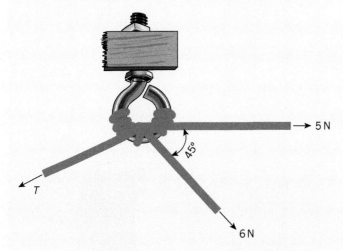

Use a free body diagram, drawn to scale, to find the tension, *T* (in newtons), that produces a resultant downward force of 10 N. *(3 marks)*

2 A hoist is used to raise bricks to higher levels on a building site.

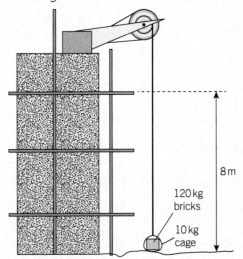

a Calculate the total weight (in newtons) of the bricks and the cage.
(gravitational field strength *g* = 10 N/kg)   *(2 marks)*

b Calculate the work done (in joules) by raising the cage of bricks to a height of 8 m.   *(2 marks)*

c It takes 10.4 seconds for the hoist to raise the cage of bricks to 8 m. Calculate:

  i the power (in watts) produced by the hoist.
(2 marks)

  ii the average momentum of the cage of bricks as it rises to 8 m. Give the unit.   *(3 marks)*

3 The motion of a bouncing ball is captured by a camera. The camera takes three photographs in a short period of time. The ball bounces back to a height lower than it was released.

Use ideas about energy, force, and momentum to explain why the height of the ball changes from when it is released to when it reaches the top of its first bounce. You may use a calculation in your answer.   *(6 marks)*

Learning outcomes

After studying this lesson you should be able to:

* explain how to stretch, bend, or compress an object
* describe the difference between elastic and plastic deformation caused by stretching forces
* describe the relationship between force and extension for a spring
* calculate the spring constant.

Specification reference: P2.3a, P2.3b, P2.3c, P2.3e

Figure 1 *The elastane in a cycling shirt makes it stretch.*

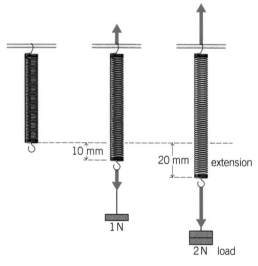

Figure 3 *Stretching a spring.*

How many stretchy items of clothing, such as a cycling shirt (Figure 1), do you own?

How do you change the shape of an object?

Forces can compress, stretch, or bend objects. You need more than one force to do this.

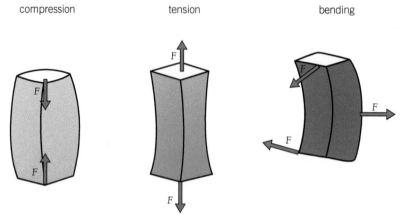

Figure 2 *You need two (or more) forces to compress, stretch, or bend an object.*

Some materials stretch but do not return to their original shape, such as modelling clay. In science we say they are **plastic**. They are deformed or distorted when you apply forces (Figure 2) and stay that way when you remove the forces.

Many modern fabrics are **elastic**. They *do* return to their original shape when you remove the forces.

> **A** State whether a rubber band is plastic or elastic.

What happens when you stretch a spring?

In 1660, Robert Hooke was investigating what happens when he stretched materials. He found that springs were special (Figure 3).

A graph of force against extension for a spring (Figure 4) is a straight line up to a certain point – force and extension have a **linear relationship** up to this point. This point is called the **limit of proportionality**.

The point marked X on the graph is the **elastic limit**. Below the elastic limit, if you remove the force, the spring returns to its original length. Above the elastic limit it does not return to its original length – it is permanently deformed.

> **B** Describe the method that you would use to obtain accurate and repeatable results to collect data to plot a graph of force against extension for a spring.

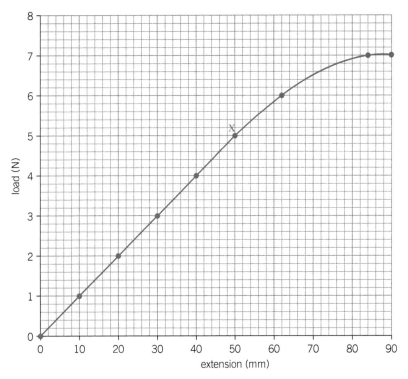

Figure 4 *Graph of force against extension for a spring. X marks the limit of proportionality.*

How do you calculate the spring constant?

If you double the force on a spring, its extension doubles. The extension of a spring is **proportional** to the force until you reach limit of proportionality. This is **Hooke's Law**. You need to recall and apply:

force exerted by a spring (N) = spring constant (N/m) × extension (m)

The gradient of the linear section of the graph of force against extension is the **spring constant**. The spring constant tells you how stiff the spring is, or how difficult it is to stretch.

Calculating the spring constant

Use information from the graph in Figure 4 to calculate the spring constant.

Step 1: Identify a point on the line below the limit of proportionality and read off the values of force and extension.

force = 4 N

extension = 40 mm = 0.04 m

Step 2: Make the spring constant the subject of the equation and calculate it.

$$\text{spring constant} = \frac{\text{force}}{\text{extension}}$$

$$= \frac{4\,\text{N}}{0.04\,\text{m}}$$

$$= 100\,\text{N/m (1 significant figure)}$$

Hooke's Law graphs are straight lines through (0, 0), until the limit of proportionality. So $y = mx$, where y = force and m = spring constant.

Figure 5 *A mechanical engineer tests the behaviour of a lorry part.*

Study tip

You must use values of extension (not length) in metres (not centimetres or millimetres) when you calculate the spring constant.

1 Calculate the force required to stretch a spring with a spring constant of 100 N/m so the extension is 2 cm. *(2 marks)*

2 A graph of force against extension starts to curve at a force of 10 N. The spring has stretched from 5 cm to 8 cm.
   a Calculate the spring constant. *(4 marks)*
   b Estimate the limit of proportionality (force). *(1 mark)*

3 State and explain whether a stiff spring has a large spring constant or a small spring constant. *(2 marks)*

4 a Explain why you might expect to plot force on the x-axis of a force–extension graph. *(1 mark)*
   b Explain why it is helpful to plot force on the y-axis of a force–extension graph instead. *(1 mark)*

Learning outcomes

After studying this lesson you should be able to:

- describe the difference between a linear and a non-linear relationship for force and extension
- calculate the work done in stretching.

Specification reference: P2.3d, P2.3f

Why do they weigh you before you do a bungee jump (Figure 1)?

How do you calculate the energy transferred in stretching a spring?

You do work when you stretch a spring because you exert a force over a distance. The force that you apply changes as the spring stretches or compresses. You need to be able to apply this equation:

energy transferred in stretching (J)
$$= 0.5 \times \text{spring constant (N/m)} \times (\text{extension (m)})^2$$

Energy transferred is also 'work done'.

A Explain why you cannot use the equation work = force × distance to calculate the work done in stretching.

Figure 1 *You need to know how far a bungee cord will stretch to do a bungee jump safely.*

Calculating energy transferred

A spring is 4.0 cm long and has a spring constant of 50 N/m. Calculate the energy transferred when it is stretched to a length of 7.5 cm.

Step 1: Calculate the extension in metres.

extension = final length − original length

$$= 7.5\,\text{cm} - 4.0\,\text{cm}$$

$$= 3.5\,\text{cm}$$

$$= 0.035\,\text{m}$$

Step 2: Use the formula for energy transferred to find the answer.

energy transferred = $0.5 \times$ spring constant $\times$ (extension)^2

energy transferred = $0.5 \times 50\,\text{N/m} \times (0.035\,\text{m})^2$

$$= 0.9\,\text{J (2 significant figures)}$$

What happens when you stretch other materials?

To ensure that you are not injured, a bungee company measures your weight and then uses a graph to work out the extension of the cord.

The graph for an elastic band (Figure 2) shows that there is a **non-linear relationship** between force and extension.

You cannot use an elastic band in a newtonmeter. You need a spring because it obeys Hooke's Law.

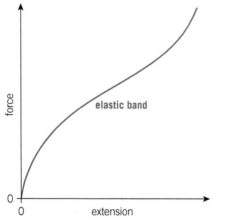

Figure 2 *The graph of force against extension is not a straight line for an elastic band.*

As you blow up a rubber balloon at first it is difficult. The rubber is quite stiff. Once you have started blowing it up, it requires less force to produce an extension. Finally it becomes stiffer again.

You should be able to link this description to the shape of the graph in Figure 2.

The shape of the graphs in Figure 3 shows you the relationship between force and extension for two more materials.

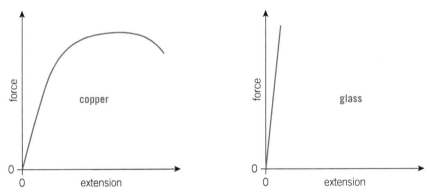

Figure 3 *Force–extension graphs for copper and glass.*

B Explain why there is no elastic limit marked on the graph for the elastic band.

The graph for glass shows a linear relationship, just like the initial part of the graph for a spring.

All materials store energy when they deform. Scientists design materials that transfer the energy back when they regain their shape – just like your Achilles tendon (Figure 4). Tennis rackets are made of materials that do this very well. In other situations, such as the design of crash barriers, you may not want the material to return to its original shape. The material used in crash barriers is permanently deformed on impact.

1 Calculate the work done in stretching a spring that has a spring constant of 75 N/m so that its extension is 0.001 m. *(2 marks)*

2 🔲 Using the graphs of force against extension, on these two pages and P2.3.1, compare what you would observe when you stretch a spring with what you would observe when you stretch glass. *(5 marks)*

3 Calculate the compression of suspension springs on a lorry that each store 5 J if the spring constant is 10^5 N/m. *(2 marks)*

4 🔲 Some pens work when you push down on the button at the top of them (Figure 5). There is a spring inside. Estimate the energy stored in the spring when you push down. *(6 marks)*

Go further

If you stretch and release a rubber band many times it gets warm. Find out why.

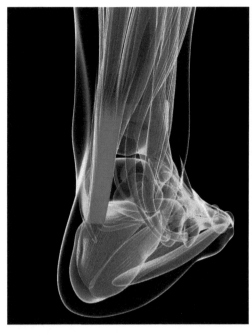

Figure 4 *You do work on your Achilles tendon and then it does work on you to help you run.*

Figure 5 *Many everyday objects, such as retractable pens, contain springs.*

When you calculate work done, 🔲 start by squaring the extension, then multiply by the spring constant, and then multiply by 0.5.

Learning outcomes

After studying this lesson you should be able to:

- explain what is meant by gravitational field, gravity force, and weight
- recall and apply the equations for gravity force and potential energy
- state g and acceleration due to gravity.

Specification reference: P2.3g, P2.3h, P2.3i

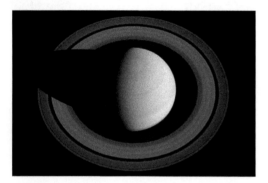

Figure 1 *Saturn.*

Synoptic link

You calculated weight using weight = mass × *g* at Key Stage 3.

Figure 2 *The mass of the astronaut does not change as he moves from the Earth to the Moon, but his weight does.*

Saturn (Figure 1) exerts a gravity force on you equal to the gravity force exerted on you by the car parked outside your house.

What is a gravitational field?

A **gravitational field** is a region where a mass experiences an attractive force. All matter has a gravitational field that causes attraction. You need to recall and use:

gravity force (N) = mass (kg) × gravitational field strength (N/kg)

Gravitational field strength, *g*, or **gravity constant, *g*,** is a measure of the force on a 1 kg mass when it is in a gravitational field due to another mass. Mass does not change, but the force on the mass depends on the field.

A gravitational field is a region where a mass experiences an attractive force. The same size force acts on each object. The force is bigger if:

- the mass of one or both of them is bigger
- the distance between them is smaller.

Calculating gravity force

A spacecraft has a mass of 60 kg and is in the gravitational field of a planet where gravitational field strength is 27 N/kg. Calculate the gravity force on the spacecraft.

Step 1: Write down what you know.

mass = 60 kg

gravitational field strength = 27 N/kg

Step 2: Use the equation to calculate the gravity force.

gravity force = mass × gravitational field strength

= 60 kg × 27 N/kg

= 1600 N (2 significant figures)

A Suggest what happens to *g* as you move away from the planet.

What is weight?

Weight is what we call the force of the Earth on an object, such as you, when it is on the Earth's surface. You measure weight using scales, or with a newtonmeter.

weight (N) = mass (kg) × gravitational field strength (N/kg)

On the surface of the Earth, *g* is 10 N/kg. The value of *g* depends on the mass of the Earth and the radius of the Earth.

Weight is also what we call the gravity force of planets and moons on objects on their surfaces. On the Moon (Figure 2), *g* is 1.6 N/kg. On Jupiter, *g* is 27 N/kg. On Saturn, *g* is 10.4 N/kg, but Saturn is a long way away, so the effect of the gravity force on you is very small.

B Suggest one reason why *g* is smaller on the Moon than on Earth.

What is the acceleration due to gravity?
The symbol *g* is also used for the acceleration due to gravity.

gravity force (N) = mass (kg) × gravitational field strength (N/kg)

and

resultant force (N) = mass (kg) × acceleration due to gravity (m/s²)

Acceleration due to gravity, *g* (also called the acceleration of free fall), is 10 m/s² on the Earth. A more precise measurement is 9.81 m/s² or 9.81 N/kg.

What is gravitational potential energy?
When you lift an object in a gravitational field you transfer energy to a gravity store. This energy is called **gravitational potential energy** (Figure 3). You need to recall and use:

gravitational potential = mass × height × gravitational field
energy (J)   (kg)   (m)   strength (N/kg)

Calculating gravitational potential energy
Calculate the energy transferred to a gravity store when a man of mass 70 kg goes from the ground floor to the 40th floor of a skyscraper. Each floor is 3.0 m high.

Step 1: Write down what you know.

mass = 70 kg

height = 40 floors × 3.0 m/floor

= 120 m

Step 2: Use the equation to calculate the energy transferred.

gravitational potential energy = 70 kg × 120 m × 10 N/kg

= 84 000 N m

= 84 000 J (2 significant figures)

1 Calculate the weight of an astronaut, of mass 70 kg, on the Moon. *(2 marks)*
2 Estimate the change in energy in a gravity store when you get into bed. *(2 marks)*
3 Explain why you should label the downwards force arrow on an object 'weight' not 'gravity'. *(2 marks)*
4 There is a point between the Earth and the Moon where the force of the Earth on an object is equal to the force of the Moon on the same object. Suggest and explain whether this point is closer to the Earth, or closer to the Moon, or half way between them. *(2 marks)*

Study tip
g has two names – gravitational field strength and gravity constant. *g* also refers to the acceleration due to gravity.

Study tip
Remember that a newton-metre and a joule are equivalent.

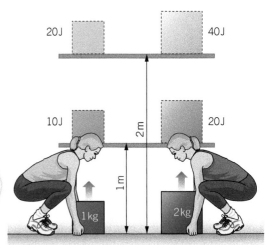

Figure 3 *The change in gravitational potential energy, or energy transferred to a gravity store, depends on the mass of the object and the change in height.*

Go further
Find out what Newton's Law of Gravitation is, and use it to work out the size of the force of Saturn on you.

Weights on other planets
1 Put one 100 g mass in a small box and label it 'Earth'. This has a weight of 1 N on Earth.
2 Seal the box.
3 Take seven more boxes and work out how much mass you need to put in each box to make them feel as they would if you took the 100 g mass to each planet.

Summary questions

1 a There is a gravitational _____ around all objects. This is stronger around more _____ objects.

b Your weight depends on your mass and the _____ _____ _____, so your weight is _____ on different planets.

c Choose the value closest to the acceleration due to gravity on Earth:

$0.1 \, \text{m/s}^2$ $1.0 \, \text{m/s}^2$ $10 \, \text{m/s}^2$ $300\,000 \, \text{km/s}^2$

2 a Complete the sentences by matching the phrases. Write the matched letters and numbers to show your answer.

  A To bend, stretch, or compress a   **1** plastic.
      piece of foam you need …

  B If the foam returns to its original   **2** more than one
      shape we say it is …   force.

  C If the foam does not return to its   **3** elastic.
      original shape we say it is …

b Select which statement, or statements, apply to a _linear relationship_ between force and extension:

  A The graph of force against extension is not a straight line.

  B If the force doubles the extension doubles.

  C Force and extension have this relationship for a elastic.

  D Force and extension have this relationship for a spring.

  E Force is proportional to extension.

c i A spring in a toy has a spring constant of 200 N/m. Calculate the force required to stretch it by 0.01 m.

  ii Calculate the energy transferred in stretching the spring using the equation:

$$\text{energy transferred in stretching} = \frac{1}{2} \times \text{spring constant} \times \text{extension}^2$$

3 Giant bungee bouncers are great fun. They are like baby bouncers but much bigger.

The bungee cords are made of rubber.

a i Sketch a force–extension graph for rubber.

  ii Explain why you cannot use the equation in **2 d** to calculate the energy stored in the rubber.

b A girl bounces up to a height of 8 m. If her mass is 50 kg, and $g = 10 \, \text{N/kg}$, calculate the gravitational potential energy.

c She can hang between the bungee cords without touching the trampoline. The angle between the bungee cords is 90°. Use a free body diagram and scale drawing to calculate the tension in the bungee cords. Remember each cord contributes to the force that balances her.

Revision questions

1 A steel paperclip of mass 5×10^{-4} kg is fixed to a bench by a piece of flexible lightweight thread.
It attracts to a permanent magnet, which is also fixed.

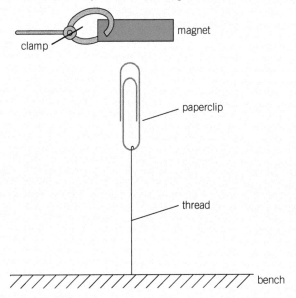

a Use ideas about forces to explain why the paperclip does not fall to the bench. *(4 marks)*

b i The mass of the paperclip is centred at a point 0.3 m above the bench. Calculate the potential energy (in joules) of the paperclip.
(gravitational field strength $g = 10$ N/kg) *(2 marks)*

ii The magnet is removed and the paperclip falls. **H**
Use your answer to **b i** to calculate the velocity (in m/s) of the paperclip as it hits the bench.
(3 marks)

2 The horizontal lightweight beam shown below rests on a pivot. The beam is balanced.

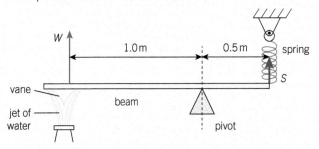

Acting on the beam is a force W, produced by a jet of water hitting a vane, and a force S, produced by the tension in a spring attached to a stationary hook.

a State why the beam is balanced. *(1 mark)*

b i The extension x of the spring is 0.06 m.
The spring constant k of the spring is 250 N/m.
Calculate the tension S (in newtons) in the spring.
(2 marks)

ii Use your answer to **b i** to calculate the force W (in newtons) produced by the jet of water. *(2 marks)*

c The flow rate of water hitting the vane is 0.3 kg/s. **H**
Use the equation
change of momentum = force × time
to calculate the velocity (in m/s) of the water.
(3 marks)

P2.1 Motion

- Describe how to measure distance and time.
- State and use the equation linking speed, distance, and time, and convert between units.
- Explain the difference between a scalar and a vector, including displacement and velocity.
- Explain what acceleration is, and state and use the equation for acceleration.
- Interpret distance–time graphs and use a distance–time graph to calculate speed.
- Interpret velocity–time graphs and use a velocity–time graph to calculate acceleration.
- Use a velocity–time graph to calculate the distance travelled.
- State and use the equation linking kinetic energy, mass, and velocity.
- Use the equation that links initial velocity, final velocity, acceleration, and distance travelled.

P2.2 Newton's laws

- Explain how forces arise, and describe contact and non-contact forces.
- Use vector diagrams to show resolution of forces. **H**
- Draw and interpret free body diagrams to explain the motion of objects in equilibrium.
- Describe and apply Newton's Second Law, and state and use the equation for force.
- Use free body diagrams to analyse situations where there is a resultant force on an object.
- Explain why objects move in a circle.
- Give examples of everyday situations where forces act, including skydivers and cars.
- State and apply Newton's Third Law.
- Describe what momentum is, and state and use the equation for momentum. **H**
- Apply and use equations to calculate the momentum or speed of objects in collisions.
- State and use the equation for work, and convert between newton-metres and joules.
- State and use the equation linking power, energy or work, and time.

P2.3 Forces in action

- Describe the difference between plastic and elastic behaviour when you deform an object.
- Describe and explain the shape of a force–extension graph for a spring.
- State and use the equation linking force, extension, and spring constant.
- Describe the difference between a linear and a non-linear relationship for force and extension, e.g., for materials such as rubber, copper, and glass.
- Use the equation for the work done in stretching a spring.
- Explain what is meant by gravitational field, gravity force, and weight.

Newton's Laws

Newton's First Law ◀ IF THERE IS NO RESULTANT FORCE
- an object remains at rest or moving at a steady speed (equilibrium) unless an external force acts on it

Newton's Second Law ◀ IF THERE IS A RESULTANT FORCE
- an object accelerates (there is a change in speed)

$$\text{force (N)} = \text{mass (kg)} \times \text{acceleration (m/s}^2\text{)}$$

Newton's Third Law
- for every action there is an equal and opposite reaction
  → forces come in pairs
- forces in an interaction pair:
  – are the same size
  – act in opposite directions
  – act on two different objects

Motion

- speeds are found if you know distance (e.g., using a ruler) and time (e.g., using a stopwatch):

$$\text{average speed (m/s)} = \frac{\text{total distance (m)}}{\text{time (s)}}$$

vector	**scalar**
- has magnitude and distance	- has magnitude only example:
- example:	– distance
– displacement	– speed
– velocity	

Distance–time graphs

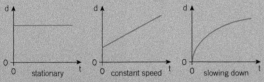

stationary   constant speed   slowing down

- gradient gives you speed

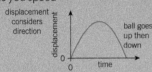

displacement considers direction

ball goes up then down

Velocity–time graphs

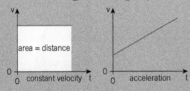

area = distance

constant velocity   acceleration

- gradient gives you acceleration

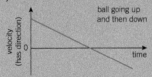

ball going up and then down

velocity (has direction)

$$\text{acceleration (m/s}^2\text{)} = \frac{\text{change in speed (m/s)}}{\text{change in time (s)}}$$

Equation of motion

$$(\text{final velocity (m/s)})^2 - (\text{initial velocity (m/s)})^2$$
$$= 2 \times \text{acceleration (m/s}^2\text{)} \times \text{distance (m)}$$

Forces

- examples = friction, weight, upthrust, drag
- measured in N
- can be contact/non-contact
- shown force arrow indicating size and direction

Free body diagrams [H]

- forces on leaf from two *different* pairs

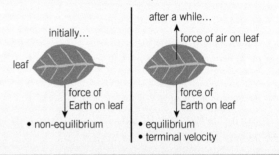

initially...

leaf

force of Earth on leaf

- non-equilibrium

after a while...

force of air on leaf

force of Earth on leaf

- equilibrium
- terminal velocity

Momentum [H]

- momentum is conserved
- momentum before = momentum after

Forces in action

energy transferred in stretching (J) = 0.5 × spring constant (N/m) × (extension (m))^2

force exerted by spring (N) = spring constant (N/m) × extension (m)

gravity force (N) = mass (kg) × gravitational field strength (N/kg)

weight (N) = mass (kg) × gravitational field strength (N/kg)

gravitational potential energy (J) = mass (kg) × height (m) × gravitational field strength (N/kg)

P2 Forces

P3 Electricity and magnetism
P3.1 Static and charge
P3.1.1 Electrostatics

Learning outcomes

After studying this lesson you should be able to:

- describe what charge is, and why we do not normally see its effects
- describe how to produce static electricity, and sparking
- explain how the transfer of electrons between objects can explain the phenomenon of static electricity.

Specification reference: P3.1a, P3.1b, P3.1c

Figure 1 *Lifting a footprint.*

A forensic scientist (Figure 1) uses electrostatics to 'lift' footprints at a crime scene so they can be photographed.

What is charge?

You may have felt a small shock from a car door, or seen lightning. You can explain what is happening if you know about **electric charge**. Some of the particles in atoms are charged:

- Protons have a positive charge.
- Electrons have a negative charge.

Charge is a property of matter just like mass. You know that atoms are neutral overall. They have no charge because there are equal numbers of protons and electrons. Like charges repel and unlike charges attract (Figure 2).

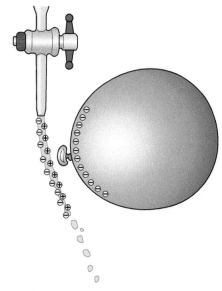

Figure 2 *A charged balloon attracts water.*

> **A** Describe an experiment you have seen that shows that like charges repel and unlike charges attract.
>
> **B** Explain why you do not normally experience static electricity.

Study tip

You should always explain static by talking about the movement of electrons, not positive charges.

How do you produce static electricity?

When you rub two insulators together you can transfer *electrons* from one insulator to the other (Figure 3). Positive charges do not move. One object ends up with extra electrons, and the other with not enough electrons to cancel out the positive charge.

The charge on each object is what we call '**static electricity**' or 'static'.

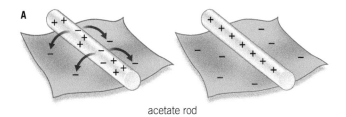

acetate rod

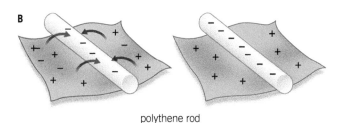

polythene rod

Figure 3 *Electrons move from one insulator to the other.* **3A** *Electrons move from the acetate rod to the cloth, leaving the rod positively charged.* **3B** *Electrons move from the cloth to the polythene rod, leaving the rod negatively charged.*

To discharge an object you need to remove the charge. You connect it to something that allows the charges to flow – like a piece of metal, or you when you touch a car door.

Sparks also discharge charged objects such as a Van der Graaf generator, or clouds (Figure 4). A spark is a flow of charge, or a **current**, through the air.

Figure 4 *Air conducts electricity, and the current through it heats the air and makes the spark that you see and hear.*

1 A student has a collection of insulating rods marked **A** and **B**. She takes a rod marked **A**, rubs it with a cloth, and hangs it up by some cotton thread.
   a When she brings another charged rod also marked **A** near to the first rod, the first rod moves away. Explain why. *(2 marks)*
   b When she brings a charged rod marked **B** near to the first rod, the first rod moves towards it. Explain why. *(2 marks)*
   c Write down and explain what would happen if she used two rods marked **B**. *(2 marks)*

2 Describe the differences between a rod that is charged positively and a rod that is charged negatively. *(2 marks)*

3 **a** Describe how to charge a balloon. *(1 mark)*
   b Explain why the balloon becomes negatively charged. *(1 mark)*
   c Sketch diagrams to explain why a charged balloon sticks to the wall. *(2 marks)*

4 ⊘ At a crime scene a forensic scientist lays a plastic sheet over a footprint and rubs the sheet.
   a Suggest why the dirt from the footprint sticks to the sheet. *(4 marks)*
   b Explain why the sheet should not be made of metal. *(2 marks)*

Synoptic link

You can learn more about protons and neutrons in C1.2 *Atomic structure.*

Learning outcomes

After studying this lesson you should be able to:

● describe what current is, and the conditions for a current to flow

● compare the current in different parts of a closed loop

● recall and use the relationship between quantity of charge, current, and time

● describe how to measure current.

Specification reference: P3.1d, P3.1e, P3.1f

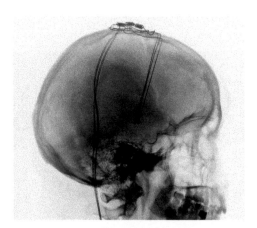

Figure 1 *An X-ray of electrodes in a brain.*

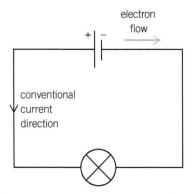

Figure 3 *The movement of negative charges in one direction is the same as the movement of positive charges in the opposite direction.*

Doctors can use electrodes to produce a current in a patient's brain (Figure 1). This can help to relieve pain.

What is current and how do you model it?

The little shock that you can experience when you touch a car door is the movement of electrons through your body. This is a current.

Current is the rate of flow of charged particles, or charge. In the metal wires that you use to make circuits the charges that move are electrons. Each electron has a very small charge, but there are large numbers of them in the wires.

To make a current flow you need a **cell** or a **battery**, or a power supply, as well as a complete circuit. The current everywhere in a single closed loop is the same.

A Explain why a current cannot usually flow in a vacuum.

Modelling electricity

You can model an electric circuit with a loop of rope, as in Figure 2. A person pulling the rope represents the battery, the movement of the rope represents the current, and someone gripping the rope represents a circuit component.

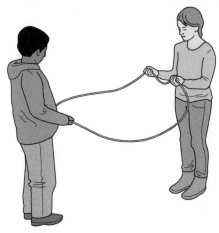

Figure 2 *You will find a loop of rope useful to model what is happening in a circuit.*

Which way does current flow?

When you draw the direction of electric current on a circuit diagram, you draw it going in the direction of the positive terminal of the battery to the negative terminal (Figure 3). This is called **conventional current**. This is opposite to electron flow.

B Suggest whether the colour of insulation on a wire affects the current in a circuit. Give a reason for your decision.

How do you calculate with current?

You need to be able to recall and apply:

$$\text{charge flow (C)} = \text{current (A)} \times \text{time (s)}$$

Charge is measured in **coulombs** (C), current is measured in **amperes** or amps (A), and time is measured in seconds. Small currents are measured in **milliamps** (mA), and $1\,\text{mA} = 1 \times 10^{-3}\,\text{A}$.

Calculating charge

Calculate the charge flowing in 2 minutes for a toy electric car that needs a current of 14 mA.

Step 1: Convert the quantities to standard units.

$$\text{time} = 2\text{ minutes} \times 60 \text{ seconds/minute}$$
$$= 120 \text{ seconds}$$
$$\text{current} = 14\,\text{mA}$$
$$= 14 \times 10^{-3}\,\text{A}$$

Step 2: Calculate the charge.

$$\text{charge flow} = \text{current} \times \text{time}$$
$$= 14 \times 10^{-3}\,\text{A} \times 120\,\text{s}$$
$$= 1.7\,\text{C (2 significant figures)}$$

You can also use the equation to calculate the current that flows.

Calculating current

Calculate the current through the air in a lightning strike if a charge of 300 C flows in 0.01 s.

Step 1: Write down what you know.

$$\text{charge} = 300\,\text{C}$$
$$\text{time} = 0.01\,\text{s}$$

Step 2: Change the subject of the equation and calculate the current.

$$\text{current} = \frac{\text{charge}}{\text{time}}$$
$$= \frac{300\,\text{C}}{0.01\,\text{s}} = 30\,000\,\text{A (1 significant figure)}$$

This is an enormous current.

1. Describe the difference between charge and current. *(2 marks)*
2. Calculate the charge flowing in a circuit of a torch that is left on for 2 hours if the current is 0.4 A. *(2 marks)*
3. Calculate the current flowing in your finger when you touch a car if a charge of 0.1 µC flows in 0.2 ms. $1\,\mu\text{C} = 1 \times 10^{-6}\,\text{C}$. *(2 marks)*
4. The charge on the electron is very, very small, $1.6 \times 10^{-19}\,\text{C}$.
   a. Calculate how many electrons you need for a charge of 1 C. *(2 marks)*
   b. Calculate the number of electrons that travel past a point per second to produce a current of 2.0 mA. *(2 marks)*

Figure 4 *The current in the wires in a toaster is about 5 A.*

Electricity and magnetism

Summary questions

1 a Select the correct equation for calculating charge flow:

charge flow = current × time

$$\text{charge flow} = \frac{\text{current}}{\text{time}}$$

$$\text{charge flow} = \frac{\text{time}}{\text{current}}$$

  ii Write down the unit of charge.

  b Write down the meanings of the following terms.

  charge   current   potential difference   resistance

2 Use the words and phrases from the box to complete the sentences below.
Use each word once, more than once, or not at all.

electrons	conductors	iron	negative
insulators	positive	protons	neutrons
no	plastic	friction	some

  a Static electricity is the imbalance between
  _____ and _____ charge. It is
  caused by the movement of _____.

  b Every atom contains three types of particle. They are
  _____ with a positive charge, electrons with
  a _____ charge and _____ with
  _____ charge.

  c _____ are materials that don't hold tight to
  their electrons and electrons have an easy time moving
  through them. An example is _____.

  d _____ are materials that hold tight to
  their electrons and don't allow them to move in and
  out. An example is _____.

3 a Describe and explain how you charge a polythene
  rod negatively.

  b Describe and explain what happens when you bring
  the rod near some very small pieces of paper on
  the desk.

  c Two negatively charged polythene rods will repel.
  Use the idea of an electric field to explain why.

4 a Calculate the charge transferred when a current of
  0.1 A flows through a bulb in 10 seconds.

  b Calculate the charge transferred when a current of
  2 mA flows through a bulb in 1 minute.

  c Calculate the current flowing if a charge of 450 C is
  transferred in 10 minutes.

  d Calculate how long it would take to transfer a charge
  of 6.2 C if the current is 2.5 A.

5 David says that 'current' flows from the positive to the
negative terminal of a cell in a simple circuit, but Sunita
says it is the other way round. Explain how they can
both be 'correct'.

6 In a thunderstorm clouds become charged by air
moving inside them.

  a Explain why there are two regions of charge inside a
  thundercloud.

  b The bottom of the cloud becomes negatively
  charged. Explain why the top of a tree becomes
  positively charged.

  c When lightning strikes, a charge of 0.0005 mC flows
  in half a second. Calculate the current in the air.

  d You can put a lightning conductor on a tall chimney
  so that the building is not affected by lightning.
  A rod on the chimney points up to the sky, and is
  connected to the ground by cable. Suggest and
  explain a suitable material for the rod and the cable.

7 There are examples of static electricity being formed in
lots of different situations. At a petrol station you fill up
your car with petrol, and there are ways to reduce the
hazards involved in doing so.

  a Suggest why flowing petrol becomes charged.

  b Explain why this would be dangerous.

  c If you hold the nozzle against the edge of the filling
  hole (touching the outside of the car) you are less
  likely to produce a spark. Explain why.

  d Some petrol nozzles have a metal wire connected
  from the nozzle to the ground along the fuel line.
  Explain how that would reduce the chance of
  producing a spark.

8 Read the information in the box below.

> Lightning and sparks are examples of situations
> where there is an electric current flowing. The air
> conducts. We talk about different things being
> insulators but there is only really one insulator, which
> is a complete vacuum. It is very dangerous to be
> out in a thunderstorm because you could be hit by
> lightning. The current would go through you to earth.

  a Explain why the air conducts but a vacuum does not.

  b Identify the sentence in the box above that indicates
  that your body contains charged particles.

  c Suggest and explain whether glass is a conductor or
  an insulator.

Revision questions

1 A girl rubs a balloon on her hair. This transfers charges from her hair to the balloon.

When she holds the charged balloon near a stream of water, it changes the direction of the water.

  a Give the name of the charges that are transferred from the girl's hair to the balloon. (*1 mark*)

  b Explain why the stream of water bends towards the balloon.
You may draw and label a diagram to help with your answer. (*3 marks*)

2 The waste gases of a power station contain smoke particles.
The smoke particles are removed by a *precipitator*. This contains a charged metal grid and a charged collecting plate.
Each smoke particle is neutral.

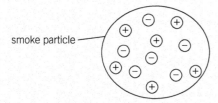

  a Explain what is meant by *neutral*. (*2 marks*)

  b The smoke particles pass through a negatively charged metal grid. They gain electrons.

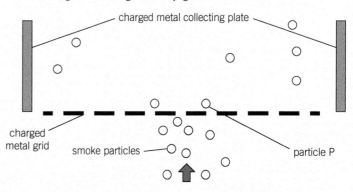

Copy and complete the diagram below to show the arrangement of charges on particle P after it has passed through the charged metal grid. (*2 marks*)

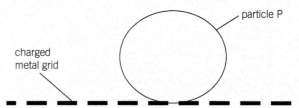

  c After passing through the grid, the smoke particles move towards the metal collecting plate. State the charge on the grid and the charge on the collecting plate. (*2 marks*)

  d The potential difference between the grid and the collecting plate is 22 000 V. The collecting plates receive a total of 0.9 C of charge every second.

    i State the current in the collecting plate. (*1 mark*)

    ii Calculate the electrical resistance (in ohms) between the collecting plates and the grid. (*2 marks*)

P3.2 Simple circuits

P3.2.1 Circuits and potential difference

Learning outcomes

After studying this lesson you should be able to:

- represent d.c. circuits with the conventions of positive and negative terminals
- use symbols that represent common circuit elements
- recall and apply the equation that links energy transferred, potential difference, and charge.

Specification reference: P3.2b, P3.2m

How much energy do you need to transfer to a patient to restart their heart (Figure 1)?

How do we draw circuits?

You use circuit symbols to draw electric circuits. You can find these symbols in the Reference material.

What is potential difference?

To make a current flow in a circuit you need a **potential difference (p.d.)**. Inside a cell or battery (Figure 2) there are substances that react to separate the charges. This makes one side of the battery positively charged and the other side negatively charged.

The positive terminal of the cell is at a higher electrical potential than the negative terminal. The potential difference, and the current that a cell can deliver, depends on the construction of the cell, not its size. Potential difference is measured in **volts (V)**. The longer line on the symbol for a cell is positive, and the shorter line is negative.

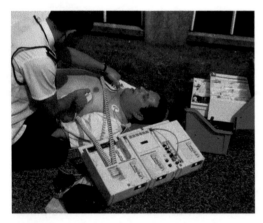

Figure 1 *A paramedic using a portable defibrillator.*

Figure 2 *The two batteries (cells) on the left have the same potential difference as the button cell on the right.*

> **A** Explain why you could say that batteries provide a push *and* a pull on the negative electrons in a wire.

When you apply a p.d. between the ends of a piece of wire, you set up an electric field in the wire. The field is set up very quickly (close to the speed of light in a vacuum), so the charged electrons start to move straight away.

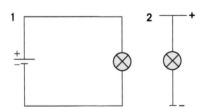

Figure 3a *You can pull apart a circuit (1)... to make a line (2)...*

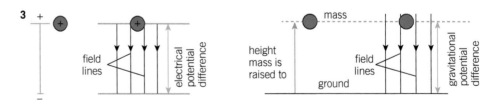

Figure 3b *...and show that electrical potential difference is similar to gravitational potential difference (3).*

You measure potential difference with a **voltmeter**.

How do you model potential difference?

In the rope model you can show the work done by the battery by pulling the rope. The work done by the charges in the component is the work done on the person's hand holding the rope. The charges do very little work in the wires.

B   Suggest what is 'used up' when a current flows.

What is the link between potential difference, energy, and charge?

When you connect a voltmeter across a component in the circuit you measure the work done or **energy** transferred by the charges in the component. We call this transferring energy electrically. You need to recall and apply:

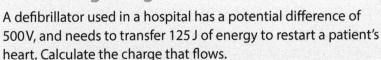
energy transferred (J) = potential difference (V) × charge (C)

Calculating charge

A defibrillator used in a hospital has a potential difference of 500 V, and needs to transfer 125 J of energy to restart a patient's heart. Calculate the charge that flows.

Step 1: Write down what you know.

potential difference = 500 V

energy transferred = 125 J

Step 2: Change the subject of the equation to charge.

$$\frac{\text{energy}}{\text{potential difference}} = \frac{\text{potential difference} \times \text{charge}}{\text{potential difference}}$$

$$\frac{\text{energy}}{\text{potential difference}} = \text{charge}$$

Step 3: Calculate the charge.

$$\frac{\text{energy}}{\text{potential difference}} = \text{charge}$$

$$\frac{125\,\text{J}}{500\,\text{V}} = \text{charge}$$

charge = 0.25 C (3 significant figures)

Voltage and current

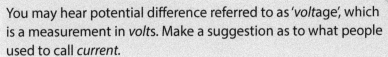

You may hear potential difference referred to as '*voltage*', which is a measurement in *volts*. Make a suggestion as to what people used to call *current*.

Figure 4 *Electric eels can produce a potential difference of about 600 V to stun their prey.*

Study tip

When you draw circuits with cells it is helpful to draw them with the cell or battery at the side of the circuit, not the top. This reminds you that a battery 'lifts up' charge.

1 Explain why the electrons in the wires of a circuit move.   (*2 marks*)

2 Explain the difference between current and potential difference.   (*2 marks*)

3 Calculate the energy transferred when a charge of 3 mC moves through a potential difference of 1 kV.   (*2 marks*)

4 **a** Compare gravitational potential energy and (electrical) potential energy (Figure 3).   (*2 marks*)

   b Suggest how you might calculate electrical potential energy for a charge in an electric field.   (*2 marks*)

P3.2.2 Series and parallel circuits

Learning outcome

After studying this lesson you should be able to:

- describe the differences between series and parallel circuits.

Specification reference: P3.2a

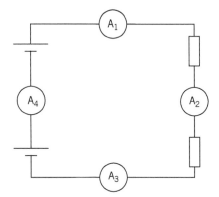

Figure 2 *Ammeters should be in the loop because charge needs to flow* **through** *them.*

Figure 3 *This is an analogue ammeter. It shows the current using a needle on a scale.*

Why would the voltmeter in Figure 1 read zero?

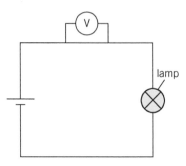

Figure 1 *A circuit with a voltmeter.*

How do you measure current in series circuits?

You have learned that a **series circuit** has only one loop, and the current is the same everywhere (Figure 2). You measure the current in a circuit with an **ammeter** (Figure 3).

> **A** Use the rope model to explain why the current in a series circuit is the same everywhere.

How do you measure potential difference in series circuits?

A voltmeter (Figure 4) measures a 'difference' – the (electrical) potential difference. You need to connect the voltmeter to *both sides* of a component (Figure 5).

A voltmeter measures the 'rise in potential' across a cell or battery. It can also measure the 'drop in potential' across a component. There is very little 'drop' across the wires, so the voltmeter in Figure 1 reads zero.

Figure 4 *You can use a digital meter as a voltmeter to measure p.d. You need to work out which terminals to use.*

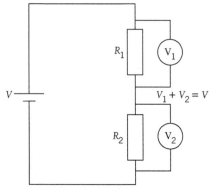

Figure 5 *The voltmeters are measuring the drop in potential across the resistors.*

> **B** Explain why the reading on the voltmeter in Figure 1 is zero.

You end up at the bottom of the 'potential hill', or 0V, so the readings on the voltmeters always add up to the reading across the cell.

What happens in parallel circuits?

It is helpful to think of a **parallel circuit** as having more than one loop (Figure 6).

In a parallel circuit each loop can be worked independently. This is what happens in your house. You do not have to have all the lights on at once.

If you measure the current at different points in a parallel circuit, the currents in the loops add up to the current near the battery (Figure 7).

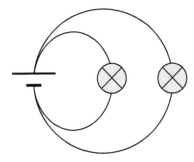

Figure 6 *A parallel circuit with two loops.*

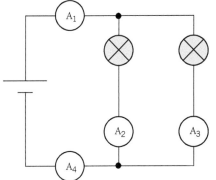

Figure 7 *Ammeter readings:*
$A_1 = A_4 = A_2 + A_3$

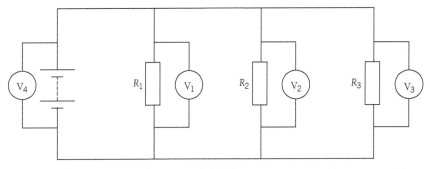

Figure 8 *If you measure the potential difference across each component then you find it is the same. Each component 'sees' the potential difference of the cell.*

It is helpful to think of a parallel circuit like the diagram in Figure 9.

● Resistor 1 and resistor 2 are both directly connected to the cell.

● If you *add* the current at b and the current at c you get the current at a.

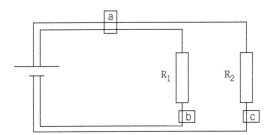

Figure 9 *A way of thinking about a parallel circuit.*

1 In Figure 5 the potential difference of the cell is 6V, and the reading on V_1 is 2V. Calculate the reading on V_2. *(2 marks)*

2 In Figure 7 suggest when the reading on A_2 and A_3 would be the same, and when they would be different. *(1 mark)*

3 A student adds another resistor in parallel to the circuit in Figure 7. Suggest and explain what happens to the readings on each of the four ammeters. *(2 marks)*

4 **a** Predict the potential difference across an ammeter in a series circuit. Explain your answer. *(2 marks)*

   b Predict the current through a voltmeter connected in parallel with a component in a series circuit. Explain your answer. *(2 marks)*

Connecting an ammeter

You connect an ammeter so that the negative (black or 'com') terminal is nearest the negative terminal of the battery. If you do not then the reading on the meter is negative, or the needle goes to the left of zero.

Synoptic link

You have drawn circuit diagrams at Key Stage 3.

You can find a full list of the electrical symbols you will need to know in the *Reference materials*.

Learning outcomes

After studying this lesson you should be able to:

- recall that current (I) depends on both resistance (R) and potential difference (V)
- recall and apply the relationship between I, R, and V
- explain that for some resistors the value of R remains constant but that for others it can change as the current changes.

Specification reference: P3.2c, P3.2d, P3.2e

A gap in a circuit means no current flows. Can air conduct electricity (Figure 1)?

Figure 1 *The resistance of the air is so high it takes millions of volts to make it conduct.*

What does the current depend on?

The current in a circuit depends on the potential difference of the cell or battery and the **resistance** of the components. Resistance is measured in **ohms** (Ω).

Modelling resistance

In the rope model, resistance is modelled by the person gripping the rope.

- If the person grips the rope more tightly and the other person pulls with the same force then the rope will move more slowly.
- To keep the same speed the person pulling the rope would have to pull harder.

A Translate the two statements above into statements about current, potential difference, and resistance.

Resistance of a wire

You can take measurements of current and potential difference to find out how the resistance of a piece of resistance wire varies with length.

You need to do a risk assessment because wires get hot.

1 Connect a cell, a piece of resistance wire, and an ammeter in series.

2 Connect a voltmeter in parallel with the length of resistance wire in the circuit.

3 Take measurements and calculate the resistance.

4 Change the length of the wire and repeat your measurements.

This experiment gives you practice in connecting ammeters and voltmeters correctly.

How do you calculate resistance?

You cannot *choose* the current, only the potential difference and resistance of your circuit. The current is the *dependent* variable.

$$\text{current (A)} = \frac{\text{potential difference (V)}}{\text{resistance } (\Omega)}$$

You can rearrange this equation to calculate resistance or potential difference:

$$\text{resistance} = \frac{\text{potential difference}}{\text{current}}$$

You need to recall and apply:

$$\text{potential difference} = \text{current} \times \text{resistance}$$

The symbol equation is:

$$V = I \times R$$

Calculating resistance

If you hold the ends of a 1.5 V battery in your fingers, a current of about 10 µA (microamps) flows through you. Calculate your resistance. $1\,\mu A = 1 \times 10^{-6}\,A$.

Step 1: Write down what you know, in standard units.

$$V = 1.5\,V$$

$$I = 10 \times 10^{-6}\,A$$

Step 2: Calculate the resistance.

$$R = \frac{V}{I}$$

$$= \frac{1.5\,V}{10 \times 10^{-6}\,A}$$

$$= 1.5 \times 10^{5}\,\Omega\ (= 150\,000\,\Omega)\ \text{(2 significant figures)}$$

Figure 2 *Resistors are used in most electronic devices, such as computer circuit boards.*

Why does the resistance of some components change?

A metal is made up of positively charged ions arranged in a regular pattern (Figure 3). The ions are formed when electrons leave the outer shells of metal atoms. These delocalised electrons are free to move through the structure of the metal. Resistance is produced when electrons collide with the ions in the lattice. This explains why the resistance of some components changes with current.

Figure 3 *Electrons in a wire are free to move in the electric field produced by the potential difference.*

B Suggest why a thicker wire has a lower resistance.

A **variable resistor** (Figure 4) is a circuit component you can use to change the amount of wire or other resisting material. You use a variable resistor every time you use a dimmer switch.

Electrical intensity and current

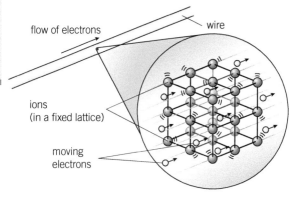

The letter I is used instead of C, for current, because the scientist who discovered electricity called it electrical 'intensity'.

Figure 4 *If you increase the resistance the current decreases for the same p.d.*

1 Explain why potential difference is not the dependent variable. *(1 mark)*

2 Calculate the resistance of a wire with a current through it of 18 mA when the potential difference across it is 6 V. *(2 marks)*

3 The potential difference between the bottom of a thundercloud and the ground is about 1000 MV. The resistance of the air is about $10^{15}\,\Omega$. Calculate the current in the air when lightning strikes. *(2 marks)*

4 A current of 1 A in the human body is extremely dangerous.
   a Estimate the p.d. needed to produce this current. *(2 marks)*
   b Suggest why you are unlikely to be injured by an electric current in your house. *(1 mark)*

Study tip

You only need to remember one of these equations, then you can rearrange it. The rope model helps you remember:

$$I = \frac{V}{R}$$

Learning outcomes

After studying this lesson you should be able to:

- explain the design and use of circuits to explore how resistance changes with current
- use graphs to explore whether circuit elements are linear or non-linear
- use graphs and relate the curves to the function and properties of resistors, lamps, and diodes.

Specification reference: P3.2f, P3.2g, P3.2h

Figure 1 *A blue LED.*

Figure 2 *You need to use a voltmeter and an ammeter to produce a characteristic graph.*

Table 1 *Results for plotting a characteristic graph.*

p.d. (V)	Current (A)	Resistance = V/I (Ω)
0	0	–
1	0.1	1
2	0.2	1
3	0.3	1
−1	−0.1	1
−2	−0.2	1
−3	−0.3	1

Why is one 'leg' of a light-emitting diode (LED) longer than the other one (Figure 1)?

How do you get measurements for a graph of current and potential difference?

A graph of current against potential difference is called a **characteristic graph**. You collect data for the graph by taking measurements of the current flowing through a component for different potential differences. Then you reverse the battery or power supply connections and repeat the measurements.

When you have recorded your measurements you can:

- calculate the resistance from each pair of measurements
- plot a characteristic graph with potential difference on the *x*-axis and current on the *y*-axis.

A Draw a circuit diagram for the circuit in Figure 2.

What is the characteristic graph for a resistance wire or a resistor?

Table 1 shows some results for a piece of resistance wire or fixed resistor. These results are plotted in the graph in Figure 3.

The wire is a **linear circuit element**. Its resistance does not change as you change the potential difference (Figure 3).

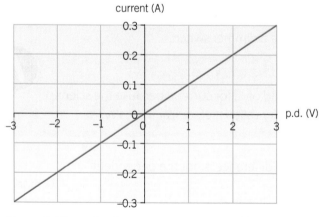

Figure 3 *The ratio of current to potential difference does not change.*

B Explain why you cannot calculate resistance for the first set of measurements in Table 1.

You use resistance wire or a resistor in a circuit if you need the resistance to be constant.

What is the characteristic graph for a lamp?

In 1827, George Ohm discovered that metal wires were linear elements. He said that the current is proportional to the potential difference if the temperature does not change. This is Ohm's Law.

If the wire gets hot then the resistance varies and the graph is not a straight line (Figure 5). For a **non-linear circuit element** the resistance is not constant.

Figure 4 *You use a circuit like this to get data to plot a characteristic curve.*

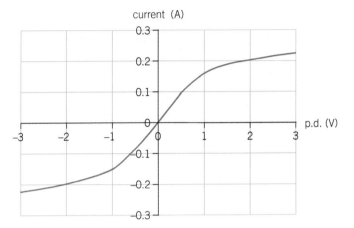

Figure 5 *A characteristic graph for a wire in a light bulb.*

The electrons in a wire collide with the ions in the wire. The ions vibrate more as the wire gets hotter. Hot wires can be used in lamps. As that happens there are more collisions. The wire heats up more. The current *decreases* as the potential difference increases.

What is a diode, and what does its characteristic graph look like?

A **diode** is a component that only allows a current to flow one way. Some diodes emit light. There are light-emitting diodes (LEDs) in most of the electronic devices that you use. The long leg of an LED should be connected to the positive terminal of a battery (Figure 6).

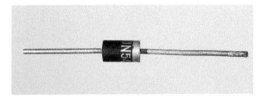

Figure 6 *You have to connect the silver end of this diode to the negative terminal.*

Avoiding zero errors

If an analogue meter does not read zero before you connect it there will be an error in all of your measurements, called a zero error. If you have a zero error due to one of your meters your graph will not go through the origin, (0, 0).

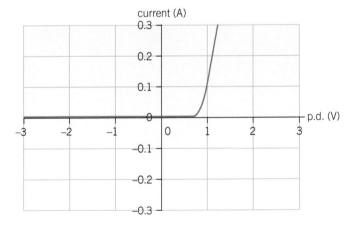

Figure 7 *A characteristic graph for a diode.*

As you apply a potential difference in the 'forward' direction very little current flows. Then the current suddenly increases (Figure 7). If you reverse the potential difference there is no current. You use a diode if you want the current to flow only in one direction.

1 You have a 'mystery' component. Describe how you would work out whether it was a linear or non-linear circuit element. *(3 marks)*

2 Suggest how you could model a diode in the rope model of a circuit. *(2 marks)*

3 **a** Take a reading from the graph in Figure 5 to calculate the resistance of the lamp at potential differences 1 V and 2 V. *(4 marks)*
  b Explain whether the resistance is proportional to the potential difference. *(2 marks)*

4 Describe and explain the resistance of the diode in the 'reverse' direction. *(2 marks)*

Learning outcomes

After studying this lesson you should be able to:

- use graphs to explore whether circuit elements are linear or non-linear
- use graphs and relate the curves produced to the function and properties of thermistors and LDRs.

Specification reference: P3.2g, P3.2h

Figure 1 *The most common type of digital thermometer is the ear thermometer.*

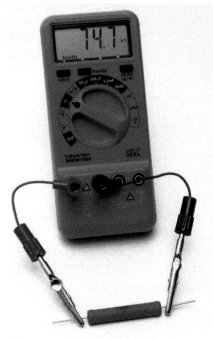

Figure 3 *You can connect a component to a multimeter to measure resistance directly.*

How does a digital thermometer work (Figure 1)?

What is a thermistor?

At the end of many digital thermometers is a **thermistor**. The resistance of a thermistor depends on temperature.

Thermistors come in different shapes and sizes (Figure 2), and detect different ranges of temperature.

 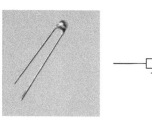

Figure 2 *A thermistor, a bead thermistor, and the circuit symbol for a thermistor.*

A thermistor is not like a piece of wire. It is made of a semiconducting material, such as silicon. Electrons in the atoms of a **semiconductor** do not need much energy to escape from the atom to form the current.

A State an important use of a thermistor.

How does the resistance of a thermistor change with temperature?

You can measure the resistance of the thermistor by measuring the current through it and the potential difference across it (Figure 3).

If you put a thermistor in a beaker of cold water and heat the water up the resistance of the thermistor decreases (Figure 4).

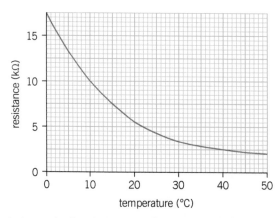

Figure 4 *A graph of resistance and temperature for a thermistor.*

As you heat the thermistor many electrons gain enough energy to escape from the atoms in the semiconductor.

For a certain potential difference:

- at low temperatures, the current is small, so the resistance of the thermistor is high
- at higher temperatures, the current is high, so the resistance of the thermistor is low.

If there are more electrons moving per second for a particular potential difference, the current will be bigger. A bigger current for the same potential difference means the resistance is smaller.

You will have many thermistors in your house. They are used to monitor the temperature in ovens and refrigerators, and help to prevent your laptop or tablet from overheating.

B Use the graph in Figure 4 to estimate the resistance of the thermistor at room temperature.

What is an LDR?

The resistance of a **light-dependent resistor (LDR)** changes with light intensity. It is a circuit component that is also made of a semiconducting material (Figure 5). In the LDR, light causes electrons to be released into the circuit to increase the current.

 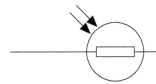

Figure 5 *A light-dependent resistor, and the circuit symbol for a light-dependent resistor.*

How does the resistance of an LDR change with light intensity?

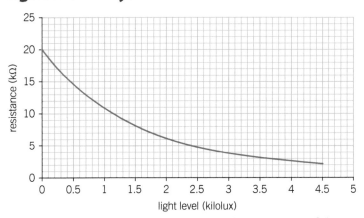

Figure 6 *As the light intensity increases the resistance of the LDR decreases.*

The shape of the graph for an LDR (Figure 6) is the same as the shape of the graph for a thermistor (Figure 4). As the intensity of the light increases, more electrons are released in the semiconductor and the resistance decreases. LDRs are used to automatically control lights in a building.

Go further

Find out how semiconducting materials are used to make diodes.

Using a multimeter

A digital multimeter can be used to measure current, potential difference, or resistance. You need to check which of the three terminals to use.

1 Use the graph in Figure 4 to suggest the effect on the resistance of the thermistor of doubling the temperature. *(2 marks)*

2 Describe the difference between the cause of resistance in a wire and the cause of resistance in a thermistor. *(2 marks)*

3 Suggest how and why the material in a thermistor used in a medical thermometer is different from the material used in an oven. (Hint: atoms in different semiconductors need different amounts of energy to release electrons from the atoms.) *(2 marks)*

4 Suggest why the graphs of resistance against temperature, and of resistance against light level, eventually level off. *(2 marks)*

Learning outcomes

After studying this lesson you should be able to:

- explain the net resistance of two resistors in series, and the net resistance of two resistors in parallel
- calculate the currents, potential differences, and resistances in d.c. series and parallel circuits
- apply equations relating potential difference, current, and resistance.

Specification reference: P3.2i, P3.2j, P3.2m

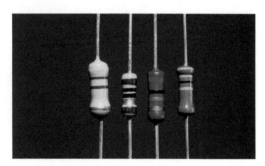

Figure 1 *A selection of resistors.*

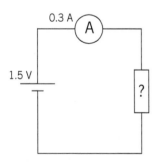

Figure 2 *All of the rest of the circuit is in the 'mystery' box.*

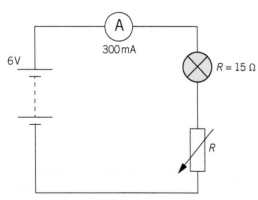

Figure 3 *A series circuit.*

How can you put resistors together and get *less* resistance (Figure 1)?

What is net resistance?

In the circuit in Figure 2 you can calculate the resistance of the box without knowing what is in it. This is the **net resistance**. If you changed the components, or the arrangements of the components, then the current could change. The net resistance would be different.

A Calculate the net resistance in Figure 2.

Suppose there is a lamp in the box.

If you add another identical lamp in *series*:

- the current *decreases*
- the net resistance *increases*.

If you add another identical lamp in *parallel*:

- the total current *increases*
- the net resistance *decreases*.

In a series circuit the net resistance increases. In a parallel circuit the net resistance decreases.

How do you analyse series circuits?

You know that in a series circuit:

- the current is the same everywhere
- the p.d.s across each component add up to the p.d. across the battery
- $V = I \times R$.

When you analyse circuit problems you may need to do calculations that involve many steps. The first thing to do is to write down what you know.

Suppose you wanted to find the resistance of the variable resistor for the circuit in Figure 3. Table 1 shows how to analyse a series circuit.

Table 1 *Analysing a series circuit (Figure 3).*

The strategy	What you are using
If you know the current and the resistance you can: • work out the p.d. across the lamp.	$V = I \times R$
If you know the p.d. across the lamp and the cell you can: • work out the p.d. across the variable resistor.	$V_{VR} = V_{cell} - V_{lamp}$
If you know the p.d. across the variable resistor and the current through it you can: • work out the resistance of the variable resistor.	$R = \dfrac{V}{I}$

B Calculate the p.d. across the lamp for the circuit shown in Figure 3.

How do you analyse parallel circuits?

You know that in a parallel circuit:

- the p.d. is the same across each loop
- the current in each loop adds up to the current near the battery
- $V = I \times R$.

Suppose you wanted to find out the resistance of the lamp in the circuit in Figure 4. Table 2 shows how to analyse a parallel circuit.

Table 2 *Analysing a parallel circuit (Figure 4).*

The strategy	What you are using
If you know the p.d. across the resistor and across the lamp, and if you know the resistance, you can: • work out the current through the resistor.	$I = \dfrac{V}{R}$
If you know the current near the battery you can: • work out the current through the lamp.	$I_{lamp} = I_{battery} - I_{resistor}$
If you know the p.d. across the lamp and the current through it you can: • work out the resistance of the lamp.	$R = \dfrac{V}{I}$

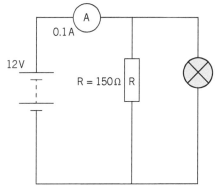

Figure 4 *A parallel circuit.*

Calculating net resistance

Calculate the net resistance of the circuit in Figure 4.

Step 1: Write down the potential difference and the total current.

potential difference = 12 V

total current = 0.1 A

Step 2: Use the equation for resistance to calculate the net resistance.

$$R = \frac{V}{I}$$

$$= \frac{12\,V}{0.1\,A}$$

$$= 120\ \Omega$$

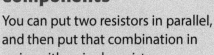

Figure 5 *The net resistance of two lamps in parallel is less than that of one lamp on its own.*

1 Explain the difference between the resistance of a component and the net resistance of a circuit. *(2 marks)*

2 Describe how you can connect resistors together to get less resistance. *(2 marks)*

3 **a** Calculate the resistance of the variable resistor in the circuit in Figure 3. *(3 marks)*

 b Compare the ratios of the resistances and the ratios of the potential differences across the components. *(3 marks)*

4 In the circuit in Figure 4 you replace the single lamp with two lamps in the same loop.

 a Suggest and explain what happens to the net resistance of the circuit. *(3 marks)*

 b Calculate the resistance of each lamp. *(6 marks)*

Combining circuit components

You can put two resistors in parallel, and then put that combination in series with a single resistor.

Alternatively, you can put two resistors in series in one branch of a parallel circuit, and a single resistor in the other branch of the circuit.

Which has the bigger net resistance?

Connect an ammeter near the power supply, and find the potential difference across the battery.

Calculate the net resistance of each circuit.

Learning outcomes

After studying this lesson you should be able to:

- explain the design and use of circuits containing thermistors, LDRs, and other circuit components for measurement and testing purposes
- calculate the currents, potential differences, and resistances in d.c. series and parallel circuits, such as those used for testing or monitoring
- apply equations relating potential difference, current, and resistance.

Specification reference: P3.2j, P3.2k, P3.2m

Figure 1 *How will the control system know the temperature and light level?*

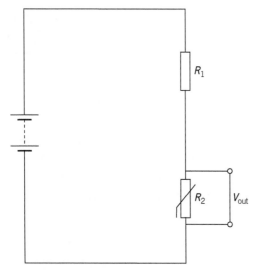

Figure 2 *A circuit that measures temperature.*

In smart buildings sensors continually adjust the lighting and heating (Figure 1). How do sensing circuits work?

How can you measure temperature with a circuit?

Thermistors can be used in **sensing circuits** to produce a potential difference that changes with temperature. This means that you can use a sensing circuit to operate a heater or the air conditioning in a house, school, or office.

The output potential difference in Figure 2 will depend on the potential difference of the battery and the magnitude of each resistor. V_{out}, as measured by a voltmeter, will depend on the temperature.

A State the value of V_{out} in Figure 2, assuming the resistors are equal and the battery has a p.d. of 6V.

Calculating potential difference in a sensing circuit

The p.d. of the battery in Figure 2 is 12 V. R_1 is 10 Ω, and R_2 is 30 Ω. Calculate V_{out}.

Step 1: Calculate the net resistance.

$$\text{net resistance} = 10\,\Omega + 30\,\Omega$$
$$= 40\,\Omega$$

Step 2: Calculate the current.

$$\text{current} = \frac{\text{p.d.}}{\text{resistance}}$$
$$= \frac{12\,V}{40\,\Omega}$$
$$= 0.3\,A$$

Step 3: Calculate the p.d. across R_2.

$$\text{p.d.} = \text{current} \times \text{resistance}$$
$$= 0.3\,A \text{ (2 significant figures)} \times 30\,\Omega$$
$$= 9.0\,V$$

Go further

Find out how pressure sensors work and where you need to use one. There are two clues in Figures 1 and 3!

Calculating changes of potential difference in a sensing circuit

In a sensing circuit in a coffee machine, the battery has a potential difference of 12 V. The fixed resistor has a resistance of 10 kΩ. Calculate the reading on the voltmeter when the thermistor is:

- at room temperature with a resistance of 100 kΩ
- in the hot water used to make coffee with a resistance of 20 kΩ.

Step 1: Write down what you know:

potential difference of supply = 12 V

fixed resistor = 10 kΩ = $10 \times 10^3 \, \Omega$

resistance of thermistor at room temperature = 100 kΩ = $100 \times 10^3 \, \Omega$

resistance of thermistor when hot = 20 kΩ = $20 \times 10^3 \, \Omega$

Step 2: Calculate the net resistance in the circuit when the thermistor is at room temperature:

net resistance = fixed resistance + resistance of thermistor

$$= 10 \times 10^3 \, \Omega + 100 \times 10^3 \, \Omega$$
$$= 110 \times 10^3 \, \Omega$$

Step 3: Calculate the current in the circuit.

$$\text{current} = \frac{\text{potential difference}}{\text{resistance}}$$
$$= \frac{12 \, V}{110 \times 10^3 \, \Omega}$$
$$= 1.1 \times 10^{-4} \, A \text{ (2 significant figures)}$$

Step 4: Calculate the potential difference across the thermistor when it is at room temperature:

potential difference = current × resistance

$$= 1.1 \times 10^{-4} \, A \times 100 \times 10^3 \, \Omega$$
$$= 11 \, V$$

Step 5: Repeat the method for the thermistor when it is hot:

potential difference = 8.0 V (2 significant figures)

How do you make other measurements of the environment?

You can see that the circuit in Figure 2 measures temperature because it contains a thermistor. If you replaced the thermistor with a different component then you could monitor a different quantity (Table 1).

Table 1 *Using different components in a sensing circuit.*

If you replaced the thermistor with...	...that has a resistance that changes with...	...then you could monitor...
an LDR	light level	the light level in a greenhouse
a variable resistor	how much it turns	the position of a door
a pressure sensor	the force applied to it	whether there is a burglar in your house

Figure 3 *Sensors in a smart refrigerator can monitor what you have and make a shopping list for you.*

1 Suggest and explain what will happen to the current in the circuit in Figure 2 as the thermistor heats up. (2 marks)

2 For the thermistor in the second example, show that V_{out} when the thermistor is hot is 8 V. (4 marks)

3 You replace the thermistor in the circuit in Figure 2 with an LDR. It has a resistance of 10 kΩ in the dark and 5 kΩ in the light. Use ratios to work out the change in resistance between light and dark. (6 marks)

4 Suggest and explain why you need to choose a 'suitable' resistance for the fixed resistor. (1 mark)

Learning outcomes

After studying this lesson you should be able to:

- explain the link between power, p.d., and current, and the energy changes over a given time
- apply equations relating potential difference, current, quantity of charge, resistance, power, energy, and time.

Specification reference: P3.2l, P3.2m

Why would you choose a higher power setting on your microwave oven to pop your popcorn (Figure 1)?

Figure 1 *On some microwave ovens you can select the power as well as the time.*

What is power?

You need a current to work your microwave oven or power shower. You select some of the appliances in your house because of their **power**. You can buy a high-power hair dryer, or one with a lower power.

You are choosing the energy transferred per second. Power is measured in **watts (W)**. Large powers are measured in **kilowatts (kW)** or **megawatts (MW)**. You might choose the higher-power appliance because you can use it for a shorter time to get a job done.

How do you calculate electric power with current and resistance?

In an electrical circuit:

- the current is the rate of flow of charge – it tells you the amount of charge flowing through a component per second
- the potential difference tells you the energy transferred by each charge.

$$\text{potential difference} = \frac{\text{energy transferred}}{\text{charge}}$$

and

$$\text{current} = \frac{\text{charge}}{\text{time}}$$

> **A** Show that multiplying potential difference by current gives the energy transferred per second.

You need to be able to recall and apply the equation for power:

$$\text{power (W)} = \text{potential difference (V)} \times \text{current (A)}$$

An electrical device with a high power will transfer a lot of energy per second.

You need to be able to recall and use:

$$\text{energy transferred (J, kWh)} = \text{power (W)} \times \text{time (s)}$$

Power and brightness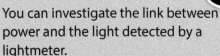

You can investigate the link between power and the light detected by a lightmeter.

1 Set up a series circuit with a lamp, an ammeter, and a power supply, then connect a voltmeter in parallel with the lamp.

2 Place a lightmeter a fixed distance away and write down the reading on the lightmeter.

3 Turn on the lamp to the lowest potential difference and record the new reading on the lightmeter, the current, and the p.d.

4 Increase the p.d. and repeat.

5 Calculate the power for each setting.

6 Plot a graph of power against light level, and explain the shape of the graph.

Calculating current using power and p.d.

A 1 kW microwave oven works on a potential difference of 230 V. Calculate the current through it.

Step 1: Write down what you know:

power = 1 kW = 1000 W

potential difference = 230 V

Step 2: Make current the subject of the equation and calculate it.

$$\frac{power}{potential\ difference} = \frac{potential\ difference \times current}{potential\ difference}$$

$$\frac{power}{potential\ difference} = current$$

$$\frac{1000\,W}{230\,V} = current$$

current = 4.3 A (2 significant figures)

How is power related to current and resistance?

You can eliminate potential difference from the power equation. This is called 'substitution'.

You know that   potential difference = current × resistance.

This means that:

$$power = potential\ difference \times current$$
$$= (current \times resistance) \times current$$
$$= current^2 \times resistance$$

You need to be able to recall and apply this equation. You can write it as:

$$P = I^2R$$

B Show that you get a power of approximately 1000 W if you use I^2R and the information in the first example.

1 Explain why a 10 W light bulb appears brighter than a 5 W light bulb. *(1 mark)*

2 A power shower has a rating of 10 kW. Calculate the energy transferred per second. *(2 marks)*

3  You plug in two light bulbs to a power supply on 12 V. Bulb A has a resistance of 10 Ω, and bulb B has a resistance of 3 Ω.
   a Calculate the power of each bulb. *(8 marks)*
   b Explain why there are two ways of working out the answer to part **a**. *(1 mark)*

4 Two kettles have different powers, 1000 W and 500 W, but work with the same potential difference.
   a Compare the current flowing in each kettle. *(1 mark)*
   b Compare the resistances of the kettles. *(1 mark)*

Figure 2 *Electrical devices that transfer little energy by heating, such as a DVD player, have a much lower power than devices that transfer more energy by heating, such as a hair dryer.*

Calculating current

A small motor that turns in a DVD player (Figure 2) has a resistance of 50 Ω, and a power of 5 W. Calculate the current.

Step 1: Write down what you know.

power = 5 W

resistance = 50 Ω

Step 2: Make current the subject of the equation, and calculate it.

$$\frac{power}{resistance} = \frac{current^2 \times resistance}{resistance}$$

$$\frac{power}{resistance} = current^2$$

$$\sqrt{\frac{power}{resistance}} = current$$

$$\sqrt{\frac{5\,W}{50\,\Omega}} = current$$

current = 0.3 A   (1 significant figure)

Study tip

If you learn how to substitute one equation into another you don't need to remember so many equations.

You need to give an appropriate number of significant figures in your answers. Explain why there are 2 significant figures in the first example, and 1 significant figure in the second.

Electricity and magnetism

P3.2 Simple circuits

Summary questions

1 a Match the quantity to the unit and the meter that you use to measure it. Write the matched letters and numbers to show your answer.

Quantity	Unit	Meter(s)
a current	**1** volts	**x** ammeter
b potential difference	**2** ohms	**y** ammeter + voltmeter
c resistance	**3** amps	**z** voltmeter

b Write down definitions for:
i potential difference **ii** resistance.

2 a i Calculate the charge transferred when a current of 0.15 A flows through a lamp in 10 seconds.
ii Calculate the potential difference across the lamp if it has a resistance of 40 Ω.
iii Use your answers to **a i** and **a ii** to calculate the energy transferred in 10 seconds.
iv Calculate the power of the lamp.
b Explain why the wire in the bulb glows.
c A motor in a circuit has a current of 0.8 A through it, and a resistance of 10 Ω. Calculate the power of the motor.

3 a i Describe the difference between a series and a parallel circuit.
ii Explain how you know that the light bulbs in your house are connected in parallel and not in series.
b A green lamp has a resistance of 3 Ω, and a blue lamp has a resistance of 5 Ω.
i When they are connected in series, a current of 1.5 A flows through them. Calculate the p.d. across each lamp.
ii Calculate the energy transferred per second by each lamp.
iii Calculate the potential difference of the power supply.
iv Compare the brightness of each colour of bulb when they are connected in parallel.

4 The owner of some tropical fish wants to monitor the temperature in the fish tank. She decides to use a thermistor.
a Explain why she has chosen this circuit component.
b Explain how she can use a power supply, resistor, thermistor, and voltmeter to monitor temperature.

c Write down and explain whether the circuit would be more sensitive at high or low temperatures. You may want to use Figure 1 to help you explain.

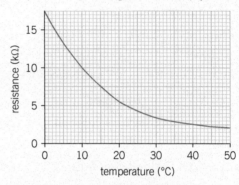

Figure 1 *A graph of resistance and temperature for a thermistor.*

d A similar type of circuit component is a light-dependent resistor (LDR). Suggest a use of a circuit containing an LDR.

5 ∞ Compare circuit A containing two bulbs and a battery, for which if one bulb breaks the other goes out, with circuit B, a sensing circuit designed to detect changes in light level.

6 ∞ Look at the graph (Figure 2).

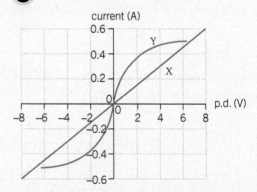

Figure 2 *A graph of current against p.d.*

a i Suggest what component X is.
ii Calculate the resistance of component X.
b i Component Y is either a lamp or a diode. Write down which it is.
ii Explain your choice.
c Write down which component is non-linear.
d Sketch a circuit diagram that you can use to take measurements to plot the graphs in Figure 2.

Revision questions

1 Hannah is investigating the resistance of a light-emitting diode (LED).
She connects a battery to a resistor in series with the LED.

a Hannah adds an ammeter and a voltmeter to her circuit to measure the resistance of the LED. Copy and complete the circuit that she should use.

(2 marks)

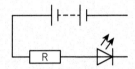

b Use the diagram below to read and record the current and potential difference of Hannah's circuit.

(2 marks)

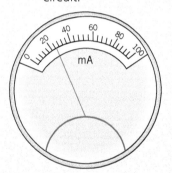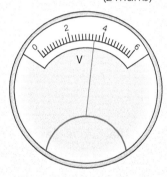

c Use the meter readings to calculate the resistance (in ohms) of the LED.

(2 marks)

d Hannah reconnects the battery to reverse the direction of the current.
Explain what happens to the LED.

(2 marks)

2 A circuit contains a thermistor in parallel with a lamp.

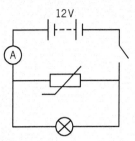

a i The switch is closed and the lamp shines brightly. As the temperature of the thermistor increases, the current in the thermistor changes. Explain how the current in the thermistor changes. *(2 marks)*

ii The brightness of the lamp does not change as the temperature of the thermistor increases. Explain why the brightness of the lamp does not change. *(2 marks)*

b i At 25 °C the current in the thermistor is 0.024 A. Calculate the resistance of the thermistor. Give the unit. *(3 marks)*

ii The power dissipated by the lamp is 2 W. Calculate the current (in amperes) in the lamp. *(2 marks)*

iii Calculate the total current (in amperes) in the circuit. *(1 mark)*

Learning outcomes

After studying this lesson you should be able to:

- describe the attraction and repulsion between unlike and like poles for permanent magnets
- describe the difference between permanent and induced magnets
- describe how the magnetic field of a magnet shows the strength and direction of magnetic forces
- explain the behaviour of a magnetic compass.

Specification reference: P3.3a, P3.3b, P3.3c, P3.3d

Figure 2 *Iron filings show the shape of the field between two attracting magnets.*

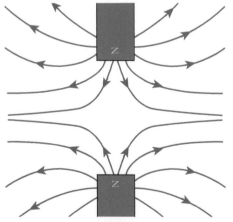

Figure 3 *You can model a magnetic field by drawing magnetic field lines. The arrow direction shows the force on a north pole. The magnets are repelling.*

The magnetic north pole moves about 30 miles a year, and once every 500 000 years the magnetic poles flip (Figure 1). This could happen in your lifetime.

 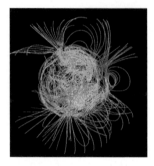 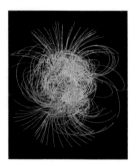

Figure 1 *Computer models help scientists to show how events, such as the flipping of the Earth's magnetic field, could happen.*

How do magnetic fields explain the behaviour of magnets?

As you know, *like* poles *repel* and *unlike* poles *attract*, just like electric charges. You can explain the movement of magnets with **magnetic field lines**. Field lines are a way of modelling a field (Figures 2 and 3). Field lines represent magnetic flux, and the number of field lines passing through a particular area is called magnetic flux density. We also call this magnetic field strength.

The magnets move in the direction that makes the field lines shorten. The density of the field lines shows you the strength of the magnetic field.

A Draw a diagram that shows attracting magnets with field lines, including arrows to show the direction of the field.

What is an induced magnet?

A steel paperclip is attracted to a magnet (Figure 4) even though the paperclip is *not* a **permanent magnet**. It is an **induced magnet**.

In the **domain** model of magnetism a permanent magnet is made up of many small magnetic regions (domains) that all line up. Steel, or iron, has regions that are *not* lined up, but when they are in a magnetic field they *do* line up (Figure 5).

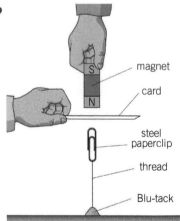

Figure 4 *You can hold up a paperclip with a magnet, and the card does not affect it.*

In some (hard) magnetic materials, the domains continue to be lined up when you remove the magnetic field. In other (soft) magnetic materials the domains return to their original direction.

B Describe how you could show that an object stays magnetic when you remove the magnetic field.

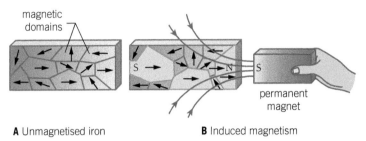

A Unmagnetised iron   **B** Induced magnetism

Figure 5 *How magnetism is induced in iron.*

Why do compasses point 'north'?

If you hang a magnet up it will line up so that one end of it points towards the **magnetic north pole** (Figure 6). This point on the surface of the Earth is *not* the same as the North Pole, which is the point about which the Earth spins. A **compass** (Figure 7) points towards the magnetic north pole. It is a 'north-seeking' pole.

The Earth behaves as if it has a large bar magnet at its centre. This is a model of the Earth and its magnetic field. Scientists are not sure what causes the field. It could be produced by convection currents in the molten iron core of the Earth.

Many compasses are 'weighted' so that they lie horizontally. They need to be weighted because the Earth's magnetic field is like that of a bar magnet. The angle between the field lines and a line horizontal to the surface of the Earth is the 'dip'. It is 90° at the north and south magnetic poles, and zero at the 'magnetic equator'. In the UK the field has a dip of about 70°.

Go further

You can levitate a frog in a strong magnetic field. Find out how.

1 Explain how you know from Figure 8 that the magnetic field of a bar magnet is stronger near the poles. *(1 mark)*
2 Explain why the model of the Earth's magnetic field as a bar magnet has the *south* pole of the magnet near the *north* pole of the Earth. *(2 marks)*
3 Describe the behaviour of a compass as you move from the equator to the magnetic north pole. *(2 marks)*
4 Suggest why the paperclip falls when you insert a magnetic material between the card and the paperclip. *(2 marks)*

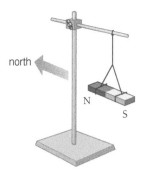

Figure 6 *The north pole of a magnet points towards the magnetic north pole.*

Figure 7 *A compass needle lines up with the magnetic field of the Earth.*

Study tip

Larger permanent magnets are not necessarily stronger magnets.

Magnetic fields are three-dimensional, not two-dimensional.

Synoptic link

You learned about electric field lines in P3.1.1 *Electrostatics*.

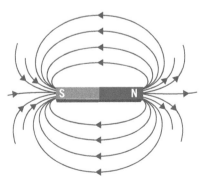

Figure 8 *The magnetic field around a bar magnet.*

Learning outcomes

After studying this lesson you should be able to:

- describe how to show that a current can create a magnetic effect
- describe the directions of the magnetic field around a conducting wire
- recall how the strength of the field depends on the current and the distance from the conductor
- explain how solenoid arrangements can enhance the magnetic effect.

Specification reference: P3.3e, P3.3f, P3.3g

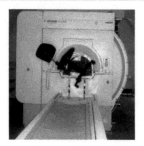

Figure 1 *The electromagnets in an MRI scanner are strong enough to pull furniture across a room.*

Engineers who build magnetic resonance imaging (MRI) scanners have to be very careful. The electromagnets inside them can pull chairs and fire extinguishers across the room (Figure 1).

What is the magnetic field around a wire?

An MRI scanner needs to produce a very strong magnetic field. The field is stronger than any produced by a permanent magnet.

In 1820, Hans Christian Oersted discovered that there is a magnetic field around a wire that is carrying a current (Figure 2). Oersted investigated this field in more detail.

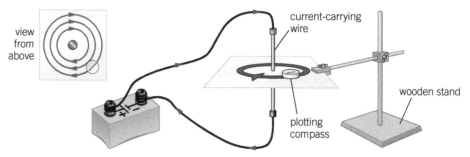

Figure 2 *You can use a compass to investigate the field around a wire.*

He found that if the current was coming towards you the field lines were anticlockwise (Figure 3).

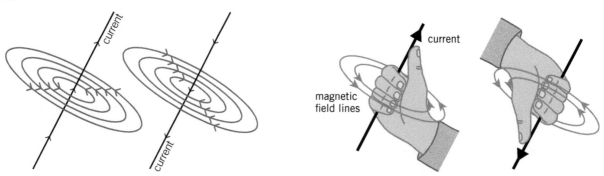

Figure 3 *You can use your right hand to work out the direction of a magnetic field around a current.*

A Describe another method, apart from using a compass, which you could use to show the magnetic field around a wire.

What does the strength of the field around a wire depend on?

The strength of the field, which is called magnetic field strength, or magnetic flux density, depends on:

- the magnitude of the current: a bigger current = a stronger field
- the distance from the wire: nearer the wire = a stronger field (Figure 4).

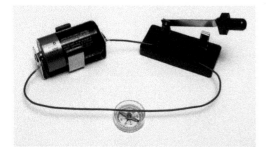

Figure 4 *The compass needle will move when you close the switch.*

The strength of a magnetic field is measured in **teslas (T)**. The strength of the Earth's magnetic field is about 0.01 mT. The strength of the field 1 cm from a wire carrying a current of 5 A is about 0.1 mT. A very strong permanent magnet has a magnetic field near its poles of about 1 T.

How does a solenoid enhance the magnetic effect?

You can make a loop of wire that carries a current. The magnetic field in the centre is a straight line (Figure 6).

> **B** Explain why the strength of the field in the centre of the card in Figure 6 is double the strength of the field due to the single wire shown in Figure 2, if the wires carry the same current.

Many parallel loops make a coil, or **solenoid**. Adding together many fields produces a much *stronger* field than that of a single wire. You can make the field even stronger by putting a magnetic material inside the core (Figure 7). The field produces an induced magnet.

You can make an electromagnet that is *much* stronger than any permanent magnet. The electromagnets used in MRI scanners have a strength of 10 T, and the strongest continuous magnetic field produced is over 40 T.

You can model the direction of the current in wires using darts (Figure 8).

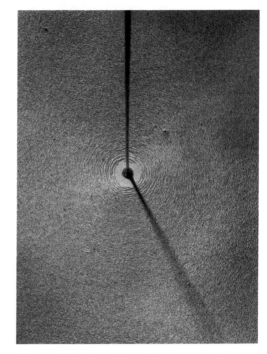

Figure 5 *The iron filings line up near the wire, but not a long way from it, showing that the field gets weaker.*

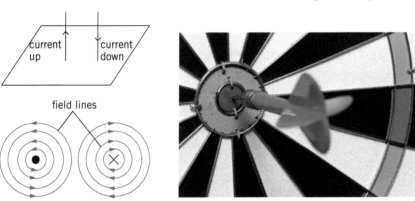

Figure 8 *If the dart is coming towards you then you see the point. If the dart is going away from you then you see the feathers, or flight.*

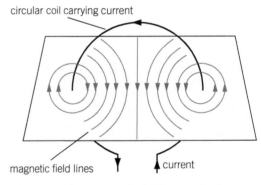

Figure 6 *The magnetic field around a loop of wire.*

1 Describe how you can show that there is a field around a solenoid. *(1 mark)*

2 Describe how you can use a compass to show that the magnetic field of a current-carrying wire is larger than the field strength of the Earth. *(2 marks)*

3 **a** Explain why the field at the centre of the solenoid in Figure 8 is greater than the field due to a single wire carrying the same current. *(2 marks)*

 b Suggest and explain what would happen to the strength of the field at the centre of the solenoid if you decreased the distance from the centre to each side of the coil of the solenoid. *(3 marks)*

4 Suggest and explain how the strength of the magnetic field changes if you double the distance from a wire. (Hint: the field is cylindrical.) *(2 marks)*

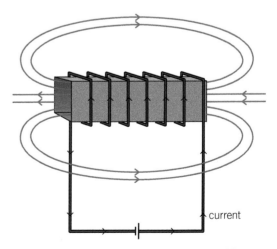

Figure 7 *The field around a solenoid is like the field around a bar magnet.*

Learning outcomes

After studying this lesson you should be able to:

- describe how a magnet and a current-carrying conductor exert a force on one another
- show how Fleming's left-hand rule represents the directions of the force, the current, and the magnetic field
- apply the equation that links the force on a conductor to the magnetic flux density, the current, and the length of conductor.

Specification reference: P3.3h, P3.3i, P3.3j

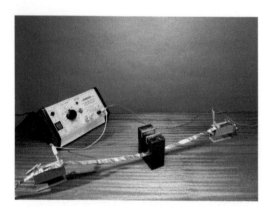

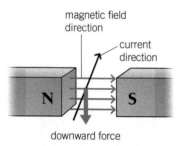

Figure 2 *When you pass a current through the foil in the magnetic field the foil moves down.*

magnetic field direction

current direction

N   S

downward force

movement of foil

What does a force of 0.2 micronewtons have to do with current (Figure 1)?

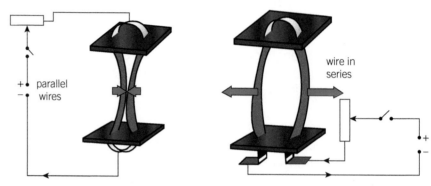

Figure 1 *Wires carrying currents attract or repel.*

What happens when you combine fields?

You can combine the field due to a wire with the field due to a permanent magnet (Figure 2). This produces a force on the wire.

A Write down the angle between the field and the force.

Why is there a force on the wire?

If you work out what is happening in the combined fields you can predict what will happen to the wire. When you put two fields together that are in the same direction they add up, but if they are in opposite directions they will cancel out.

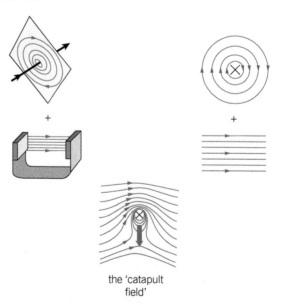

the 'catapult field'

Figure 3 *The force on a wire creates a catapult field.*

In Figure 3 the current is into the paper and the uniform field is left to right. You get a 'catapult field' with 'stretched' field lines above the wire and fewer stretched lines below it.

The wire moves down, and all the field lines straighten. The movement of the wire has acted to shorten the field lines. The current, magnetic field, and force are all at right angles to each other.

You can remember which way the wire moves by:

● drawing the fields and combining them, or

● using **Fleming's left-hand rule**.

Figure 4 shows how you can use your left hand to work out the direction of the force.

B Write down which way the wire in Figure 2 would move if you reversed the field direction *and* the current direction.

How do you calculate the size of the force?

You know that the strength of the field around a wire depends on the current through it. The force on the wire depends on the current, the field that it is in, and the length of wire in the field (assuming the wire and the field are at 90°). You need to be able to apply this equation:

force on a conductor (at right angles to a magnetic field) carrying a current (N)
= magnetic flux density (T) × current (A) × length (m)

This is how scientists define one ampere (amp). One amp is the size of current that produces a force of 0.2 micronewtons on two wires 1 metre apart. You saw how parallel wires carrying current experience forces in Figure 1. You do not have to learn this definition.

1 Calculate the force on a 0.10 m piece of wire in a field of 0.75 T that carries a current of 3.0 A. *(2 marks)*

2 Use Fleming's left-hand rule to work out the direction of the force on each wire in diagrams **A** and **B** of Figure 5. *(2 marks)*

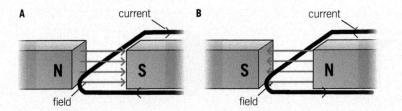

Figure 5 *What is the direction of the force on each wire?*

3 Two parallel wires carry current. Suggest why there is a force on each wire. *(3 marks)*

4 **a** Estimate the current that you would need to hold up a wire 100 m long in the Earth's magnetic field. The density of copper is about 9000 kg/m³. The copper wire has a cross-sectional area of 1×10^{-6} m². Assume $g = 10$ N/kg. Earth's magnetic flux density = 0.1 mT. *(3 marks)*

   b Explain why this method of supporting wires is probably not a good idea. *(1 mark)*

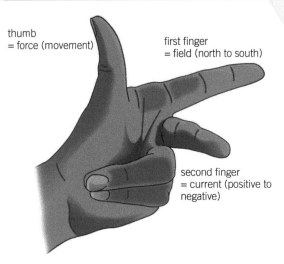

Figure 4 *Start by lining up your first finger with the field, then put your second finger in line with the current. The direction of your thumb tells you the direction of the force.*

Calculating current

Calculate the current in a wire of length 20 cm in a flux density of 0.30 T when there is a force of 0.32 N.

Step 1: Write down what you know:

length = 20 cm = 0.20 m
magnetic flux density = 0.30 T
force = 0.32 N

Step 2: Make current the subject of the equation and calculate the answer:

$$\text{force} = \text{magnetic flux density} \times \text{current} \times \text{length}$$

$$\frac{\text{force}}{\text{magnetic flux density} \times \text{length}} = \text{current}$$

$$\frac{0.32\,\text{N}}{0.30\,\text{T} \times 0.20\,\text{m}} = \text{current}$$

current = 5.3 A (2 significant figures)

Study tip

When you use Fleming's left-hand rule, remember:

● thuMb = movement

● First finger = field

● seCond finger = current.

Learning outcome

After studying this lesson you should be able to:

- explain how to use the force exerted from a magnet and a current-carrying conductor to make an electric motor rotate.

Specification reference: P3.3k

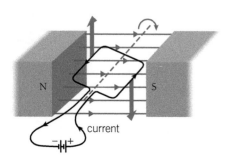

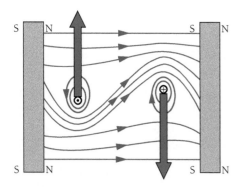

Figure 2 *You can see that the forces arise because there are two catapult fields.*

It would be hard to make robots, such as the robot dog in Figure 1, without electric motors. Why do motors rotate?

Figure 1 *Motors help the robot dog to walk and wag its tail.*

You can already buy robotic vacuum cleaners. Robots do surgery in hospitals and make cars in factories. Robots of the future could lift patients out of bed and take them to surgery.

If you want a robot to move you need to use an electric **motor**.

A Name a device that you use in your house that contains an electric motor.

How can you get a coil of wire to spin?

A motor needs to spin. You know that a combination of magnetic fields can cause a force on a wire that has a current flowing in it.

You can make a very simple motor by making a piece of wire into a loop, and placing the loop in a magnetic field (Figure 2). When you connect the wire to a battery a current flows. One side of the wire goes upwards and the other goes downwards.

However, this motor would not spin very well. The coil will start to rotate back the other way as soon as it passes the vertical position.

B Describe what happens when you reverse the magnets in Figure 2.

How does an electric motor work?

You need a way to keep the current moving in on the right and out on the left all the time, but still allowing the coil to spin. You can do this with a **split-ring commutator**.

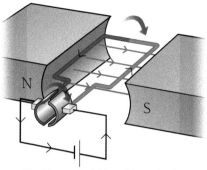

A The blue part of this coil is pushed upwards and the red half downwards. (Check with Fleming's left-hand rule.)

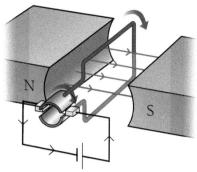

B No current, but the coil continues to turn because of its own momentum.

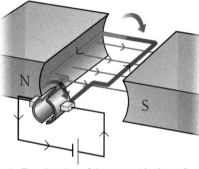

C The direction of the current in the coil and commutator is reversed. Now the blue part is pushed downwards and the red half upwards.

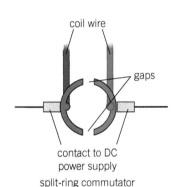

coil wire

gaps

contact to DC power supply

split-ring commutator

Figure 3 *How a motor works.*

The split-ring commutator (Figure 3) enables the current to flow the same way from the battery, but change to different halves of the coil as it spins.

This makes sure that the force on the left-hand side of the coil is always upwards, and the force of the right-hand side of the coil is always downwards.

You can change the speed of the motor by changing:

- the magnitude of the current flowing in the coil
- the strength of the magnetic field
- the number of coils of wire
- the length of the coil.

1 Describe the role of the split-ring commutator in a motor. (*2 marks*)
2 Explain in terms of magnetic fields why increasing the current increases the force on the coil. (*2 marks*)
3 Draw a catapult field diagram (as in Figure 2) for the coil when it is at position **C** in Figure 3. (*2 marks*)
4 **a** Suggest why some motors may use electromagnets rather than permanent magnets. (*1 mark*)
   b Suggest and explain why bigger motors produce a bigger force on the coil. (*2 marks*)

Figure 4 *An engineer adjusts the propeller of a robotic helicopter used for surveying forests.*

Go further

Michael Faraday built a motor shortly after Oersted's discovery. Find out how it worked.

Electricity and magnetism

P3.3 Magnets and magnetic fields

Summary questions

1 a Every magnet has a _____ pole and a _____ pole. _____ poles repel and _____ poles attract.

   b You can represent a magnetic field with magnetic field lines, with arrows on them from the _____ pole to the _____ pole to show the direction of the field.

   c If the magnetic field lines are closer together the magnetic field is _____, which happens near the _____ of a permanent magnet.

2 a Describe the difference between a permanent magnet and an induced magnet.

   b The word 'magnet' comes from a region in Greece (Magnesia) where naturally occurring magnetic rocks were found. Suggest and explain why naturally occurring rocks might be magnetic.

3 You put a plotting compass near a wire connected to a battery, with a switch in the circuit open.

   a i When no current flows in the wire the compass needle points towards a particular point on the Earth's surface. Write down the name of this point.

     ii Explain why the needle points that way.

   b You press the switch and a current flows. Copy Figure 1 and sketch the magnetic field around the wire.

Figure 1 *Copy and sketch the magnetic field around the wire.*

   c Write down what would happen to the magnetic field pattern if the current was reversed.

   d Write down how your diagram shows that the magnetic field gets weaker as you move away from the wire.

   e Write down one way that you could make the magnetic field stronger.

4 a Explain what is meant by a solenoid.

   b i Describe how to make a solenoid that you could use to pick up pieces of magnetic material.

     ii Suggest a use of a solenoid.

   c Explain why the field due a solenoid is stronger than the field due to a single piece of wire carrying the same current.

5 a i Look at diagrams **A** and **B** of Figure 2 and use Fleming's left-hand rule to work out the direction of the force on the wire.

Figure 2 *What is the direction of the force one each wire?*

     ii Write down the direction of the current in the wire in diagram **C** that would produce a downwards force on the wire.

   b Calculate the force on 20 cm of wire carrying a current of 2 A in a field of 0.03 T. Use:

force on a conductor
= magnetic field strength × current × length

   c Compare the size of the force with the weight of a piece of A4 paper that has a mass of 1 g. ($g = 10$ N/kg)

6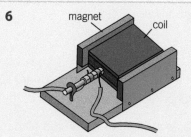

Figure 3 *Part of an electric motor.*

A student wraps a coil of wire around a block that can spin in a magnetic field.

   a Describe and explain what the student needs to do to make it into a motor.

   b Explain in terms of magnetic field lines why the coil spins.

   c Describe two ways to make the motor spin in the opposite direction.

   d Write down the effect on the motor of:

     i increasing the current

     ii using weaker magnets

   e i Suggest how, when you connect a motor in a circuit, you could tell that you are using a motor that contains an electromagnet not a permanent magnet.

     ii Suggest why a motor may use an electromagnet not a permanent magnet.

     iii Suggest why a motor might use a permanent magnet not an electromagnet.

Revision questions

1 A student investigates the strength of the magnetic field at the pole of a permanent magnet.
 She counts the number of steel paperclips the magnet will hold. She increases the separation between the magnet and the paperclips by inserting pieces of card.

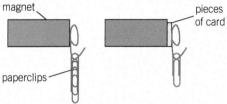

 a i Explain how a permanent magnet is able to attract a steel paperclip. (*2 marks*)
 ii Explain the differences, if any, that the student would find in her results if she tested the centre of the permanent magnet instead of the pole. (*2 marks*)
 iii State the useful property of card that makes it a suitable material for increasing the separation between the magnet and the paperclips. (*1 mark*)
 b The student presents her results in a graph.

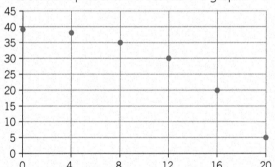

 i State the labels that should be added to the axes of the graph. (*2 marks*)
 ii Write a conclusion about the results of this experiment. (*2 marks*)
 c Describe how a plotting compass can be used to investigate the magnetic field around a permanent magnet. Use a diagram to illustrate your answer. (*3 marks*)

2 A plotting compass can be used to investigate the magnetic field surrounding a current-carrying wire.

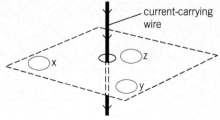

 a Copy the diagram and draw the direction of the plotting compass arrow at positions x, y, and z. (*3 marks*)
 b Describe the shape of the magnetic field around the wire. (*1 mark*)
 c State the factors that affect the strength of the magnetic field around the wire. (*2 marks*)

3 Pipelines can be installed beneath roads, rivers, and other obstacles by drilling boreholes. One method of controlling the direction of the drill is a *magnetic guidance system*.
 a Use ideas about plotting compasses to suggest how a magnetic guidance system works to keep the drill on the right course. (*3 marks*)
 b One manufacturer claims that their system is accurate to 1.5 m in 2 km. Calculate this accuracy as a percentage. (*1 mark*)

4 A demonstration of the motor effect is shown in the diagram. A rider made of copper sits on two rods, also made of copper. The rider is free to move. A direct current flows through the rods and rider in the direction shown. **H**

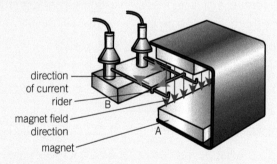

 The magnetic field strength B is 0.2 T, the current I is 0.5 A, and the length of the rider, l, in the magnetic field is 3 cm.
 a i Give the name of the unit of magnetic field strength. (*1 mark*)
 ii Use $F = B \times I \times l$ to find the force (in newtons) exerted on the rider. (*2 marks*)
 iii Explain which way the rider moves due to the force exerted on it.
  You may illustrate your answer with a diagram. (*3 marks*)
 b The power supply to the rider is replaced by one that provides an alternating current (a.c.) at 50 Hz. Explain what effect this has on the movement of the rider. (*3 marks*)

P3.1 Static and charge

- Describe what charge is, and how insulators can be charged.
- Describe what current is, and describe how to measure current.
- State and use the equation linking current, charge, and time.
- Explain what potential difference (p.d.) is, and state and use the equation for p.d.

P3.2 Simple circuits

- Describe the differences between series and parallel circuits.
- Describe how to connect meters in circuits.
- Describe what happens to current and p.d. in series and parallel circuits.
- Define resistance, and state and use the equation linking resistance, p.d., and current.
- Describe how to take measurements to plot graphs of current and p.d.
- Interpret graphs for wires, lamps, and diodes.
- Interpret the graph of resistance against temperature for a thermistor and an LDR.
- Explain what net resistance is, and explain net resistance in series circuits.
- Do calculations involving p.d., current, and resistance in series and parallel circuits.
- Make calculations of the output of a sensing circuit.
- Explain what power means, and how it relates to p.d. and current.
- State and use the equation linking electrical power, p.d., and current.
- State and use the equation linking energy transferred, electrical power, and time.

P3.3 Magnets and magnetic fields

- Describe how magnets behave and link this behaviour to magnetic field lines.
- Describe the difference between permanent and induced magnetism.
- Explain the behaviour of compasses.
- Describe evidence for a magnetic field around a wire.

- Describe the factors affecting the strength and direction of the magnetic field around a wire.
- Explain why the field of a solenoid is bigger than the field of a wire.

H

- Describe the forces between a magnet and a current-carrying conductor.
- Use Fleming's left-hand rule.
- Apply the equation for the force on a current-carrying conductor in a magnetic field.
- Describe how you can use a current-carrying wire and magnets to make a coil rotate.
- Explain why the coil rotates in terms of magnetic fields.

Simple circuits

Current

- conventional current and electron flow are in opposite directions

moving charge = current

charge flow (C) = current (A) × time (s)

Current in series	Current in parallel
current the same all around the circuit	current in branches added to give total current

Potential difference (p.d.)

energy transferred (J) = potential difference (V) × charge (C)

p.d. in series	p.d. in parallel
p.d. is shared	p.d. across each branch = supply p.d. (each is connected to the supply)

Electrical power

- energy transferred by a current per second (electrical working)
- J/s = W
- p.d. (V) = energy transferred per charge
- current (I) = charge flowing per second
- VI = energy transferred per second

power (W) = p.d. (V) × current (I)

power (W) = (current (I))^2 × resistance (R)

Characteristic graphs

- plot current and p.d. in positive and negative direction
- find resistance using ratio of p.d. to current, not gradient

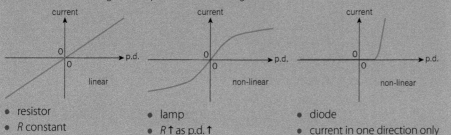

- resistor
- R constant

- lamp
- R↑ as p.d. ↑

- diode
- current in one direction only

Simple motors

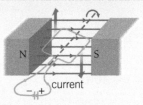

H

- ↑ current, stronger field, ↑ wire (length and number of coils) make coil spin faster
- split-ring commutator keeps coil spinning

LDRs and Thermistors

- made of semiconductor
- electrons released to produce more current
- used in sensing circuits
- monitors temperature (V changes as temperature changes)

Electric fields

- around charges
- field lines model force
- lines show direction of force on positive charge
- lines like elastic bands (try to straighten)

Static electricity

- + and + repel
- – and – repel
- + and – attract
- charging by friction
- gain or loss of electrons

Magnetic fields

- magnetic field lines = model
- arrows show direction of force
- behave like elastic bands (flux)
- could also be gravitational or electric field lines

Earth's magnetic field
- like a bar magnet in the middle

Permanent and induced magnetic fields
- **permanent** magnetic materials, permanently magnetic
- **induced** metal (e.g., steel paper clip) made into magnet

Currents and Fields

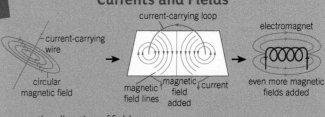

- notice direction of field
- field gets weaker further from wire

- strong magnet you can turn on and off
- stronger with ↑ coils, ↑ current, added core

P3 Electricity and magnetism

Currents and Forces

H

- field lines try to straighten → force on wire
- shown by Fleming's Left Hand Rule

force on a conductor carrying a current (N) = flux density (T) × current (A) × length (m)

Resistance

- all materials have resistance (R)
- changing R changes current (↑R → ↓current)
- metals get hot when charge flows through due to collisions between electrons and fixed lattice

$$\text{current (A)} = \frac{\text{p.d. (V)}}{\text{resistance (Ω)}}$$

Learning outcomes

After studying this lesson you should be able to:

- describe wave motion in terms of amplitude, wavelength, frequency, and period
- define wavelength and frequency
- describe differences between transverse and longitudinal waves
- describe how to use ripples on water surfaces to model transverse waves, and why ripples cannot model sound waves
- describe evidence that in both cases it is the wave and not the water or air itself that travels.

Specification reference: P4.1a, P4.1b, P4.1e, P4.1f, P4.1g

Water waves are fun to play in, but large waves, such as those during storms or tsunamis, can cause great damage by shifting huge amounts of energy (Figure 1).

Figure 1 *This railway line was washed away by waves in 2014.*

What are waves?

Every time you speak on your phone **vibrations** in your vocal cords produce **sound waves**. A wave is an oscillation that transfers energy. The microphone in your phone produces a signal that varies in the same way. Then **electromagnetic waves** are used to communicate between the two phones. Sound and water waves are **mechanical waves** and need a medium (matter) to travel through. Electromagnetic waves do not.

A Write down the names of three other types of wave.

Sound waves are **longitudinal**. The direction of vibration of individual air molecules is the same as the direction of the wave. Figure 2 shows the motion of air molecules when the wave is moving through the air. In **transverse** waves the direction of vibration is at right angles to the direction of travel of the wave (Figure 3). If you make a transverse wave on a spring the individual coils move up and down but the energy is transferred horizontally.

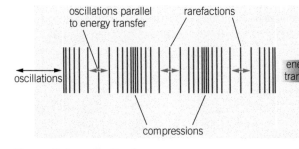

Figure 2 *Longitudinal wave.*

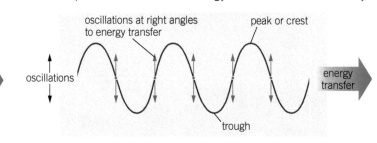

Figure 3 *Transverse wave.*

What are wave properties?

Table 1 shows other properties of waves, some of which are shown in Figures 4 and 5.

Table 1 *Properties of waves.*

Property	Definition	Symbol	Unit
amplitude	distance from the middle to the top (crest) or bottom (trough) of a wave	A	depends on the wave (e.g. metres or volts)
wavelength	distance from one point on a wave to the same point on the next wave.	λ (lambda)	metres, m
frequency	number of waves, or oscillations, per second	F	hertz, Hz
time period	the time for one wave to pass a given point	T	seconds, s

Unit prefixes

You may need to use many different prefixes for frequency and wavelength, for example, MHz or μm.

There are two ways to represent a wave. A time trace shows how displacement varies with *time* at a particular position (Figure 4). A snapshot of a wave shows how displacement varies with *distance* at a particular time (Figure 5).

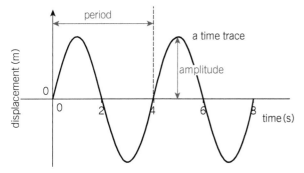

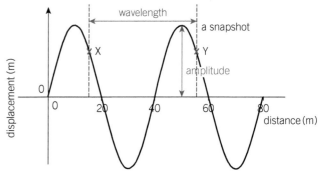

Figure 4 *The time for a wave to complete one oscillation is the time period of the wave.*

Figure 5 *The distance from one point (X) on a wave to the same point (Y) on the next wave is the wavelength.*

B Write down the time period and the wavelength for the waves in Figures 4 and 5.

In the time trace in Figure 4 you could measure the period from any point on a wave to the same point on the next wave.

On the snapshot in Figure 5 you can measure wavelength from any point on the wave to the same point on the next wave.

On either diagram you can measure amplitude from the middle to the top *or* the bottom (trough) of a wave.

Waves also have a **wave velocity**.

How do you model waves?
You have learned that you can model electric circuits with rope, and field lines with rubber bands.

Another important model is using ripples on water waves to model transverse waves. For example, you can show how waves are reflected, as shown in Figure 6.

The surface of the wave moves up and down as the wave moves through the water. You can see that by putting a small cork on the surface. The wave travels but the water does not.

This is the same for sound waves. The wave moves away from your mouth but the air does not.

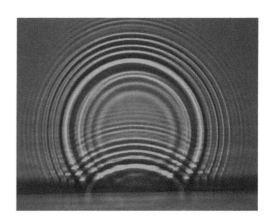

Figure 6 *Ripples in a tank show how waves are reflected.*

1 Describe how to make transverse and longitudinal waves on a long slinky spring. *(2 marks)*

2 Explain how you know that when a sound wave moves through the air the air does not move. *(1 mark)*

3 You make a transverse wave on a piece of rope.
   a Describe how you would find the wavelength. *(3 marks)*
   b Describe how you would find the amplitude. *(1 mark)*

4 A wave has a frequency of 20 kHz. Use the definitions in Table 1 to calculate the time period. *(2 marks)*

> **Study tip**
>
> Check the *x*-axis of a graph showing a wave so you know whether you can find wavelength or time period from the graph.

Learning outcomes

After studying this lesson you should be able to:

- describe and apply the relationship between frequency, wavelength, and wave velocity
- recall and apply formulae relating velocity, frequency, and wavelength
- describe how to measure the speed of ripples on water surfaces and the speed of sound.

Specification reference: P4.1c, P4.1d, P4.1f

Figure 2 *A wave on the ocean can travel very fast. A tidal wave with a velocity of 600 mph can cross the Atlantic in about 8 hours.*

Study tip

Use the example of running to help you to remember the equation for wave velocity.

The frequency of sound waves can be shown in kHz, so you must always convert to Hz before using the equation for wave velocity.
1 kHz = 1000 Hz.

You can see an aircraft that is travelling faster than sound because water droplets form a cone behind it (Figure 1).

Figure 1 *A plane travelling very fast produces a shock wave like the wake behind a boat.*

How do you calculate wave velocity?

Imagine running along a track. Your stride is 1.5 metres long and you take 2 strides each second. From this information, you could calculate that you have travelled 3 m/s.

In terms of waves, your 'stride' represents the wavelength, and the 'strides per second' represent the frequency. You need to recall and apply this equation:

$$\text{wave velocity (m/s)} = \text{frequency (Hz)} \times \text{wavelength (m)}$$

The unit of frequency is the unit of number of waves per second. There is no unit for number of waves, so 1 Hz = 1 /s.

Calculating wavelength

A singer sings a note with a frequency of 256 Hz. The velocity of sound in air is 330 m/s. Calculate the wavelength.

Step 1: Write down what you know:

frequency = 256 Hz

velocity = 330 m/s

Step 2: Make wavelength the subject of the equation and work out the wavelength.

$$\frac{\text{wave velocity}}{\text{frequency}} = \text{wavelength}$$

$$\frac{330 \text{ m/s}}{256 \text{ /s}} = \text{wavelength}$$

wavelength = 1.3 m (2 significant figures)

A Explain what would happen to the wavelength if the singer sang a note of 512 Hz.

How do you measure the velocity of ripples?

If you use a ripple tank (Figure 3), you need to know the frequency of the ripples, and their wavelength, to calculate velocity.

You can find the wavelength using a flashing light (a strobe) and a ruler, and the frequency by finding the number of rotations of the motor per second. Then you can use the equation to calculate the velocity of the waves.

How do you measure the velocity of sound?

If you time how long it takes to hear an echo (reflection) of a clap when you are at a distance from a wall you can work out the velocity of sound using the equation that links distance, velocity, and time.

B Explain how finding the velocity of sound is different from finding the velocity of ripples.

Alternatively, you can connect a pair of **microphones** a certain distance apart to an **oscilloscope** (Figure 4).

You can use the method with the microphones to measure the velocity of sound in a liquid or a solid.

Remember that sound is a longitudinal wave, so when you see the trace of a transverse wave on the screen of an oscilloscope it is showing the variation of *pressure* with time, not the sound wave itself.

The velocity of sound can vary with temperature and pressure. This is because these factors affect the velocity at which the disturbance in the wave is transferred between particles.

Modelling tsunamis

Scientists can issue tsunami warnings because they can use computer models to predict how long it will take ocean waves to reach land.

1 You make waves in a ripple tank by moving a bar up and down 2 times per second. This makes waves of wavelength 20 cm. Calculate their velocity. *(2 marks)*

2 **a** The note 'middle C' has a frequency of 256 Hz. Calculate the wavelength of middle C in water, where the velocity is 1500 m/s, and in steel, where the velocity is 5.0×10^3 m/s. *(4 marks)*
   b Explain why the note is still middle C. *(1 mark)*

3 Write down and explain whether moving your hand faster when you make a transverse wave on a slinky spring will increase the velocity of the wave on the slinky. *(2 marks)*

4 Figure 5 shows the sound pulses produced by the microphones in Figure 4. There are 10 squares for each 2 ms. Calculate the distance between the microphones. *(6 marks)* The velocity of sound in air is 340 m/s.

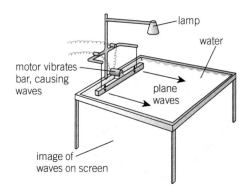

Figure 3 *You can use a ripple tank to measure the velocity of waves that you make.*

Figure 4 *You need to know the distance between the microphones and the time for the sound to travel between them to calculate velocity.*

Table 1 *The effect of temperature on the velocity of sound.*

Temperature (°C)	Velocity of sound (m/s)
15	340
25	346
35	352

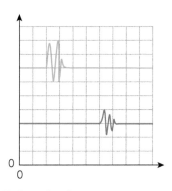

Figure 5 *Sound pulses.*

Waves and radioactivity

P4.1 Wave behaviour

Summary questions

1 Match the phrases to make sentences about waves. Write the matched letters and numbers to show your answer.

  a a sound wave moves through air…

  b a sound wave is refracted at a boundary…

  c when a sound wave is absorbed by a wall…

  1 … the wall heats up a bit.

  2 … but the air does not travel.

  3 … when it slows down.

2 What are the differences between longitudinal and transverse waves? Copy and complete the table below by writing the correct letters in each box.

Transverse waves	Longitudinal waves

  A Direction of oscillation is in the same direction as the wave motion.

  B Sound is an example of this kind of wave.

  C Light is an example of this kind of wave.

  D Oscillations are at 90° to the direction of the wave.

3 Figure 1 shows a graph of a wave with some measurements labelled.

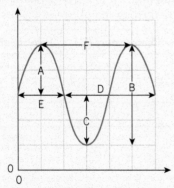

Figure 1 *A graph of a wave.*

  a Write down the letters that show the amplitude of the wave.

  b If the diagram shows a *snapshot* of the wave (displacement against distance), write down the letters that show the wavelength of the wave.

  c Write down what the letters in **b** show if the diagram shows a *time trace* (displacement against time).

  d i Explain why the diagram shows a transverse wave.

  ii Write down an example of a transverse wave in everyday life.

  e Explain why 'frequency' is not shown on the diagram.

4 **a** Select the correct equation for calculating wave speed:

  wave speed = frequency × wavelength

$$\text{wave speed} = \frac{\text{frequency}}{\text{wavelength}}$$

$$\text{wave speed} = \frac{\text{wavelength}}{\text{frequency}}$$

  b You stand on a cliff and watch waves approaching the shore. At one point there are 1.5 waves per second and the crests of the waves are 10 m apart. Calculate the speed of the wave at that point.

  c Describe how to calculate the speed of waves in ripple tank.

5 **a** Describe evidence you have observed which shows that water waves transfer energy without transferring water.

  b Describe evidence you have observed which shows that sound waves transfer energy without transferring air.

6 Calculate the speed, frequency, or wavelength of the following waves. Remember to use standard units.

  a A speed of a sound wave in water with a wavelength of 5 kHz and a wavelength of 0.3 m.

  b The frequency of a sound wave with a wavelength of 200 mm transmitted through a door where the speed of sound is 4000 m/s.

  c The wavelength of a sound wave with a frequency of 2 kHz, travelling through a metal train track where the speed of sound is 5 km/s.

Revision questions

1 Look at the following diagram of a wave.

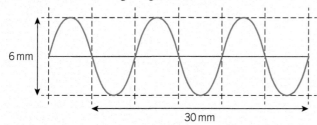

6 mm

30 mm

a What is the amplitude of the wave?
  A 3 mm   **B** 5 mm   **C** 6 mm   **D** 10 mm   *(1 mark)*

b What is the wavelength of the wave?
  A 3 mm   **B** 5 mm   **C** 6 mm   **D** 10 mm   *(1 mark)*

c The frequency of the wave is 300 Hz. What is the speed of the wave?
  A 9 m/s   **B** 15 m/s   **C** 18 m/s   **D** 30 m/s   *(1 mark)*

2 Ships use sonar to check the depth of water.
  a A ship emits waves towards the sea floor. The sound waves take 3 s to return to the ship.
    i Suggest why the waves return to the ship.
      (1 mark)
    ii Sound waves are longitudinal. Describe the differences between longitudinal and transverse waves.   *(2 marks)*
    iii The speed of sound in water is 1450 m/s. Calculate the depth of the water underneath the ship.   *(3 marks)*
  b The sound waves have a *frequency* of 200 kHz.
    i Explain what is meant by the word *frequency*.
      (2 marks)
    ii The speed of the waves is 1450 m/s. Calculate their wavelength.   *(2 marks)*

3 Here is a statement about waves.
  'Water waves transfer energy but do not carry matter.'
  Use your knowledge of waves to explain how water waves can transfer energy over large distances even though the particles in them do not move very far at all.   *(6 marks)*

Learning outcomes

After studying this lesson you should be able to:

- describe what electromagnetic waves are and what they do
- describe the main groupings of the electromagnetic spectrum and how they are different in terms of frequency and wavelength
- state the electromagnetic waves that our eyes detect
- recall and apply the relationship between speed, frequency, and wavelength for electromagnetic waves.

- state how radio waves are produced and detected. **H**

Specification reference: P4.2a, P4.2b, P4.2c, P4.2d, P4.2e, P4.2f, P4.2i

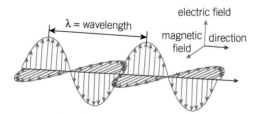

Figure 1 *The Sun emits ultraviolet waves that we can turn into a false-colour image using a computer.*

Figure 3 *An electromagnetic wave is a transverse wave.*

Our Sun is not just 'yellow' (Figure 1).

What are the waves of the electromagnetic spectrum?

When you see a rainbow you are looking at a **spectrum**. You can identify the main colours, but they merge together and there are no gaps between them. The spectrum of white light is continuous.

White light is part of a wider spectrum called the **electromagnetic spectrum** (Figure 2). We say that there are different waves in the spectrum, but we mean that there are different bands of frequencies that we call waves. Our eyes are sensitive to a narrow range of frequencies, called **visible light**, which is *not* absorbed by the atmosphere.

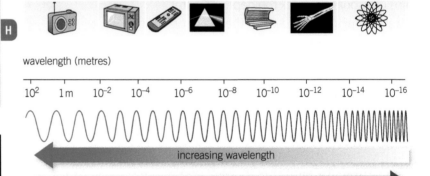

Figure 2 *The waves of the electromagnetic spectrum.*

> **A** Write down the waves of the electromagnetic spectrum in order from highest to lowest frequency.

What are electromagnetic waves?

Electromagnetic waves consist of oscillating electric and magnetic fields. The fields are oscillating in a direction at 90° to the direction of the wave (Figure 3).

All electromagnetic waves travel through a **vacuum** at 3.0×10^8 m/s. You might recognise this as the speed of light because light is part of the electromagnetic spectrum.

> **B** Write down how you know that an electromagnetic wave is transverse.

Sources such as the Sun or **microwave** ovens emit electromagnetic waves. Your skin absorbs **infrared** waves, and food absorbs microwave radiation, and both heat up.

Electromagnetic waves transfer energy from sources to **absorbers**. Some waves, such as the microwaves sent to satellites, transfer information.

How do you produce and detect radio waves? H

An oscillating potential difference across a wire makes electrons move backwards and forwards. This produces a changing electric and magnetic field, which is emitted as a **radio wave**. When the fields meet another piece of metal, such as an **aerial** (Figure 4), this makes the electrons move, which produces an electrical signal. Electromagnetic waves are also produced by the movement of electrons in atoms.

What are the frequencies and wavelengths of electromagnetic waves?

Radio waves have a wavelength that can be as long as a football pitch, but the wavelength of visible light is a fraction of a millimetre. You can use the equation for wave speed to calculate values of frequency and wavelength.

Figure 4 *Electromagnetic waves make the electrons in a metal aerial oscillate.*

Calculating frequency

The Sun emits **ultraviolet** waves with a wavelength of 320 nm. Calculate their frequency.

Step 1: Write down what you know, and convert to standard units:

wavelength = 320 nm

$$= 320 \times 10^{-9}\,m$$

$$speed = 3.0 \times 10^8\,m/s$$

Step 2: Make frequency the subject of the formula and calculate frequency:

$$\frac{wave\ speed}{wavelength} = frequency$$

$$\frac{3.0 \times 10^8\,m/s}{320 \times 10^9\,m} = frequency$$

frequency = 9.4×10^{14} Hz (2 significant figures)

Waves, rays, and radiation

Waves and rays are different ways of modelling what a source emits – radiation. Write down where you have used a ray model at Key Stage 3.

1   Write down which of these is the speed of radio waves:
    3 m/s, 340 m/s, 3 000 000 m/s, 300 000 000 m/s.   *(1 mark)*

2   **a** Suggest what we mean when we say 'the frequency of visible light'.   *(1 mark)*
    b The range of wavelengths of visible light is about 400 nm to 700 nm. Calculate the frequency range.   *(5 marks)*

3   Explain why electromagnetic waves can travel through a vacuum but sound waves cannot.   *(2 marks)*

4   Suggest and explain whether waving a charged balloon produces a radio wave.   *(4 marks)*

Study tip

For the waves of the electromagnetic spectrum the wavelengths can be very small, and the frequencies very large, so we use prefixes or powers of ten.

You need to make sure you can convert from all the different prefixes when answering questions about electromagnetic waves.

Learning outcomes

After studying this lesson you should be able to:

- describe the different ways that electromagnetic waves interact with matter
- explain how refraction is related to velocity
- describe some uses of waves in different regions of the electromagnetic spectrum
- describe which waves are dangerous and why.

Specification reference: P4.2g, P4.2h, P4.2j, P4.2k

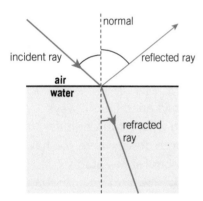

Figure 2 *When a wave hits a boundary, part of the wave is reflected at the same angle, and part of the wave is refracted (changes direction).*

Figure 3 *Your remote control communicates with your television.*

In some places it is hard to get a mobile phone signal (Figure 1). How do satellite phones work?

H

Figure 1 *You can use a satellite phone instead.*

How do electromagnetic waves interact with matter? H

Electromagnetic waves can be absorbed, reflected, transmitted, or refracted.

When electromagnetic radiation (like light) goes into another medium (like from air into glass) at an angle, it changes velocity and its direction changes (Figure 2).

You can see that electromagnetic waves interact differently with matter by looking at some uses and dangers. What happens depends on their wavelength.

How are electromagnetic waves used for communication?

Many people would find their lives very difficult without wireless devices.

Your phone communicates with transmitters using microwaves. Microwaves are also used to communicate with satellites, and for WiFi and Bluetooth® systems.

TV and radio stations transmit television and radio signals by adding sound and picture information to radio waves.

Remote controls (Figure 3) use pulses of infrared to communicate with televisions. You can also send information at high speeds using infrared pulses down optical fibres.

Ships sometimes communicate using flashing visible light and Morse code.

A Suggest an advantage of using a mobile phone compared with a flashing light.

What are other uses of electromagnetic waves?

Electromagnetic waves transfer energy in a range of situations.

In a microwave oven, the water and fat in food absorb the microwaves, which heats up the outside of the food. Conduction transfers energy to the middle.

Infrared radiation cooks food in a grill or oven. Infrared from a radiator can heat you by transferring energy to a thermal store.

Lasers in CDs, DVDs, and Blu-ray Discs™ use visible light.

Ultraviolet radiation helps to produce vitamin D, which you need for strong bones.

Forensic scientists use the fact that bodily fluids glow in ultraviolet light (Figure 4), and you can also use ultraviolet to detect forged bank notes.

Figure 4 *A forensic scientist can use ultraviolet to detect blood, semen, and saliva at a crime scene.*

B Suggest how you could show that microwaves do not 'cook from the inside out'.

Ultraviolet, **X-rays**, and **gamma rays** can damage or kill cells. This can be useful because:

- ultraviolet radiation kills bacteria in water (sterilises it)
- X-rays can kill skin **cancer** or other cancer cells
- gamma rays can kill cancer cells, and also kill bacteria on food.

Which waves are dangerous, and why?

Ultraviolet radiation can damage the DNA in the cells of your skin. The cells can grow very rapidly and cause skin cancer. If you expose your eyes to ultraviolet you can develop cataracts, which make your corneas cloudy.

X-rays can also damage your cells and cause cancer. A **radiographer** operating an X-ray machine stands behind a lead screen or in another room while the machine is on (Figure 5).

Gamma rays can also damage or kill the cells in your body.

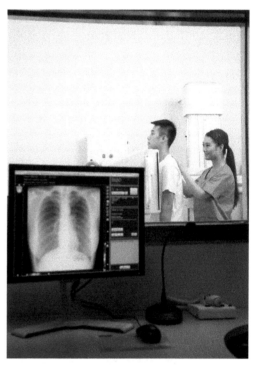

Figure 5 *A doctor uses an X-ray produced by a radiographer.*

1 Suggest why using X-rays on your feet to see if your shoes fit is a bad idea. *(1 mark)*

2 Suggest why some scientists think that using your mobile phone to make calls might affect your health. *(2 marks)*

3 Suggest a link between the number of uses of microwaves and the microwave region of the electromagnetic spectrum. *(2 marks)*

4 Discs that store data, such as CDs and DVDs, have a long continuous spiral of pits. This is how the information is stored. Suggest and explain which stores more information: a Blu-ray Disc or a CD that uses red laser light to read it. *(3 marks)*

Study tip

Always write 'microwave oven' not just 'microwave', because that could mean the wave.

Waves and radioactivity

Summary questions

1 a Choose the correct words to complete the sentences:

i Electromagnetic waves are **longitudinal/transverse** waves and travel through space at **the same velocity/different velocities**.

ii There are groupings of waves, e.g. microwaves, which indicate a range of **frequencies/velocities** in the electromagnetic spectrum.

iii Our eyes can detect only a small range called **infrared/visible light**.

iv All the electromagnetic waves transfer **energy/matter** from a source to an absorber.

b Copy and complete Table 1 with some examples of sources and absorbers.

Table 1 *Sources and absorbers.*

Electromagnetic wave	Source	Absorbed by...
microwaves	microwave transmitter	
infrared		skin
X-rays	X-ray machine	

2 a Copy and complete the sentences, choosing the correct words:

i The waves of the electromagnetic spectrum with the shortest wavelength are **radio waves/gamma rays**.

ii The waves of the electromagnetic spectrum with the smallest frequency are **radio waves/gamma rays**.

b The visible light spectrum is part of the electromagnetic spectrum. Write down the waves of the visible spectrum from lowest to highest frequency.

c Explain why we talk about radio waves as a 'group', and not 'the frequency of radio waves'.

d Describe what is oscillating in an electromagnetic wave.

3 a Calculate the frequency of radio waves that have a wavelength of 1 km. The velocity of electromagnetic waves is 300 000 km/s.

b X-rays have a wavelength that is about the diameter of an atom. Calculate their frequency.

4 a Explain what 'ionising' means.

b Write down the waves of the electromagnetic spectrum that are ionising.

c Write down a use of each of the waves in **b**.

5 a Write down the waves of the electromagnetic spectrum that produce a heating effect.

b Write down a use of each of the waves in **a**.

6 Mobile phones use microwave radiation.

a Make a list of four other devices that you use in everyday life which use electromagnetic radiation.

b Suggest why it is difficult for scientists to do experiments to find out if using a mobile phone is harmful.

7 Suggest *two* reasons why hospitals use ultrasound and not X-rays to produce an image of a fetus.

8 a Describe how radio waves are produced and detected.

b Some people are concerned about the effect of electromagnetic radiation on their health. Copy and complete Table 2.

Living near	Reason why concern would be justified	Reason why concern would not be justified
electricity pylons		
mobile phone transmitter		
nuclear power station		

Revision questions

1 **a** Which type of electromagnetic wave does not damage or kill cells?

    A X-rays   **B** gamma rays

    C radio waves **D** ultraviolet waves   (*1 mark*)

  b Which statement about electromagnetic waves is correct?

    A Electromagnetic waves are transverse waves because the oscillating electric field is at 90° to the direction of travel of the wave.

    B Electromagnetic waves are transverse waves because the oscillating magnetic field is in the same direction of travel as the wave.

    C In an electromagnetic wave, the electric and magnetic fields are constant.

    D Electromagnetic waves are longitudinal waves because the oscillating electric field is in the same direction of travel as the wave.   (*1 mark*)

  c Which statement about the uses of electromagnetic waves is correct?

    A X-rays are used for communication.

    B Gamma rays are used to kill bacteria on food.

    C Microwaves are used to sterilise water.

    D Radio waves are used to cook food.   (*1 mark*)

2 Here are four types of electromagnetic radiation:

microwaves

X-rays

ultraviolet

infrared

Put them in order of increasing wavelength, starting with the shortest.   (*2 marks*)

Learning outcomes

After studying this lesson you should be able to:

- describe what is in the nucleus of an atom, and state the charge on the nucleus
- describe what 'isotope' means
- use the correct symbols for isotopes.

Specification reference: P4.3a, P4.3b, P4.3c

About 1 in 3000 water molecules is heavier than 'normal' water. If you make ice from 'heavy water' and put it in 'normal' water what happens? (Figure 1).

Figure 1 *Ice made from 'heavy water' sinks.*

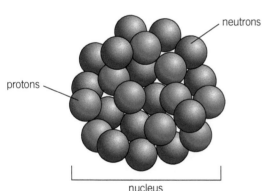

Figure 2 *The particles inside a nucleus.*

What is inside the nucleus of an atom?

Inside an atom's nucleus (Figure 2) are protons and neutrons, which are **subatomic particles**.

As Table 1 shows, protons and neutrons are much heavier than electrons. Protons and electrons have opposite charges, but the neutron has no charge.

Table 1 *Masses and charges of subatomic particles.*

Subatomic particle	Mass relative to mass of proton	Relative charge
proton	1.0000	+1
neutron	1.0000	0
electron	0.0005 (effectively zero)	−1

The charge on the nucleus of an atom depends on the number of protons in it. It is the *charge* on the nucleus that is unique to a particular element.

- If the charge on a nucleus is +1 then the element is hydrogen.
- If the charge on a nucleus is +79 then the element is gold.

A Write down the charge on a hydrogen atom with one proton and one electron in it.

Why do the nuclei of different elements have different masses?

Atoms of an element all contain the *same* number of protons.

However, the atom of an element can have a *different* number of neutrons (Figure 3). This changes the mass of the nucleus without changing the charge.

B Explain why adding neutrons to a nucleus affects the mass but not the charge.

Atoms of an element with different numbers of neutrons are called **isotopes**. Isotopes are written in the format 'carbon-12'. The number 12 refers to the *total* number of subatomic particles in the nucleus.

You can add a neutron to an atom of hydrogen to make an isotope called deuterium, or hydrogen-2. Deuterium oxide (D_2O) is called 'heavy water'. Hydrogen oxide (H_2O) is 'normal' water (Figure 4).

How do we represent isotopes?

You have learned about **mass number** and **atomic number** in Chemistry (Figure 5). You can use these numbers to work out the number of particles in a nucleus, or in a neutral atom.

carbon-12   carbon-11

Figure 3 *The mass of carbon-11 is smaller than the mass of carbon-12, but both are carbon.*

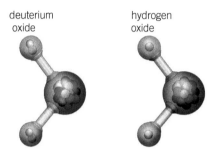

deuterium oxide   hydrogen oxide

Figure 4 *Deuterium oxide is 'heavy water' because each hydrogen atom attached to the oxygen contains a neutron. Hydrogen oxide is 'normal' water.*

Calculating the number of neutrons

Calculate the number of protons and neutrons in an atom of $^{222}_{86}$ Rn (radon).

Step 1: Write down the number of protons using the bottom number:

   number of protons = 86

Step 2: Subtract the atomic number from the mass number to find the number of neutrons:

   number of neutrons = 222 − 86

                      = 136

mass number

atomic number

$$\text{X} \quad \overset{12}{\underset{6}{\text{C}}}$$

Figure 5 *The top number is the mass number, the bottom number is the atomic number, and the letter is the chemical symbol of the element.*

1 Write down the mass numbers of the isotopes of carbon in Figure 3. *(2 marks)*

2 The atomic number of uranium is 92.
   a Calculate the difference in the number of neutrons in uranium-235, and uranium-238. *(3 marks)*
   b Explain why there are two methods of doing this calculation. *(1 mark)*

3 Suggest why isotopes are written as 'name'-'mass number' (carbon-12), and not 'name'-'atomic number' (carbon-6). *(1 mark)*

4 **a** Explain why heavy water does not have twice the mass of 'normal' water. *(1 mark)*
   b Calculate the percentage by which 'heavy water' is more massive than 'normal' water. *(4 marks)*

Go further

Some of the mass numbers of the Periodic Table are whole numbers, but most are not. Find out why.

Learning outcomes

After studying this lesson you should be able to:

- describe the types of radiation that unstable nuclei emit
- describe the different penetrating powers of alpha, beta, and gamma radiation.

Specification reference: P4.3d, P4.3l

Figure 1 Marie Curie was the first person to use the word 'radioactive'.

α particle $= {}^{4}_{2}$He

Figure 3 *An alpha particle has two protons and two neutrons.*

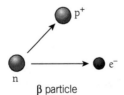

Figure 4 *An electron is produced when a neutron decays into a proton and an electron.*

Who (Figure 1) was the first person to use the word 'radioactive'? She is the only woman to win two Nobel Prizes.

What do unstable nuclei emit?

Most, but not all, of the atoms that you are made of are **stable**. This means that they do not break down, or decay.

The nuclei of atoms that are **unstable** emit **radiation** (Figure 2). This radiation can be made up of particles or waves (Table 1). Materials that emit radiation are **radioactive**.

Table 1 *Types of radiation.*

Radiation	Type	Symbol	What is it?	Equation symbol
alpha	particle	α	the nucleus of a helium atom	${}^{4}_{2}$He
beta	particle	β	a fast-moving electron	${}^{0}_{-1}$e
gamma	electromagnetic wave	γ	a wave of the electromagnetic spectrum	none
neutron	particle	n	a particle in the nucleus	${}^{1}_{0}$n

In the equation symbol in Table 1, the top number shows the mass relative to a proton, and the bottom number shows the charge.

Figure 2 Unstable atoms emit radiation from the nucleus.

> **A** Compare the charge on an alpha particle (Figure 3) with the charge on a beta particle.

A nucleus does *not* contain electrons, so where does the beta particle come from?

Neutrons are not stable. They can decay to make a proton and an electron (Figure 4).

How do you detect radiation?

You detect radiation with a Geiger–Müller tube, or **Geiger counter**. This is the device that 'clicks' when radiation enters it. Each click is a tiny current produced when the radiation ionises atoms of the gas inside the tube.

How are alpha, beta, and gamma radiation different?

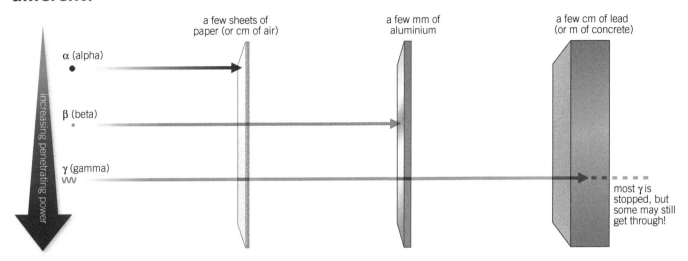

Figure 5 *Alpha, beta, and gamma radiation are invisible, but you can tell them apart by what absorbs them.*

Alpha, beta, and gamma have different **penetrating powers** (Figure 5). You can stop alpha with paper, or your skin. Beta travels through paper, but is stopped by aluminium. Gamma is the most penetrating.

B Suggest a material that could be used for lining containers that transport radioactive materials.

You can explain the differences between the penetrating powers of the different types of radiation if you know how radiation interacts with the atoms it collides with.

The radiation emitted by radioactive material is **ionising radiation**. This means that the radiation can remove electrons from atoms to produce positively charged **ions**.

Table 2 shows how the amount of ionisation that happens depends on the mass, charge, and energy of the radiation.

Table 2 *Properties of radiations.*

Radiation	Relative mass	Charge	Ionising power	Range
alpha	large	+2	high	short
beta	small	−1	medium	medium
gamma	none	none	low	long

You have to transfer energy to an atom to ionise it. Alpha particles transfer more energy to the material they are travelling through than gamma rays – this is why alpha radiation has a much shorter range.

Go further

When a neutron decays a particle other than an electron is emitted. Find out what it is and how physicists worked out it was there.

1 List the three types of radiation in order from most penetrating to least penetrating. *(1 mark)*

2 Describe how you can use a Geiger counter to work out the type of radiation that a radioactive material was emitting. *(6 marks)*

3 Suggest why you need to surround a building that contains a large amount of radioactive material, such as a nuclear reactor, with concrete as well as a thick layer of lead. *(2 marks)*

4 Suggest and explain whether neutrons are more, less, or similarly ionising to alpha particles. *(3 marks)*

P4.3.3 Nuclear equations

Learning outcomes

After studying this lesson you should be able to:

- describe in terms of particles what happens in alpha, beta, and neutron decay
- describe the changes (if any) in the mass and charge of a nucleus that emits radiation
- write balanced equations for nuclear decay using the names and symbols of common nuclei and particles.
- describe the difference between contamination and irradiation.

Specification reference: P4.3d, P4.3e, P4.3f, P4.3g, P4.3m

Figure 1 *Bananas contain an unstable isotope of potassium.*

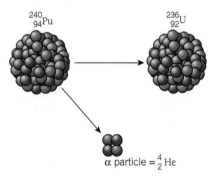

α particle $= {}^{4}_{2}\text{He}$

Figure 2 *The alpha decay of plutonium.*

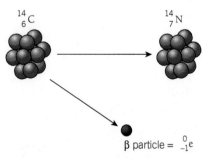

β particle $= {}^{0}_{-1}\text{e}$

Figure 3 *The beta decay of carbon.*

Bananas (Figure 1) contain potassium-40, which is unstable. The emission of beta particles changes the nucleus of potassium-40 atoms, but the emission of gamma rays does not. Why?

What happens in alpha decay?

Large nuclei are unstable. Imagine a very big nucleus containing large numbers of protons and neutrons. Two protons and two neutrons can join up to form an alpha particle, which is emitted from the nucleus (Figure 2).

You can write equations for nuclear decay, just as you can for chemical reactions.

$$ {}^{240}_{94}\text{Pu} \quad \rightarrow \quad {}^{236}_{92}\text{U} \quad + \quad {}^{4}_{2}\text{He} $$

In a nuclear decay you have to make sure that the equation is balanced.

If you read across the *top* numbers you see that they add up. There are the same numbers of protons and neutrons after alpha decay as there were before. Mass is conserved.

If you read across the *bottom* numbers you see that they add up. Charge is conserved.

> **A** Compare the charge on a uranium-236 nucleus with the charge on a plutonium-240 nucleus.

What happens in beta decay?

In beta decay a neutron decays to a proton and an electron (Figure 3). The electron is emitted as a beta particle. The number of neutrons goes *down* by one, but the number of protons goes *up* by one.

You can see what is happening using the nuclear equation:

$$ {}^{14}_{6}\text{C} \quad \rightarrow \quad {}^{14}_{7}\text{N} \quad + \quad {}^{0}_{-1}\text{e} $$

The *total* number of protons and neutrons in the nucleus (14) has not changed, so the mass does not change.

The *charge* on the nucleus has increased by +1. A particle with a charge of −1 has been emitted, so, overall, the charge before and after is the same.

> **B** Explain why beta decay produces a different element even though there is the same number of particles in the nucleus.

What happens in gamma decay?

Gamma rays are electromagnetic waves, so they do not have mass or charge. When a nucleus emits a gamma ray (Figure 4), usually alongside alpha or beta decay, the atomic number and the mass number stay the same.

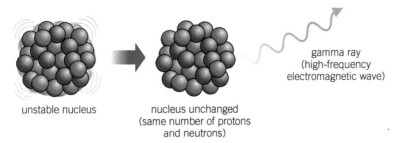

Figure 4 *Gamma decay.*

What happens in neutron emission?

When some nuclei decay they produce nuclei with large numbers of neutrons. These nuclei can emit neutrons.

An isotope of helium, helium-5, decays by neutron emission. The charge on the nucleus has not changed, so it is the same element, but the nucleus is now more stable.

$$^5_2\text{He} \rightarrow {}^4_2\text{He} + {}^1_0\text{n}$$

What is the difference between contamination and irradiation?

You have probably eaten radioactive food today, and breathed in radioactive gas. Food is just one of the sources of **background radiation** that we are exposed to all the time (Figure 5).

Contamination happens when you take radioactive material inside your body or if it is on your skin. Once you are internally contaminated, you cannot remove the radioactive material from inside you.

Irradiation happens when there is radioactive material outside your body, but the radiation can travel into your body.

In both cases, ionising radiation can damage the DNA inside your cells, which can cause cancer.

1 ✏ Compare alpha and beta decay in terms of changes to the mass and charge of a nucleus. *(4 marks)*

2 a ✏ Write down the nuclear equation for the alpha decay of a nucleus of uranium-238. *(4 marks)*

b Write down the nuclear equation for the beta decay of potassium-40. *(4 marks)*

c There is potassium in bananas. Explain why eating bananas is contamination not irradiation, and a possible hazard. *(2 marks)*

3 Describe how alpha and beta decay are similar, and how gamma and neutron decay are similar. *(2 marks)*

4 🖩 Most radioactive elements decay by a series of alpha and beta decays until they reach a stable element. The uranium-238 in **2a** decays by: α, β, β, α, α, α, α, α, β, β, α, β, β, α. Calculate the mass and charge of the stable element produced. *(7 marks)*

Writing a nuclear equation

Write down the nuclear equation for the beta decay of caesium-137 (Cs).

Step 1: Use the Periodic Table to find the atomic number of caesium.

atomic number = 55

Step 2: Find the element with an atomic number of 55 + 1.

element = barium, Ba

Step 3: Write out the equation:

$$^{137}_{55}\text{Cs} \rightarrow {}^{137}_{56}\text{Ba} + {}^{0}_{-1}\text{e}$$

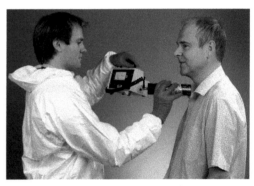

Figure 5 *Everyone is slightly radioactive because of the carbon-14 in our bodies. This isotope of carbon is produced in the atmosphere, and absorbed by plants which we eat.*

Study tip

You should always check that the mass number total and the atomic number total are the same before and after decay. Remember you can find mass numbers and atomic numbers in the Periodic Table.

Learning outcomes

After studying this lesson you should be able to:

- explain what half-life means and how it relates to the randomness of decay
- calculate the ratio of final to initial activity (net decline) after a given number of half-lives.

Specification reference: P4.3j, P4.3k

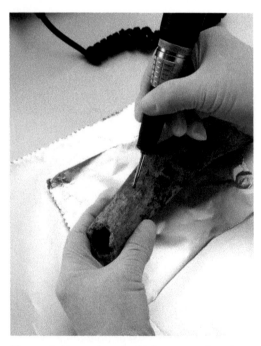

Figure 1 *Forensic scientists can work out when someone died using the level of carbon-14 in their bones and the half-life of carbon-14.*

Table 1 *Half-lives for commonly used isotopes.*

Radioactive isotope	Half-life
helium-6	0.8 seconds
radon-222	3.8 days
carbon-14	5700 years
uranium-238	4.5 billion years

Some of the carbon in the toast that you have for breakfast is carbon-14. This makes you radioactive. What happens when you die (Figure 1)?

How do you measure the activity of a radioactive material?

H If you listen to a Geiger counter detecting radiation you can hear that the material does not emit radiation in a regular pattern. The material emits radiation at **random**.

A Geiger counter can measure the radiation (photons or particles) emitted per second. This is called the **activity**, or count rate, of the sample, and is measured in **becquerels (Bq)**.

One becquerel is one count (wave or particle) per second. You can measure lower activities in counts per minute.

> **A** Convert a count rate of 6 counts per minute to a count rate in becquerels.

What is half-life?

The activity of a lump of radioactive material, such as uranium, decreases with time (Figure 2). The time it takes for the activity to halve is called the **half-life**. This is the same as the time for the nuclei of half the atoms to decay.

The probability that any one nucleus decays in one second is fixed. This means that the decay is random, and also means that the half-life is constant.

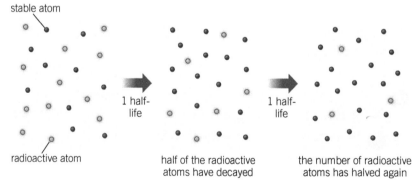

Figure 2 *After each half-life the number of radioactive atoms halves.*

Notice that the atoms that decay do not disappear. If they emit alpha or beta particles, they change to the atom of a different element. Eventually they become stable.

The half-life of a radioactive material can be very short, or very long (see Table 1). The half-lives of different isotopes of an element will all be different.

How do you calculate using half-life?

You can show how the activity of a sample changes on a graph like the one in Figure 3.

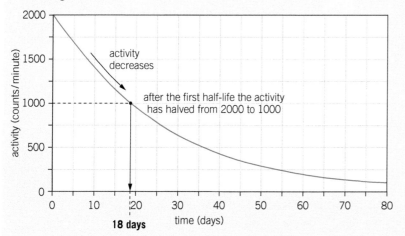

Figure 3 *The half-life of californium-253 is 18 days.*

B Write down the activity of californium-253 after 36 days. Use data from the graph in Figure 3.

How do you calculate the ratio of final to initial activity using half-life?

You can use the half-life to calculate the ratio of the final to initial activity. This is known as the net decline. For example, after one half-life the ratio will be 1:2; after two half-lives it will be 1:4.

You can calculate the fraction of material that is still radioactive using half-lives.

Calculating with half-lives

A sample of radon-222 has an activity of 100 Bq.
Calculate the activity after 11.4 days. Use data from Table 1.

Step 1: Calculate the number of half-lives.

$$\text{number of half-lives} = \frac{11.4 \text{ days}}{3.8 \text{ days/half-life}}$$

$$= 3 \text{ half-lives}$$

Step 2: Use the number of half-lives to calculate the new activity.
After 3 half-lives the activity is reduced to:

$$\frac{1}{2} \times \frac{1}{2} \times \frac{1}{2} = \frac{1}{8}$$

So, activity $= \frac{1}{8} \times 100 \text{ Bq}$

$= 12.5 \text{ Bq (3 significant figures)}$

You can see how the net decline is linked to half-lives in Figure 4.

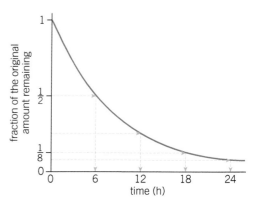

Figure 4 *The half-life of technetium-99m is 6 hours.*

1 Write down the two definitions of half-life. *(2 marks)*

2 Suggest and explain which isotope in Table 1 has the highest probability of decay per second. *(2 marks)*

3 **a** Sketch a graph of activity of a sample containing carbon-14 over 20 000 years if the initial count rate is 60 counts/minute. *(3 marks)*

 b A scientist measures a count rate of 12 counts/minute for a piece of animal bone that has been dug up. Use your graph to suggest the time since the animal died. *(1 mark)*

 c State one assumption that the scientist needs to make when working out this time. *(1 mark)*

4 You have a sample of radioactive material that decays to a stable isotope.

 a Calculate the fraction that is radioactive after 5 half-lives. *(2 marks)*

 b If the original mass of the sample was 1 g, calculate the mass of stable isotope after 5 half-lives. *(4 marks)*

Learning outcomes

After studying this lesson you should be able to:

- describe how electrons are arranged in atoms
- describe what happens when atoms absorb electromagnetic radiation
- describe what happens when atoms emit electromagnetic radiation
- describe what happens when atoms gain or lose electrons.

Specification reference: P4.3h, P4.3i

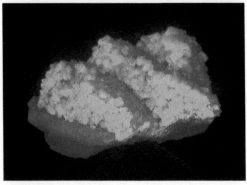

Figure 1 *Fluorite crystals on quartz glow in the dark.*

Go further

Find out how astronomers use spectra when they are investigating exoplanets (planets that orbit stars other than the Sun).

Why do some materials glow in the dark (Figure 1)?

How are electrons in atoms arranged?

Electrons are negative, and the nucleus is positive, so why do electrons not spiral into the nucleus?

Scientists have worked out that electrons can only occupy certain specified **energy levels** around the nucleus of an atom (Figure 2). Different atoms have different energy levels.

Electrons usually occupy the lowest possible energy level, at the smallest distance from the nucleus.

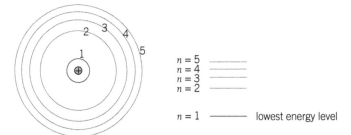

Figure 2 *A hydrogen atom has several energy levels, which we usually show as horizontal lines.*

What happens when atoms absorb electromagnetic radiation?

We have used a ray model *and* a wave model for electromagnetic radiation.

There is a third model. In the **photon** model electromagnetic radiation is emitted and absorbed as packets of energy, called photons, and the energy of each photon is proportional to the frequency.

It takes a photon of exactly the right energy to 'excite' an electron to a higher energy level. The electron moves from a lower to a higher level (Figure 3), and we say that the atom is in an 'excited' state.

A Suggest why some of the photons in Figure 3 are not affected when they hit an atom.

When light of all frequencies is passed through hydrogen gas some frequencies are absorbed. An **absorption spectrum** (Figure 4) shows a set of frequencies of radiation absorbed by an atom when excited electrons move to higher energy levels.

A photon that has enough energy can completely remove an electron from the atom. The atom is ionised. Photons of ultraviolet, X-ray, and gamma ray frequencies have enough energy to ionise atoms.

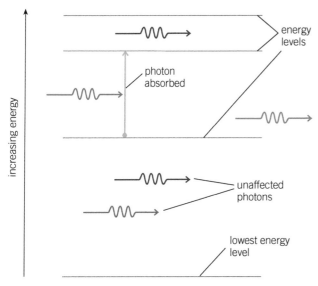

Figure 3 *When an atom absorbs a photon an electron jumps from one energy level to a higher energy level.*

Why do atoms emit radiation?

There are many ways to 'excite' electrons. For example, you can excite the electrons in the atoms of a gas by passing an electric current through it. When electrons move from a higher to a lower level they emit radiation. An **emission spectrum** (Figure 5) shows a set of frequencies of radiation emitted by an atom when excited electrons move to lower energy levels.

B Suggest a connection between the emission and absorption spectrum of hydrogen.

The frequency of radiation emitted depends on the difference in energy of the energy levels (Figure 6). The energy change can take place in one go, or two or more. If there are two changes then the emitted photons will have less energy, lower frequencies, and longer wavelengths.

The largest energy difference is from an energy level just below ionisation. The highest energy photons from a hydrogen atom are in the ultraviolet part of the electromagnetic spectrum, but carbon atoms can emit X-ray photons.

Gamma rays are the highest energy radiation, and they are emitted from nuclei. Protons and neutrons occupy energy levels in the nucleus. The energies involved are much higher, so the radiation emitted is of a higher energy.

1 Describe the difference between an 'excited' atom and an 'ionised' atom. *(2 marks)*

2 Describe in terms of the electrons what happens when:
   a photons are absorbed *(1 mark)*
   b photons are emitted. *(1 mark)*

3 Suggest and explain why hydrogen cannot emit X-ray photons. *(2 marks)*

4 Explain why some atoms can absorb ultraviolet radiation, but emit visible light (and so glow in the dark). *(4 marks)*

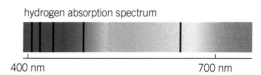

Figure 4 *You can use the particular frequencies that an atom absorbs as a sort of 'bar code' for the element.*

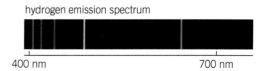

Figure 5 *The emission spectrum of hydrogen has only certain frequencies.*

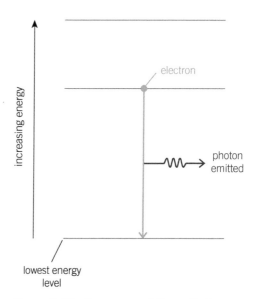

Figure 6 *The frequency of the radiation emitted depends on the difference in energy between the levels.*

Study tip

Remember that electrons move up to a higher energy level when photons are absorbed, and move down to a lower energy level when photons are emitted.

Summary questions

1 Copy and complete the following sentences.

  a The nucleus of an atom consists of positively charged _____, negatively charged _____, and _____ which have no charge.

  b The mass of the _____ and _____ are about equal, and much bigger than the mass of the _____.

  c The _____ in the nucleus, or number of _____, tells you which element it is. In a neutral atom, this is also equal to the number of _____.

  d Nuclei with the same number of protons and different numbers of neutrons are called _____.

2 **a** Copy and complete Table 1 using the words 'alpha', 'beta', 'gamma', and 'neutron'.

  Table 1 *Identify the emissions.*

Type of radiation	Phrase or symbol
	electromagnetic wave
	$^{0}_{-1}e$
	$^{1}_{0}n$
	$^{4}_{2}He$

  b Copy and complete Table 2 by ticking the correct column for each type of radioactive decay.

  Table 2 *Radioactive decay.*

Type of decay	Change of mass of nucleus?	Change of charge on nucleus?	Different element produced?
alpha			
beta			
gamma			
neutron			

3 Compare contamination and irradiation.

4 Copy and complete the following sentences, choosing from these words. You may need to use the words once, more than once, or not at all.

  least   lead   most   alpha   beta
  gamma   ionising   emitting   aluminium

  a Out of alpha radiation, beta radiation, and gamma rays, alpha radiation is the _____ penetrating.

  b Out of alpha radiation, beta radiation, and gamma rays, gamma rays are the _____ penetrating.

  c All three types of radiation are _____ radiation.

  d Gamma radiation is the least _____.

  e Beta radiation is absorbed by _____.

5 **a** Radioactive decay is random. Explain what this means.

  b Radon is an alpha-emitting gas. Write a balanced nuclear equation for the alpha decay of $^{219}_{86}Rn$.

  c Write a balanced nuclear equation for the beta decay of radioactive iodine: $^{131}_{53}I$.

6 The emission spectrum of helium contains bright lines at certain frequencies.

  a Explain how the lines are produced.

  b Describe what can happen when an atom absorbs electromagnetic radiation.

7 Describe and explain the difference between the electromagnetic radiation emitted from atoms and the electromagnetic radiation emitted from nuclei.

8 A rock contains uranium-238, which has a half-life of 4.5 billion years, and decays into thorium-234.

  a Suggest and explain whether uranium-238 decays by alpha, beta, or gamma decay.

  b Explain what half-life means.

  c Look at the graph in Figure 1. **H**

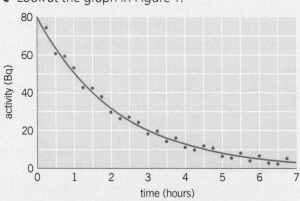

  Figure 1 *Find the half-life of this substance.*

  i Calculate the half-life.

  ii Calculate the net decline after 7 half-lives.

  iii You have 24.00 g of this uranium-238. Calculate the mass of thorium after 7 half-lives.

  iv Write down an assumption that you have made.

Revision questions

1 a Which statement about isotopes is correct?
   A Isotopes have the same atomic number and different numbers of neutrons.
   B Isotopes have the same number of neutrons and different numbers of protons.
   C Isotopes have the same atomic number and different numbers of electrons.
   D Isotopes have the same atomic number and the same number of neutrons. (1 mark)

   b The diagram shows different radiations being absorbed by different materials. Which track, A, B, C, or D, shows gamma radiation? (1 mark)

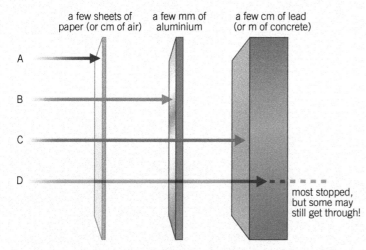

a few sheets of paper (or cm of air) a few mm of aluminium a few cm of lead (or m of concrete)

A
B
C
D

most stopped, but some may still get through!

   c Here are some decay equations. Which one correctly shows beta decay?
   A $^{90}_{38}Sr \rightarrow {}^{90}_{39}Y + {}^{0}_{-1}e$
   B $^{90}_{38}Sr \rightarrow {}^{91}_{38}Y + {}^{-1}_{0}e$
   C $^{90}_{38}Sr \rightarrow {}^{86}_{36}Kr + {}^{4}_{2}He$
   D $^{90}_{38}Sr \rightarrow {}^{89}_{38}Sr + {}^{1}_{0}n$ (1 mark)

2 Finn carries out an experiment to model radioactive decay. He starts with 100 dice and removes all of the dice showing a six. He records the number remaining and rolls the remaining dice. He repeats the process many times.
   a Explain why this is a good model for radioactive decay. (2 marks)
   b How can Finn work out the half-life of the number of dice in terms of the number of times he rolls the dice? (2 marks)
   c How can Finn improve the accuracy of his estimate of the half-life? (1 mark)

3 a Explain why atoms only absorb light at certain frequencies. (2 marks)
   b A hydrogen atom absorbs light with a frequency of 6.17×10^{14} Hz. Calculate the wavelength of the light. (speed of light = 3×10^8 m/s) (2 marks)

4 The ratio of the final to the initial activity in a radioactive sample is 1 : 64. How many half-lives is this? (2 marks) H

5 Compare the similarities and differences in alpha, beta, and gamma decay. (6 marks)

P4.1 Wave behaviour

- Describe what waves are.
- Describe properties of waves.
- Describe how to model transverse waves.
- State and use the equation linking wave speed, frequency, and wavelength.
- Describe how to calculate the speed of water waves.
- Describe how to calculate the speed of sound waves.
- Describe what happens to speed, frequency, and wavelength of a wave crossing a boundary.

P4.2 The electromagnetic spectrum

- Describe what electromagnetic waves are.
- Name the waves of the electromagnetic spectrum.
- State the electromagnetic waves that our eyes detect.
- Use the wave equation for electromagnetic waves.
- State how radio waves are produced and detected.
- Describe some uses of waves in different regions of the electromagnetic spectrum.
- Describe which waves are dangerous and why.
- Explain why electromagnetic waves are refracted. **H**
- Describe the different ways that electromagnetic waves interact with matter.

P4.3 Radioactivity

- Describe what is in the nucleus of an atom.
- Describe what 'isotope' means.
- Use the correct symbols for isotopes.
- Describe the types of radiation that unstable nuclei emit.
- Describe the different penetrating powers of alpha, beta, and gamma radiation.
- Describe in terms of particles what happens in alpha, beta, and neutron decay.
- Write balanced equations for nuclear decay.
- Explain what half-life means.
- Interpret graphs of activity against time.
- Calculate the ratio of final to initial activity after a given number of half-lives. **H**
- Describe what happens when atoms absorb electromagnetic radiation.

- Describe what happens when atoms emit electromagnetic radiation.
- Describe the difference between contamination and irradiation.

Uses and Hazards

- background radiation mainly from natural sources (e.g., rocks, radon, cosmic rays)
- some medical sources (e.g., tracers, radiotherapy, gamma knife)
- need to choose isotopes with short half-lives for medical purposes
- use protective clothing/screens for medical staff

Irradiation

- external source

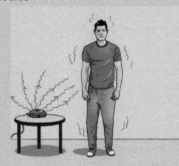

Contamination

- inside or on the body usually more hazardous

Wave behaviour

Longitudinal

Transverse

Modelled using ripples

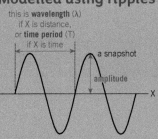

this is **wavelength** (λ)
if X is distance,
or **time period** (T)
if X is time

a snapshot

amplitude

X

wave speed = frequency × wavelength
(m/s)   (Hz)   (m)

The electromagnetic spectrum

radio waves	micro-waves	infrared (IR)	visible light	ultraviolet (UV)	X-rays	gamma rays

← increasing wavelength

increasing frequency →

made by and detected with oscillators in electric circuits **H**	the only group our eyes detect	different absorption useful in hospitals (broken bones)	gamma camera detects gamma rays emitted by tracer **H**

all transfer energy and travel at 3.0×10^8 m/s in a vacuum (speed of light)

P4 Waves and radioactivity

Half-life

- over time the activity of a source decreases
- different materials have different half-lives

- ratio of final to initial activity: **H**

  1:1 → 1:2 → 1:4 → 1:8

  each arrow represents a half-life

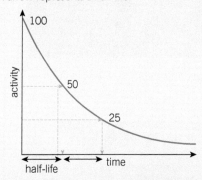

Radiation in and out of atoms

- energy levels for electrons
- electrons can be excited and move up, then move down energy levels
- electromagnetic radiation → photons

Absorption spectrum

- black lines are seen
- for example, hydrogen absorption spectrum:

400 nm   700 nm

Emission spectrum

- coloured lines are seen
- for example, hydrogen emission spectrum:

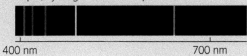

400 nm   700 nm

Isotopes and radiation

Isotopes

- different number of neutrons
- same proton number

Radiation

- particles or waves emitted from unstable nuclei
- ionising radiation damages living cells, which can lead to cancer

Nuclear equations

- alpha decay
- beta decay
- gamma decay → no change to type of element → excited nucleus releases energy

Learning outcomes

After studying this lesson you should be able to:

- describe energy stores and transfers
- explain what an energy store is
- describe the law of conservation of energy.

Specification reference: P5.1a

Figure 1 *Angel Falls waterfall, Venezuela.*

Figure 2 *As a skier skies down a mountain the energy in a gravitational potential store decreases.*

The temperature of the water at the bottom of the world's highest waterfall, Angel Falls (Figure 1), is higher than the water at the top.

What is energy?

Energy is a quantity (a number in **joules**) that tells you what *is possible*, but does not tell you what *will happen*. For example, when you fill a car with petrol there is an amount of energy associated with the fuel and oxygen. It means that some things are possible when the fuel burns, such as reaching a certain speed or travelling a certain distance.

The amount of energy will not tell you where you are going, or how fast you are travelling. Forces and physical processes explain *why* things happen.

What types of energy stores do we use?

We keep track of energy using the idea of **energy stores**. Each store is associated with an equation, so you can do a calculation.

Table 1 *Energy stores.*

Type of store	Example of store	Related equation you have learned so far
chemical potential	a pile of coal with oxygen glucose in your muscles with oxygen	none
thermal	a hot bath	$\Delta E = mc\Delta T$ change in energy = mass × specific heat capacity × temperature difference
kinetic	a moving car	$E = \frac{1}{2}mv^2$ energy = $\frac{1}{2}$ mass × speed²
gravitational, or **gravity** potential	a skier at the top of a hill (Figure 2)	$E = mgh$ energy = mass × gravitational field strength × height
elastic potential	a stretched elastic band	$E = \frac{1}{2}kx^2$ energy = $\frac{1}{2}$ spring constant × extension²
nuclear	hydrogen in the Sun (fusion) a lump of uranium-245 (fission)	none

A store is not a place, like a cupboard, and energy is not something that you put in it, like water in a bottle. We use the idea of a store to indicate the amount of energy in joules. You can calculate this value.

A Explain the difference between a fuel and an energy store.

How is energy transferred?

Energy is transferred between stores

- **mechanically** (with forces)
- electricallly (with an electric current)
- **heating** by particles
- heating by radiation.

We can use equations to calculate energy transfered mechanically or electrically (Figure 3).

- mechanically: work done = force × distance
- electrically: energy transferred = electrical power × time

You need to remember and apply the above equations.

You can calculate the change in energy in a thermal store using:

change in thermal energy = m × specific heat capacity × change in temperature.

You need to be able to apply this equation.

B Calculate the work done when a force of 10N acts over 10cm.

What is the conservation of energy?

Energy is a quantity that is conserved. The **Law of Conservation of Energy** says:

Energy cannot be created or destroyed. Energy can only be transferred between stores.

If you have a **closed system** then there is no net change in energy. No external forces act on a closed system, and the system itself is not heated or cooled, although the components in the system can be heated or cooled as long as there is no transfer of energy into or out of the system.

An analogy for energy

We often use analogies to explain things. Energy is a bit like money (Figure 4). If you know how much you have at the start of a shopping trip, and how much you spent, you know how much you have now. Money, like energy, is conserved.

Figure 3 *Transferring energy electrically heats the pool and makes bubbles in the jacuzzi.*

Figure 4 *You can use money as an analogy to explain energy.*

Study tip

Energy is not a substance, like a liquid or a fuel, or a process. It is a number that you can calculate.

Study tip

If you see 'thermal energy' it is a shorthand for energy in a thermal store. There are no types of energy.

1 Describe the difference between energy in a store and energy transfer. *(1 mark)*
2 In these three situations the energy in the store is decreasing. Name the store in each situation:
   a a cup of tea cooling down **b** a woman on a bungee cord that is getting shorter **c** wood burning on a fire. *(3 marks)*
3 Suggest and explain which type of energy transfer applies to stretching an elastic band. *(2 marks)*
4 Suggest why the water is warmer at the bottom of a waterfall. *(5 marks)*

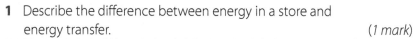

Learning outcomes

After studying this lesson you should be able to:

- describe all the changes involved in the way energy is stored when a system changes for common situations, such as an object being accelerated by a constant force
- describe the changes in energy involved when a system is changed by work done by forces
- make calculations of the energy changes associated with changes in a system using the equation for mechanical work
- use a common scale to show the overall redistribution of energy in the system
- calculate the amounts of energy associated with a moving body.

Specification reference: P5.1b, P5.1c, P5.1d, P5.1e

Figure 1 *Drag cars need to be able to reach a high speed in a short amount of time.*

Figure 2 *You increase the energy in a chemical potential store when you refill your car.*

You need to transfer a large amount of energy to win a drag race (Figure 1).

How do you analyse a situation using energy?

To do an energy analysis you need to:

- choose two points in a process
- identify which stores have more or less energy in them at those points
- work out which type of transfer has transferred the energy between stores.

It helps to think about the physical situation first.

How do you analyse situations involving constant forces?

A drag racer has a powerful engine, which exerts a *constant* force on the car over the distance of the race. This situation is analysed in Table 1.

Table 1 *Energy analysis for a car.*

	Point 1 – start of the race	Transfer	Point 2 – end of the race
Physical situation	stationary car more fuel + oxygen	an engine exerts a *constant* force	moving car at the end of the track less fuel + oxygen
Energy analysis	*no* energy in the **kinetic** store *more* energy in the **chemical potential** store	mechanically	*some* energy in the **kinetic** store *less* energy in the **chemical potential** store

A Write down the equation for transferring energy mechanically.

You transfer energy mechanically from a chemical potential store (such as the fuel in the car, and oxygen; Figure 2) to a kinetic store. You can show this on an energy analysis diagram like the one in Figure 3.

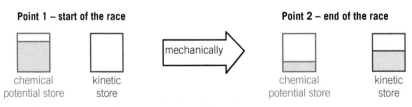

Point 1 – start of the race ..... mechanically ..... Point 2 – end of the race

chemical potential store   kinetic store   chemical potential store   kinetic store

Figure 3 *Energy analysis diagram for a drag race.*

In a closed system, the decrease in energy in the chemical potential store is equal to the increase in energy of the kinetic store because of the mechanical work done.

Calculating speed

A drag racer, starting from rest, exerts a force of 4 kN over a distance of 300 m. Calculate the work done. If the mass of the racer is 300 kg, calculate the final speed.

Step 1: Write down what you know and the equations for energy stores, or transfers involved:

force = 4 kN = 4000 N

distance = 300 m

mass = 300 kg

work done = $F \times d$

$E = \frac{1}{2}mv^2$

Step 2: Calculate the work done:

work done = $F \times d$

$= 4000\,\text{N} \times 300\,\text{m}$

$= 1.2 \times 10^6\,\text{J (or N m)}$

Step 3: Make speed the subject of the equation for energy in the kinetic store and calculate it using the equation kinetic energy $= \frac{1}{2}mv^2$

$E = \frac{1}{2}mv^2$

$v = \sqrt{\dfrac{2E}{m}}$

$v = \sqrt{\dfrac{2 \times 1.2 \times 10^6\,\text{N m}}{300\,\text{kg}}}$

$v = 90\,\text{m/s (1 significant figure)}$

You can choose *any* two points for an energy analysis, depending on what you want to calculate.

In reality, some energy is transferred to the thermal store of the surroundings because of friction, sound, or air resistance (Figure 4).

An energy analysis using equations for the energy in the stores involved in the process allows you to calculate how the energy in each store changes. You can make comparisons if you calculate energy in the same units. Here we use joules.

B Write down what happens to the temperature of the air as the drag racer moves through it.

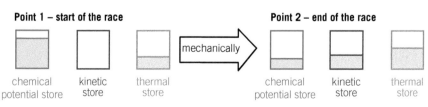

Figure 4 A more realistic energy analysis – some energy is transferred to a thermal store of the surroundings.

1 Explain how the diagram in Figure 3 shows that energy is conserved. *(1 mark)*

2 **a** A quad bike engine exerts a force of 800 N over a distance of 20 m. Calculate the final speed of the bike if it has a mass of 300 kg. *(4 marks)*

   b Write down an assumption that you have made to do this calculation. *(1 mark)*

3 **a** The drag racer in the *Calculating speed* example actually reaches a speed of 80 m/s at the end of the race. Explain why. *(1 mark)*

   b Calculate the energy transferred to the thermal store. *(4 marks)*

4 **a** You can escape the gravitational field of the Earth if you leave the Earth at 11 km/s. Calculate the distance over which you would need to use the drag racer engine to reach that speed. *(4 marks)*

   b Suggest why the drag racer is unlikely to reach this speed. *(2 marks)*

Learning outcomes

After studying this lesson you should be able to:

- describe all the changes involved in the way energy is stored when a system changes for common situations, such as a vehicle slowing down
- describe the changes in energy involved when a system is changed by work done by forces
- make calculations of the energy changes associated with changes in a system using the equation for mechanical work
- use a common scale to show the overall redistribution of energy in the system
- calculate the amounts of energy associated with a stretched spring.

Specification reference: 5.1b, P5.1c, P5.1d, P5.1e

Figure 1 *A thermogram of a car.*

Figure 2 *A springboard and vault.*

The brakes on a car get hot, as the thermogram in Figure 1 shows. A large amount of energy is transferred when you brake.

How do you analyse situations involving braking?

Brakes can exert a force on a car, and the work done by the brakes can slow a car down, transferring energy from the kinetic store (of the moving car) to the thermal stores of the brake pads and surroundings. Eventually the brake pads heat the surroundings (Table 1).

Table 1 *Energy analysis for a braking car.*

	Point 1 – a moving car	Transfer	Point 2 – a stationary car
Physical situation	a moving car cool surroundings	the brakes exert a force over a distance	a stationary car warmer surroundings
Energy analysis	kinetic store thermal store	mechanically heating by particles, heating by radiation	kinetic store thermal store

A Write down the equation you would use to calculate the change in energy in a thermal store.

Calculating force

A drag racer comes to a stop over a distance of 50 m. Calculate the force exerted by the brakes. The energy in the kinetic store before braking is 1.2×10^6 J.

Step 1: Write down what you know:

energy in kinetic store = 1.2×10^6 J

distance = 50 m

Step 2: Use the equation for work done to calculate the force.

work done by brakes = $F \times d$

$$force = \frac{W}{d}$$

$$= \frac{1.2 \times 10^6 \text{ J}}{50 \text{ m}}$$

$$= 24\,000 \text{ N (2 significant figures)}$$

How do you analyse situations involving springs?

A gymnast jumps, lands, and compresses a springboard before a vault (Figures 2 and 3). Table 2 shows one possible energy analysis.

Table 2 *Energy analysis for a gymnast.*

	Point 1 – gymnast in the air above springboard	Transfer	Point 2 – gymnast momentarily stationary on compressed springboard
Physical situation	uncompressed spring gymnast running and jumping	gymnast exerts a *changing* force over a distance	compressed spring stationary gymnast at a lower height
Energy analysis	elastic potential store kinetic store gravitational potential store	mechanically	elastic potential store kinetic store gravitational potential store

You can use the equation for work, or for energy stored in a spring, $E = \frac{1}{2}kx^2$, to do calculations.

In reality, some energy is transferred to the thermal store of the surroundings due to sound and air resistance.

B Explain why, in reality, the gymnast would not reach the same height as her original jump after the spring extends.

Calculating energy

Calculate the energy transferred to the elastic potential store of the springboard if the spring compresses by 30 cm, and the spring constant is 35 kN/m.

Step 1: Write down what you know.

compression (equivalent to extension) = 30 cm = 0.3 m

spring constant = 35 kN/m

Step 2: Use the spring equation to calculate the energy transferred.

$$E = \frac{1}{2}kx^2$$
$$= \frac{1}{2} \times 35 \times 10^3 \text{ N/m} \times (0.3 \text{ m})^2$$
$$= 1600 \text{ J (2 significant figures)}$$

Figure 3 *Energy in a kinetic store is transferred to an elastic potential store.*

1 Explain why the energy analysis of the braking car is 'realistic'. *(1 mark)*

2 Calculate the energy transferred to the elastic potential store of a spring in the suspension of a car which compresses by 1 cm. The spring constant is 100 kN/m. *(2 marks)*

3 **a** Estimate the force that a cyclist travelling at 6 m/s needs to apply to the brakes to bring the bicycle to a stop in a distance of 15 m. Ignore air resistance and friction. *(4 marks)*

 b Suggest and explain how air resistance and friction affect your answer to **a**. *(2 marks)*

4 Explain why it is not possible to calculate the increase in temperature of the surroundings when a car brakes. *(2 marks)*

Study tip

By doing the analysis of changes to the physical situation first you can work out which calculations you need to do.

Go further

Find out the difference between bicycle brakes, car brakes, and the brakes you need on racing cars.

Learning outcomes

After studying this lesson you should be able to:

- describe all the changes involved in the way energy is stored when a system changes for common situations, such as an object projected upwards or up a slope
- describe all the changes involved in the way energy is stored when a system changes for common situations, such as a moving object hitting an obstacle
- describe the changes in energy involved when a system is changed by work done by forces
- use a common scale to show the overall redistribution of energy in the system
- calculate the amounts of energy associated with a moving body
- calculate the amounts of energy associated with an object raised above ground level.

Specification reference: 5.1b, P5.1c, P5.1d, P5.1e

How does a tennis player (Figure 1) know how fast to throw the ball when serving?

How do you analyse situations involving gravity?

Imagine that you are a tennis player throwing a ball upwards (Figure 1). Table 1 analyses the situation.

Table 1 *Energy analysis for throwing a ball upwards.*

	Point 1 – as the ball leaves your hand	Transfer	Point 2 – when the ball stops momentarily
Physical situation	a moving tennis ball close to the Earth	the Earth exerts a force over a distance	a stationary tennis ball further from the Earth
Energy analysis	kinetic store / gravitational potential store	mechanically	kinetic store / gravitational potential store

In this situation there are two ways of working out the energy transferred.

You can use:

- work done = force × distance
  = weight of ball × change in height
  = mass × gravitational field strength × change in height
- (in a gravity field) potential energy
  = mass × gravitational field strength × change in height

The work done and the change in energy are the same.

> **A** Explain why you have to use the *change* in height when you do calculations involving a gravitational potential store.

Figure 1 *At the top of the throw the ball is stationary and the kinetic store is empty.*

Calculating with energy

A ball leaves your hand at 5.0 m/s. Calculate the height above your hand that it reaches. Assume that $g = 10\,\text{m/s}^2$.

Step 1: Write down what you know, and the equations for energy stores or transfers involved:

$v = 5.0\,\text{m/s}$

$g = 10\,\text{m/s}^2$

$E = \dfrac{1}{2}mv^2$ and $E = mg\Delta h$

Step 2: Put the equations together and change the subject to what you need to find:

$E = \dfrac{1}{2}mv^2 = mg\Delta h$

then $2 \times \frac{1}{2}mv^2 = 2mg\Delta h$ so $mv^2 = 2mg\Delta h$

Then $\frac{mv^2}{m} = \frac{2mg\Delta h}{m}$ so $v^2 = 2g\Delta h$

and then $\frac{v^2}{2g} = \frac{2g\Delta h}{2g}$ so $\frac{v^2}{2g} = \Delta h$

change in height, $\Delta h = \dfrac{(5\ \text{m/s})^2}{2 \times 10\ \text{m/s}^2}$

$= 1.3\ \text{m}$ (2 significant figures)

In reality the system is *not* closed, and some energy will end up in a thermal store because of air resistance (Figure 2).

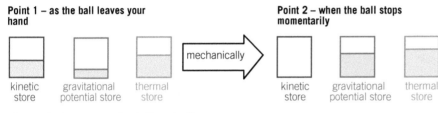

Point 1 – as the ball leaves your hand

Point 2 – when the ball stops momentarily

mechanically

kinetic store / gravitational potential store / thermal store → kinetic store / gravitational potential store / thermal store

Figure 2 Energy analysis for a ball.

You can use the same analysis for objects rolling up a slope. You need to use the *vertical* height, *not* the distance up a slope.

B Explain why you have to use the vertical distance.

How do you analyse situations in which objects hit obstacles?

When a moving object hits an obstacle it might bounce or stop. If you drop your sunglasses on a sandy beach (Figure 3) they stop (Table 2).

Figure 3 *Sunglasses fall when you let them go.*

Table 2 *Energy analysis for falling sunglasses.*

	Point 1 – just before the sunglasses land	Transfer	Point 2 – when the sunglasses have stopped moving
Physical situation	moving sunglasses — cooler sand and air	the Earth exerts a foce over a distance	stationary sunglasses — warmer sand and air
Energy analysis	kinetic store / thermal store	mechanically — heating by radiation	kinetic store / thermal store

There are many different ways of analysing situations involving objects hitting obstacles depending on your choice of point 1 and point 2.

1 State whether a ball thrown upwards will reach a larger or smaller height if there is air resistance. *(1 mark)*

2 **a** A pair of sunglasses has a mass of 25 g, and is travelling at 2 m/s just before it hits the sand. Calculate the energy transferred to the thermal store of the surroundings. *(2 marks)*
  b Explain why the energy analysis of the sunglasses falling *is* the realistic situation. *(1 mark)*

3 You push a trolley up a ramp and let go immediately. The trolley reaches a vertical height above the desk of 40 cm.
  a Calculate how fast it was going when you let it go. *(2 marks)*
  b Explain why you do not need to know the mass of the trolley. *(1 mark)*

Energy

Summary questions

1 **a** Write down the Law of Conservation of Energy.

b Write down which of these are types of energy store:

thermal   kinetic   sound   light
chemical potential   electrical
gravitational potential

2 Copy and complete Table 1. For each situation suggest an appropriate store for each column:

Table 1 *Energy stores.*

	Amount of energy in this store goes down...	Amount of energy in this store goes up...
a toy car projected up a slope		
a tennis ball hitting a tennis racket		
a battery-operated toy train being accelerated by a constant force		
a cyclist slowing down		
bringing water to the boil in a kettle using a gas camping stove		

3 **a** Write down the equation for work done.

b Write down the equation for energy transferred by an electric current.

4 Here are some different ways that you can transfer energy between stores:

using an electric current   heating   using a force

For each of the following situations write down a suitable method of transferring energy between the stores.

a From an elastic potential store of a bungee jumper who is stationary with the cord extended at the bottom of a jump, to the gravitational potential store of the same jumper with the cord slack at the top of the jump.

b From a chemical potential store of coal and oxygen in a power station to a thermal store of the hot wire in a toaster.

c From the thermal store of the hot wire in a toaster to the thermal store of the hot toast.

5 **a** **i** In one energy analysis, the temperature of a hot potato of mass 0.1 kg decreases by 30 K. If the specific heat capacity of the potato is 3.43 J/kg °C calculate the change of energy in the thermal store of the potato. Use the equation:

change in energy in a thermal store = mass × specific heat capacity × change in temperature

ii Suggest the store that has more energy in it now.

b **i** In another analysis, a girl on a trampoline stretches 50 springs by 1 cm when she comes to a stop at the bottom of a jump. If the spring constant of one spring is 500 N/m, calculate the total energy in the elastic potential store of the springs. Use the equation:

energy transferred in stretching = 0.5 × spring constant × (extension)^2

ii Assuming that the system is closed, calculate the speed of the girl on the trampoline if all the energy in the elastic potential store is transferred to a kinetic store. Her mass is 60 kg.

iii Suggest how some of the energy is transferred to the surroundings.

6 **a** A learner driver has to do an emergency stop as part of their driving test.

i The mass of the car is 1500 kg. It is moving at 20 m/s at point 1, and is stationary at point 2. Copy and complete Table 2.

Table 2 *Energy analysis for an emergency stop.*

	Point 1 – moving car	Transfer	Point 2 – stationary car with cool brakes
Physical situation			
Energy analysis			

ii Calculate the change in energy of the kinetic store.

b One way that energy is transferred is by sound when the breaks squeal. Write down one other type of transfer in this situation.

7 Every year there is a cheese-rolling contest in Gloucestershire, where competitors race a rolling cheese of mass 4 kg down a hill. Complete an energy analysis (as in **6**) for the cheese, making clear your start point and end point (which can be wherever you like!).

Revision questions

1 a Which formula is used to calculate kinetic energy?

A $E = \frac{1}{2}mv^2$

B $E = Fd$

C $E = \frac{1}{2}kx^2$

D $E = mgh$ *(1 mark)*

b A fly swatter uses energy in the elastic potential store of a spring to launch a small object to swat flies.

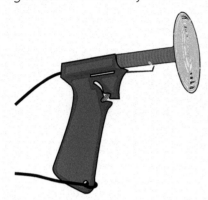

Which diagram shows the energy stores correctly? *(1 mark)*

A point 1: before the swatter is fired   point 2: after the swatter is fired

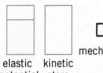 mechanically

elastic potential store   kinetic store   elastic potential store   kinetic store

B point 1: before the swatter is fired   point 2: after the swatter is fired

 mechanically

elastic potential store   kinetic store   elastic potential store   kinetic store

C point 1: before the swatter is fired   point 2: after the swatter is fired

 mechanically

elastic potential store   kinetic store   elastic potential store   kinetic store

D point 1: before the swatter is fired   point 2: after the swatter is fired

 mechanically

elastic potential store   kinetic store   elastic potential store   kinetic store

c What happens to the energy in the elastic potential store of the spring when you halve the stretch of the spring?

A the energy stored quadruples

B the energy stored doubles

C the energy stored decreases by a half

D the energy stored decreases by three quarters *(1 mark)*

2 a What happens with regard to energy in a closed system? *(2 marks)*

b Explain why, in terms of energy, most systems are not closed. *(2 marks)*

3 A spring is extended 20 cm and stores 4 kJ of energy. Calculate the spring constant of the spring. *(3 marks)*

4 A stone with a mass of 500 g is dropped off the top of a vertical cliff. The cliff is 200 m high.

a Calculate the decrease in potential energy as the stone falls.
Assume that $g = 10$ m/s^2. *(3 marks)*

b Calculate the speed of the stone when it hits the ground. *(3 marks)*

c Describe all the changes involved in the way energy is stored from when the stone is dropped to just before it hits the ground. *(6 marks)*

d What happens to the energy of the stone when it hits the ground? *(1 mark)*

Learning outcomes

After studying this lesson you should be able to:

- describe the changes in energy involved when a system is changed by work done when a current flows
- make calculations of the energy changes associated with changes in a system using the equation for transferring energy electrically
- use a common scale to show the overall redistribution of energy in the system
- use kWh to measure energy use in electrical appliances in the home
- describe, with examples, the relationship between the power ratings for domestic electrical appliances and how this is linked to the changes in stored energy when they are in use.

Specification reference: P5.1c, P5.2c

Figure 1 *Half of the energy transferred electrically to run the Internet is used to cool down Internet computers.*

Figure 2 *The meter does not measure energy in joules because 1 joule is a tiny amount of energy. It measure kWh.*

About 2% of the energy transferred by electrical work globally is used to run the Internet (Figure 1).

How does an electric current transfer energy?

In electrical devices, energy is transferred when charge moves:

- from a chemical potential store of a battery, or
- from a chemical potential or nuclear store of the fuel in a power station used to produce mains electricity.

Electrons in the wire produce light, or a heating effect, or make a motor turn, and energy is transferred.

A Name one device in your kitchen that contains an electric motor.

What does the power rating of an appliance mean?

Electrical devices, such as microwave ovens or hair dryers, have a **power rating** in watts (W) or kilowatts (kW). This tells you the *rate* at which they transfer energy between stores.

A larger power rating means the appliance will transfer *more* energy per second when you use it. Your battery goes flat faster, or fuel in a power station is used up more quickly.

The energy transferred by electrical appliances is measured with a meter (Figure 2).

For domestic appliances we use the **kilowatt-hour** as the unit of energy transferred electrically. It is the energy transferred by a 1 kW appliance switched on for one hour. You need to remember these equations:

$$\text{(electrical) work done (kWh)} = \text{power (kW)} \times \text{time (h)}$$

$$\text{power} = \frac{\text{(electrical) work done}}{\text{time}}$$

Calculating electrical work done

Calculate the number of joules in 1 kWh.

Step 1: Write down power and time:

$$1\text{ kW} = 1000\text{ W}$$

$$1\text{ h} = 3600\text{ s}$$

Step 2: Calculate the electrical work done:

$$\text{electrical work done} = \text{power} \times \text{time}$$

$$= 1000\text{ W} \times 3600\text{ s}$$

$$= 3\,600\,000\text{ J (1 significant figure)}$$

Calculating energy transferred

Calculate the energy transferred by a 10 kW shower that you use for 15 minutes.

Step 1: Write down what you know from the question. Convert to standard units:

power = 10 kW

$$\text{time} = \frac{15\,\text{minutes}}{60\,\text{minutes}}\text{h} = 0.25\,\text{h}$$

Step 2: Use the equation to calculate the answer, including the correct unit:

energy transferred = 10 kW × 0.25 h

= 4.0 kWh (2 significant figures)

B Write down which is bigger: 1 MJ or 1 kWh.

What do you pay for when you pay your electricity bill?

You are charged for each kWh, or unit, that you use (Figures 3 and 4).

Calculating cost

Calculate the cost of using a 10 kW shower for 15 minutes. The cost of one unit is 10p per kWh.

Step 1: State what you know from the question. Use the number of kWh of energy transferred from the example *Calculating energy transferred*.

cost of one unit = 10p per kWh

energy transferred = 4 kWh

Step 2: Use the equation to calculate the answer, including the correct unit:

cost of energy transferred = 4 kWh × 10p/kWh

= 40p (2 significant figures)

Figure 3 *Drills are less powerful than ovens, so cost less to run if you use them for the same amount of time.*

Electricity Statement

Electricity Readings						
Meter Serial no.	Read Date	Read Type		Read	Last Read	Units Used
		Removal		28619	28170	449
		Smart		1749	0	1749
Total units						**2198 kWh**

Electricity Charges 05 Jan 2010 - 30 Jun 2010				
Electricity supply standing charge	177 days	22.0p per day	£	38.94
Electricity total unit charge	2198.0 kWh	8.085p per kWh	£	177.71
Total supply charges			£	**216.65**
VAT @5.00%			£	10.83
Total cost of electricity			£	**227.48**

Figure 4 *An electricity statement.*

1 Name two devices that work with a battery, and two devices that work from the mains (other than the device that you named in question **A**). *(4 marks)*

2 **a** Calculate the power in kW of an oven that transfers 18 kWh to cook a chicken in 2 hours. *(2 marks)*

b Calculate the cost of cooking the chicken if 1 unit costs 10p. *(2 marks)*

3 Suggest and explain one reason for buying a hairdryer with a higher power rating. *(2 marks)*

4 Suggest and explain whether using higher-power devices is cheaper, more expensive, or costs the same as using lower-power devices. *(6 marks)*

Study tips

Be careful not to confuse kW (power) and kWh (energy transferred).

Avoid using the term 'electrical energy', but use 'energy transferred electrically' instead. There are no 'types' of energy.

Learning outcomes

After studying this lesson you should be able to:

- describe all the changes involved in the way energy is stored when a system changes for bringing water to a boil in an electric kettle
- describe the changes in energy involved by work done when a current flows
- make calculations of energy changes using the equation for transferring energy electrically, and by heating
- use kWh to measure energy use in electrical appliances in the home
- describe how, in different domestic devices, energy is transferred from batteries or the a.c. from the mains.

Specification reference: P5.1c, P5.2b, P5.2c

Figure 1 *An electric pickle.*

Figure 2 *You can heat water using energy transferred electrically (in a kettle), or with radiation (in a microwave oven).*

Figure 3 *Your phone battery will run down quickly if you take a large number of photos.*

A pickle glows when a current passes through it (Figure 1).

What do electrical appliances do?

An electrical appliance transfers energy electrically from chemical potential stores. An electrical device changes electrical transfer to other forms of energy transfer to do a particular job.

For example, a microwave oven is a device that changes energy transfered electrically to energy transfer by heating (Figure 2). The current produces microwaves which heat food.

With a hairdryer, energy transferred electrically produces heating by radiation (infrared) and energy transferred mechanically (the fan and air move) to dry your hair.

If you use a higher-power mains device the amount of fuel at a power station goes down faster. The screen of your phone requires a high power, so if it is on then the battery will drain quickly (Figure 3).

A Write down the equation for calculating energy transferred electrically.

How do appliances change the energy in stores?

Appliances transfer energy between stores (Table 1).

Table 1 *Appliances transfer energy.*

Appliance	Running off	Store that has *less* energy after the appliance has been used	Store that has *more* energy after the appliance has been used
television	mains	chemical potential (fuel and oxygen)	thermal store (surroundings)
DVD player	mains	chemical potential (fuel and oxygen)	kinetic (turntable when it speeds up)
smartphone	battery	chemical potential (battery)	thermal store (surroundings)

When a current flows in a wire, the wire heats up. This means that energy is always transferred to a thermal store when you use an electrical appliance. This energy is wasted.

Energy stores

Identify the stores involved when you use a battery-operated fan at a steady speed.

Step 1: Identify the start and end points.

Point 1: The fan is running.

Point 2: The fan has stopped.

Step 2: Identify the stores.

kinetic (of fan), chemical (of battery), thermal (of surroundings)

How do you analyse systems where a current flows?

You can burn wood to heat water, but using an electric current is a clean way to transfer energy. Table 2 shows the energy transfers when you use an electric kettle (Figure 4) that runs off the mains.

Table 2 *Energy analysis for an electric kettle.*

	Point 1 – when you turn the kettle on	Transfer	Point 2 – when the water boils
Physical situation	cold water in the kettle, more fuel/oxygen	a current flows and heats an element in the kettle	boiling water in the kettle, less fuel/oxygen
Energy analysis	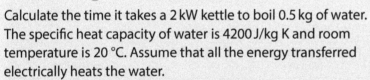 chemical potential store / thermal store – water	energy transferred electrically, heating by radiation, heating by particles	chemical potential store / thermal store – water

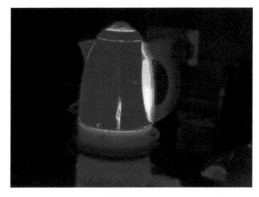

Figure 4 *The kettle heats the surroundings so not all of the energy from the chemical potential store is transferred to the water.*

B State one other thermal store that will be filled up as the kettle heats the water.

Calculating time to heat water

Calculate the time it takes a 2 kW kettle to boil 0.5 kg of water. The specific heat capacity of water is 4200 J/kg K and room temperature is 20 °C. Assume that all the energy transferred electrically heats the water.

Step 1: Write down what you know and the equations relating to the stores or transfers involved:

power = 2 kW = 2000 W

mass = 0.5 kg

specific heat capacity = 4200 J/kg K

$E = mc\Delta T$, and $E = P \times t$

temperature difference = (100 °C – 20 °C)

= 80 °C

Step 2: Calculate the change in energy in the store of the water:

$E = mc\Delta T$

= 0.5 kg × 4200 J/kg K × 80 °C

= 168 000 J

Step 3: Use the energy and power to calculate the time.

$E = P \times t$, so $t = \dfrac{E}{P}$

$t = \dfrac{160\ 000\ \text{J}}{2000\ \text{W}}$

= 80 seconds (2 significant figures)

Study tip

Remember to change from kW to W when you do calculations involving energy transferred electrically.

You need to be able to apply the equation relating to heating.

1 Write down how energy is transferred from the pickle (Figure 1) when a current flows through it. *(1 mark)*

2 Calculate the power of a motor that uses a current to transfer 40 000 J in 2 minutes. *(2 marks)*

3 Draw an energy transfer diagram like Table 2 for the kettle for an electric motor from the point when it is stationary until it reaches top speed (ignoring friction and air resistance). *(4 marks)*

4 **a** Draw a more realistic energy analysis diagram for a kettle. *(4 marks)*
   b An LED indicator light with a power of 1 W is on if the kettle is plugged in. Estimate how much money you would save each week if you turned the kettle off at the mains, if 1 kWh costs 10p. *(4 marks)*

5 A leaflet about electricity says 'Turning off lights when you are not using them saves energy'. Write down and explain whether this is true. *(3 marks)*

Learning outcomes

After studying this lesson you should be able to:

- describe the changes in energy involved when a system is changed by heating (in terms of temperature change and specific heat capacity)
- make calculations of the energy changes associated with changes in a system using the equation for transferring energy by heating
- use a common scale to show the overall redistribution of energy in the system
- describe, with examples, the process by which energy is dissipated, so that it is stored in less useful ways
- explain ways of reducing unwanted energy transfer.

Specification reference: P5.1c, P5.2a

Figure 1 *Food, like this breakfast, gives you fuel.*

You need to burn fuel (Figure 1) to maintain a constant body temperature.

How is energy transferred to or from a thermal store?

You can increase the energy in a thermal store by heating. This usually means:

- burning a fuel, or
- using an electric current to transfer energy from a fuel.

A temperature difference produces a transfer of energy from a hot object (such as the bottom of a frying pan) to a cold object (such as a sausage in the pan). Any temperature difference produces a transfer of energy, which continues until the objects are in equilibrium.

A Write down what 'in equilibrium' means.

How do you analyse systems where things heat up or cool down?

Storage heaters in a house contain a large piece of concrete that heats up during the night. During the day it cools down and heats your house.

Table 1 *Energy analysis for a storage heater.*

	Point 1 – at the start of the day	Transfer	Point 2 – at the end of the day
Physical situation	a hot piece of concrete a cold room	the radiator gets hot, emits radiation, heats the air	a cool piece of concrete a warm room
Energy analysis	thermal store – concrete thermal store – room	heating (infrared, conduction, convection)	thermal store – concrete thermal store – room

B Explain why you can analyse the situation *only* in terms of the change in energy in the thermal stores and *not* using the transfer.

What is energy dissipation?

We have fuels, and power stations that use fuels to produce mains electricity. We also have batteries.

We have appliances, such as televisions or washing machines, which do useful jobs.

But after we have finished watching television, or put our clean clothes away, what has happened to the energy that was in the chemical potential or nuclear store?

The radiation transferred by the television has been absorbed by the surroundings (you, the walls, etc.), which heats them up.

The hot clothes or machines have cooled down and heated the surroundings.

You cannot easily use the energy in the surroundings. It has been **dissipated**, and is no longer in a store that is very useful.

Table 2 *Energy is dissipated.*

Transfer	Effect	So energy ends up in...
friction between parts of a car engine	the parts of the engine head up	the thermal store of the engine parts
conduction between water in a kettle and the plastic of the kettle	the plastic of the kettle gets hot	the thermal store of the kettle
radiation from the front of a hot oven	the room that the oven is in warms up	the thermal store of the surroundings

Ultimately, the energy will end up in the thermal store of the surroundings.

● You can reduce the energy dissipated due to friction by **lubrication** (e.g. using oil).

● You can reduce the energy dissipated due to heating by **insulation** (e.g. using foam).

When you use oil you are placing a layer of fluid between two solid surfaces. The surfaces are no longer in direct contact, and friction is reduced (Figure 2). This is extremely important in car engines where the engine parts are moving very fast.

When you use an insulator you are placing a material that does not conduct very well between a hot and a cold object, so the rate of energy transfer is reduced. You insulate yourself in the winter when you wear layers of clothing, or thick clothing.

Using lubrication or insulation reduces the energy transferred to the thermal store of the surroundings, usually from a chemical store such as fuel or food.

1 Explain why the thermal store of the concrete in a storage heater is useful, but the thermal store of the surroundings is not. *(1 mark)*

2 Describe the changes to the energy in the stores for a car travelling at a *steady* speed. *(2 marks)*

3 **a** A room is not a closed system. Suggest and explain how this affects what happens when you use a storage heater. *(3 marks)*

b Explain what you can do to make your house more of a closed system. *(2 marks)*

4 Estimate the energy transferred to you by a hot water bottle. The specific heat capacity of water is 4200 J/kg K. *(4 marks)*

Calculating energy transfer

A piece of concrete in a storage heater has a mass of 100 kg, and a specific heat capacity of 880 J/kg K. The temperature of the block changes from 80 °C to 20 °C. Calculate the energy transferred between the thermal stores.

Step 1: Write down what you know, and the equation that relates to the store(s) in the analysis:

mass = 100 kg

specific heat capacity = 880 J/kg K

temperature change = 80 °C − 20 °C = 60 °C or 60 K

$E = mc\Delta T$

Step 2: Calculate the energy transferred:

$E = mc\Delta T$

$= 100 \text{ kg} \times 880 \text{ J/kg K} \times 60 \text{ K}$

$= 5.3 \times 10^6 \text{ J}$ (2 significant figures)

Figure 2 *Friction between moving parts heats a car engine.*

Learning outcomes

After studying this lesson you should be able to:

- describe how the rate of cooling depends on the thickness of walls
- describe how the rate of cooling depends on the thermal conductivity of walls.

Specification reference: P5.2g

Figure 1 *An igloo is made from blocks of ice.*

Figure 2 *The thermal image shows that the house on the right has walls that are cooler on the outside.*

Figure 4 *You can reduce energy transfer by adding thick insulation made of a material with a low thermal conductivity to your walls.*

How can living in a building made of ice (Figure 1) be warm?

Why does your house cool down?

It is winter. If you come back to your house when you have been away it might be cold if the heating is off. The walls, floor, windows, and roof transfer energy to the thermal store of the surroundings.

To maintain your house at a constant temperature you need to transfer energy *to* it. If your house is at a *constant* temperature then burning fuel (e.g. gas) to run your central heating is actually heating up the surroundings.

A Write down how you know the energy in the thermal store of your house is *not* increasing even though the heating is on.

The rate at which energy is transferred through the walls of your house depends on the thickness of the walls and what they are made of (Figure 2). It also depends on the difference in temperature between the two sides of the walls.

How does the thickness of the wall affect the rate of cooling?

Imagine two similar houses. The walls are made of the same material, but of different thicknesses. There is the same temperature difference across them.

It is a cold day, so the heating is on in both houses. Then the people in both houses switch off the heating at the same time. Both houses cool down until the temperature inside the houses is the same as the temperature outside. Figure 3 shows that the house with the thinner walls takes a shorter time to cool down. The rate of temperature drop is greater if the walls are thinner.

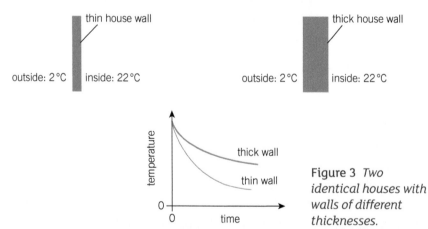

Figure 3 *Two identical houses with walls of different thicknesses.*

How does the thermal conductivity of the walls affect the rate of cooling?

In most houses there are two layers of stone or brick with insulation in between (Figure 4).

When you build walls you need to think about the **thermal conductivity** of the material you are using. This tells you how quickly energy is transferred through a wall with:

- an area of 1 m²
- a thickness of 1 m
- a temperature difference across it of 1 °C.

B Suggest one other thing you need to consider when you choose a building material for the walls of a house.

Suppose there are two identical houses with walls of different thermal conductivities (Figure 5).

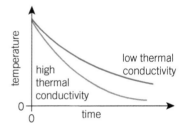

Figure 5 *Two identical houses with walls of different thermal conductivities.*

The room with walls of a *higher* thermal conductivity will cool down faster. The rate of temperature drop is greater if the thermal conductivity is higher.

Modern insulation materials have a low thermal conductivity. Table 1 shows some values of thermal conductivity for everyday materials, and aerogel (Figure 6). Aerogel is used to insulate space vehicles that travel through the atmosphere.

Ice has a low thermal conductivity, so even igloos can be warm.

1 Put these three situations in order of rate of cooling from slowest to fastest. *(1 mark)*
 A thick walls of high thermal conductivity material
 B thin walls of high thermal conductivity material
 C thick walls of low thermal conductivity material

2 Suggest two reasons why a homeowner would want to insulate the walls of his house. *(2 marks)*

3 **a** Calculate the energy transferred per second through a wall of concrete with area 1 m², thickness 1 m, if the temperature difference is 10 K. *(2 marks)*
 b Suggest how your answer would change if the thickness of the wall was 25 cm. *(4 marks)*

Table 1 *Thermal conductivities of some materials.*

Material	Relative thermal conductivity
concrete	1.00
brick	1.31
glass	0.96
wood	0.17
fibreglass (roof insulation)	0.04
foam (wall insulation)	0.03
aerogel	0.004

Figure 6 *Energy is transferred very slowly through aerogel.*

Investigating insulation

You can investigate the thermal conductivity of different materials by using them to insulate a hot object, such as a beaker of hot water, and measure the temperature drop in a fixed period of time for different materials.

You need to make sure that you control *all* the possible factors that can affect the energy transfer:

- thickness
- area
- starting temperature.

Go further

Work out why the unit of thermal conductivity is W/m K.

Learning outcomes

After studying this lesson you should be able to:

● calculate energy efficiency for any energy transfer

● explain ways of reducing unwanted energy transfer

● describe how to increase efficiency. H

Specification reference: P5.2d, P5.2e, P5.2f

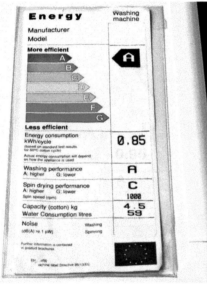

Figure 2 *Energy rating labels tell you how efficient a domestic appliance is.*

Go further

Energy ratings on an energy label range from A+++ to D. Find out what the different categories mean, and how appliances are judged.

Science and government policy

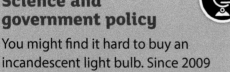

You might find it hard to buy an incandescent light bulb. Since 2009 the UK has stopped making them because they are so inefficient. This is an example of science influencing government policy.

Why has it recently become difficult to buy light bulbs with filaments (Figure 1)?

Figure 1 *The incandescent light bulb on the left of each picture gets much hotter than the LED in the middle, or the compact fluorescent light (CFL) on the right.*

What is efficiency and how do you calculate it?

More efficient devices (Figure 2) are better at transferring energy between stores that do the job we want, rather than a job we do not want.

LED lamps are much more efficient than incandescent light bulbs.

You need to be able to remember and use the equation for the **efficiency** of an appliance

$$\text{efficiency} = \frac{\text{useful output energy transfer}}{\text{input energy transfer}}$$

Efficiency tells us how good the appliance is at doing its job, and is expressed as a ratio or as a percentage. If half the input energy transfer was useful then the appliance would have an efficiency of 0.5. We say it is 50% efficient. No appliances are 100% efficient because energy is always dissipated. Some ends up in the thermal store of the surroundings – it is wasted.

A Explain why an appliance cannot be 200% efficient.

Calculating wasted energy

A 100 W filament lamp (incandescent bulb) transfers 100 J each second, but is only 10% efficient. Calculate the wasted energy.

Step 1: Write down what you know:

input energy transfer = 100 J

efficiency = 10% = 0.1

Step 2: Use the equation to calculate the useful energy output.

$$\text{efficiency} = \frac{\text{useful output energy transfer}}{\text{input energy transfer (or total energy transferred)}}$$

useful output energy transfer = efficiency × input energy transfer

= 0.1 × 100 J

= 10 J

Step 3: Subtract the useful energy output from the input energy transfer to find the wasted energy.

wasted energy = 100 J – 10 J = 90 J

The lamp heats the room much better than it lights the room.

You can use a diagram called a **Sankey diagram** to show efficiency. The width of the arrow shows the amount of energy transferred. Figure 3 shows a Sankey diagram for an electric motor that is lifting up an object on a piece of string.

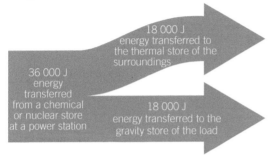

Figure 3 *The total width of the two arrows is equal to the width of the arrow at the beginning.*

B Explain why the total width of the arrows at the end is the same as the width at the beginning.

How do you increase efficiency?

If you want to *increase* efficiency you need to *reduce* the wasted energy (Figure 4).

You can:

- use insulation to reduce heating of the surroundings
- make devices from materials that reduce unwanted energy transfer
- use technology to produce devices that are better at their job, for example, LEDs.

More efficient devices operate at a lower power, so they use up fuels more slowly.

1 Calculate the efficiency of an electric motor that usefully transfers 340 J of energy for every 400 J supplied. (*2 marks*)
2 Suggest how to improve the efficiency of an oven. (*1 mark*)
3 You buy an LED that has the same light output as a 100 W incandescent lamp.
   a Use Table 1 to find the power of the LED. (*1 mark*)
   b If the efficiency of the LED is 40% calculate the useful energy output per second. (*2 marks*)
4 Explain why using LEDs might not reduce your electricity bill. (Hint: think what it will feel like to be in a room with LEDs rather than incandescent bulbs.) (*6 marks*)

Figure 4 *Each year there is a competition to find the most fuel-efficient car.*

Table 1 *Light bulbs of different powers produce the same light intensity. If the light intensity is the same they appear equally bright.*

Light intensity (lumens)	Power of incandescent light bulb (W)	Power of CFL (W)	Power of LED light (W)
800	60	15	10
1800	100	25	18
2800	150	45	16

A CFL is an energy-saving light bulb.

Study tip

Efficiency cannot be more than 100%. If you get a number greater than 100 it is incorrect.

Energy cannot be destroyed, so it is better to say 'dissipated' rather than 'lost'.

Energy

Summary questions

1 Match each word to its definition. Write the matched letters and numbers to show your answer.

Word	Definition
A efficiency	**1** transferring energy to less useful stores
B dissipation	**2** the power that the appliance is designed to work at
C lubrication	**3** reducing the work done when surfaces move over each other
D equilibrium (thermal)	**4** a percentage that shows you how much energy is usefully transferred
E power rating	**5** how we describe objects at the same temperature

2 a Explain what 'dissipation' means.

b You cook a chicken in an oven connected to the mains. Write down two ways that energy is dissipated in this process.

3 a Put these statements in order from the *most* energy transferred to the *least* energy transferred.

A a 2 kW kettle used for 10 minutes
B a 1 kW kettle used for 15 minutes
C a 2 kW kettle used for 5 minutes
D a 2 kW kettle used for 15 minutes

b Explain why we use kilowatts and hours to calculate the energy transferred by electrical devices, and not watts and seconds.

c Describe one way that energy is wasted as it is transferred to the kettle by the mains.

4 a A music player has a useful output energy transfer of 25 J for every 30 J of input energy transfer. Calculate the efficiency as a ratio and as a percentage.

b Calculate the energy dissipated by a motor with an efficiency of 80% if the input energy transfer is 1000 J.

5 a You put identical heaters into two buildings of exactly the same dimensions and turn them on for 2 hours. Building A has walls of a high thermal conductivity. Building B has walls of the same thickness but of a low thermal conductivity. After 2 hours the heaters are turned off. Copy and complete Table 1 by ticking the correct box.

Table 1 *Using identical heaters in two buildings.*

	Building A (high thermal conductivity)	Building B (low thermal conductivity)
a long time to heat up		
a low rate of transfer of energy through walls		
once heated, a short time to cool down		

b Batteries in spacecraft must not get too hot or too cold. Suggest how scientists ensure that the battery stays at a constant temperature.

6 Some people have suggested that we could save a great deal of money (and fossil fuels) by turning off the appliances that have a small LED on when they are in standby mode.

Assuming all the appliances in your house continue to transfer energy at a rate of 120 W when in standby mode:

a Estimate how much energy you would save in one year if you turned them off if the cost of one unit (1 kWh) is 10p.

b Calculate the national annual saving if there are 26 million households in the UK.

c Comment on your answer to **b** if a typical school budget is £5 million.

Revision questions

1 a Which two of the following would reduce the rate of energy transfer through the wall?

    A Use a material with a higher thermal conductivity.

    B Use a material with a lower thermal conductivity.

    C Decrease the thickness of the wall.

    D Increase the thickness of the wall.   *(1 mark)*

b An LED light bulb wastes 0.7 W when it is supplied with 5 W. What is its efficiency?

    A 14%

    B 86%

    C 93%

    D 116%   *(1 mark)*

c Which one of these is not an energy store?

    A a moving car

    B a tank of petrol

    C a charged battery

    D mains electricity supply   *(1 mark)*

2 Explain the difference between a kilowatt (kW) and a kilowatt-hour (kWh)   *(2 marks)*

3 a Describe how energy is dissipated when a car brakes.   *(2 marks)*

b State what the energy stores are before and after braking.   *(2 marks)*

4 A 60 W incandescent light bulb is replaced with a 5 W LED light bulb.
The light is used for 4 hours each day.
Calculate how much less the LED light bulb costs to run for a year than the incandescent bulb.
(Assume that electricity costs 11p per kWh and that there are 365 days in a year.)   *(3 marks)*

5 Describe all the changes involved in the way energy is stored when a gas boiler heats water.   *(6 marks)*

P5 Energy: Topic summary

P5.1 Work done

- Explain what an energy store is.
- Describe the different types of energy store.
- Describe the process that transfers energy between stores.
- Describe the Law of Conservation of Energy.
- Describe how to do an energy analysis.
- Do calculations involving energy stores and energy transferred mechanically for objects accelerating due to a constant force.
- Do calculations involving energy stores and energy transferred mechanically for objects slowing down.
- Do calculations involving energy stores and energy transferred mechanically for objects being stretched.
- Do calculations involving stores and work done with objects hitting obstacles.
- Do calculations involving stores and work done with the force of gravity.
- Describe how a current transfers energy.

P5.2 Power and efficiency

- State and use the equation linking power in kW, energy transferred in kWh, and time in h.
- Describe what a power rating means.
- Describe how power rating links to energy transferred between stores.
- Describe how to analyse situations in terms of energy when a current flows in an appliance.
- Do calculations involving stores and electric power.
- Describe how to analyse situations in terms of energy.
- Do calculations involving stores and heating.
- Describe how the rate of cooling depends on the thickness of walls.
- Describe how the rate of cooling depends on the thermal conductivity of walls.
- Describe what efficiency means.
- State and use the equation linking efficiency and energy transfer.
- **H** Describe how to increase efficiency.

Stores and transfers

Energy stores

- **chemical potential**
- **thermal:** $\Delta E = mc\Delta T$
- **kinetic:** $E = \frac{1}{2}mv^2$
- **gravity potential:** $E = mgh$
- **elastic potential:** $E = \frac{1}{2}kx^2$

Energy transfers

- in general:

BEFORE		AFTER
a store empties	physical process(es)	other stores fill up

- energy is like money – can be calculated using equations
- energy is conserved (so if it looks like it isn't, look for a thermal store filling)

Examples

- dropping a ball (moving body):

BEFORE		AFTER
lots of energy in gravity potential store	force of Earth on ball → accelerates	lots of energy in kinetic store

- pulling a spring

BEFORE		AFTER
energy in chemical potential store ↓	force exerted → mechanical working	energy in elastic potential store ↑

- car stopping/slowing down

BEFORE		AFTER
energy in kinetic store ↓	force exerted → mechanical working	energy in thermal store ↑

- lifting an object/projecting up a slope

BEFORE		AFTER
energy in chemical potential/ kinetic store ↓	force exerted → mechanical working	energy in gravity potential store ↑

- using a kettle

BEFORE		AFTER
energy in chemical potential store ↓	force exerted → mechanical working	energy in thermal store ↑

Electrical power and cost

- current flows due to mains a.c. or battery (chemical store) → does electrical work
- some energy to thermal store (surroundings – wire gets hot)
- appliances with a higher power rating deplete chemical stores faster

$$\text{power (kW)} = \frac{\text{(electrical) work done (kWh)}}{\text{time (h)}}$$

$$\text{cost (p)} = \text{power (kW)} \times \text{time (h)} \times \text{unit cost (p/kWh)}$$

P5 Energy

Energy in houses

- temperature ↓ over time
- dependent on temperature difference and material thickness/area
- reduce energy transfer by:
  - ↑ insulation with low thermal conductivity
  - ↓ area
  - ↓ temperature difference

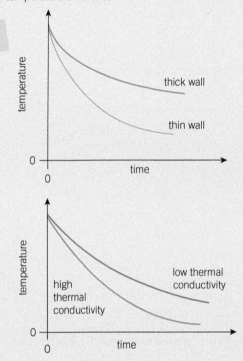

Energy analysis

Forces
- change shape/motion
- mechanical working

Particles move/vibrate
- conduction and convection

Current flows
- wires heat up, motors spin
- electrical working

EM radiation and sound
- emitted/absorbed

Efficiency

- shows ratio of desired energy transfer to total energy transferred
- efficient appliances transfer less to undesired stores (usually thermal store of surroundings)
- usually expressed as a percentage
- represented by Sankey diagram:

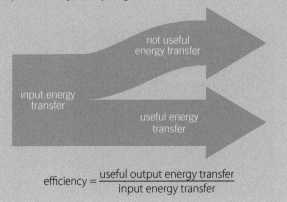

$$\text{efficiency} = \frac{\text{useful output energy transfer}}{\text{input energy transfer}}$$

P6 Global challenges

6.1 Physics on the move

6.1.1 Everyday motion

Learning outcomes

After studying this lesson you should be able to:

- describe how to measure distance and time in a range of scenarios
- recall typical speeds in a range of everyday situations
- estimate the magnitudes of everyday accelerations
- make calculations using ratios and proportional reasoning to convert units and to compute rates.

Specification reference: P6.1a, P6.1b, P6.1c

How many ways can you measure the speed of a car (Figure 1)?

Figure 1 *There are different ways of measuring speed.*

How do you measure everyday speeds?

You use a range of instruments to measure everyday speeds. To calculate speed you need to find distance and time. Table 1 has some examples.

Table 1 *Measuring speed.*

Moving object	Speed measuring system	Example of how you measure the distance	Example of how you measure the time
100 m sprinter	electronic timing	measuring tape/trundle wheel	pressure sensor to start, break laser beam to end
car on a road	speed camera	trundle wheel to find the distance between marks on the road	time between two photos
car on a road	speed gun (LIDAR)	use distance $= \dfrac{\text{speed} \times \text{time taken for a reflection}}{2}$	time between pulses
cyclist	wheel sensor (Figure 2)	wheel diameter	magnetic sensor detects one rotation
any	satellite navigation (satnav)	comparing the distance to three satellites	electronic timer

Figure 2 *The speed on the bicycle computer is calculated using a sensor on the wheel.*

A Estimate the time it takes for an athlete to run 100 m.

Calculating speed

Calculate the speed of a cyclist on a bike with wheels of diameter of 60 cm, if the time between pulses (for one rotation) is 0.3 seconds.

Step 1: Use the diameter to calculate the circumference of the wheel:

$$\text{circumference} = \pi \times \text{diameter}$$

$$= \pi \times 0.6 \text{ m}$$

$$= 1.9 \text{ m (2 significant figures)}$$

Step 2: Use the circumference and time to calculate speed:

$$\text{speed} = \frac{\text{distance}}{\text{time}}$$

$$= \frac{1.9\,\text{m}}{0.3\,\text{s}}$$

$$= 6.3\,\text{m/s}$$

Figure 3 *A cheetah can run as fast as a car on a motorway.*

How fast do everyday objects move?

A dog or cat can run at about 30 mph (the speed limit in towns), but a cheetah (Figure 3) can run at 70 mph (the motorway speed limit). Table 2 shows some typical speeds.

Table 2 *Some typical speeds.*

A person	Typical speed (m/s)	Typical speed (mph)
walking	1	2.2
running	5	11
cycling	7	15
cycling (Olympic)	20	45

Object	Typical speed (m/s)	Typical speed (mph)
strong wind	13	30
car	22	50
train	56	125
sound	330	738

B Estimate (without calculation) the speed in m/s of a car travelling at 40 mph.

How big are everyday accelerations?

You can estimate acceleration by estimating the time it takes for the object to reach a certain speed.

Calculating acceleration

Estimate the acceleration of a cyclist who reaches a top speed of 5.3 m/s (12 mph).

Step 1: Write down what you know and estimate the time it takes the object to reach the speed:

typical time to reach this speed = 10 seconds

change in speed = 5.3 m/s

Step 2: Calculate the acceleration:

$$\text{acceleration} = \frac{\text{change in speed}}{\text{time}}$$

$$= \frac{5.3\,\text{m/s}}{10\,\text{s}}$$

$$= 0.53\,\text{m/s}^2 \text{ (2 significant figures)}$$

Remember that this number means that the speed increases by 0.53 m/s for each second that the cyclist accelerates.

Precise and accurate measurements

Measurements need be both precise (have a small range, or spread, when you repeat them) and accurate (be close to the true value).

Study tip

Choose the speed of a fast object and a slow object to remember, and then you can estimate typical speeds of other objects.

When you estimate, think of the order of magnitude (1 s, or 100 s) rather than an exact value.

1 Suggest the speed of a competitive swimmer in a swimming competition. *(1 mark)*

2 Estimate the acceleration of a car that reaches a top speed of 70 mph. There are 1609 m in 1 mile. *(5 marks)*

3 Calculate the time between pulses in a speedometer system for a car with wheels of diameter 40 cm travelling at 30 mph. *(4 marks)*

4 The speed shown on a satnav is accurate, but always lower than the speed on the speedometer of a car. Suggest why. *(1 mark)*

Learning outcomes

After studying this lesson you should be able to:

- explain methods of measuring human reaction times
- recall typical human reaction times
- explain the factors that affect the distance required for road transport vehicles to come to rest in emergencies and the implications for safety.

Specification reference: P6.1d, P6.1e

Figure 1 *Some scientific studies suggest that playing some games can improve your hand–eye co-ordination, and your reaction time, which helps if you are a fighter pilot.*

Figure 2 *A person holds the ruler just above your hand then drops it. The length of ruler below your hand when you catch it indicates your reaction time.*

What is the link between games and flying a plane (Figure 1)?

What is reaction time and how do you measure it?

We do not use stopwatches to measure times in Olympic athletics races. Why not?

You see a runner passing the finish line when light reflects from the runner and hits your retina. A signal travels from your retina to your brain, and then a signal travels from your brain to your finger to press the button. This takes a certain time, called **reaction time**. Your reaction time is probably about 0.2 seconds.

A Explain why playing games cannot reduce your reaction time to zero.

One way to measure reaction time is to catch a falling ruler (Figure 2).

What is thinking distance?

If something happens when you are in the car, such as the car in front suddenly braking, it takes time before the driver's foot starts to apply a force on the brake pedal. During that time the car travels a distance called the **thinking distance**.

Calculating thinking distance

Estimate the thinking distance for a car travelling at 50 mph. There are 1609 m in 1 mile.

Step 1: Write down what you know:

$$\text{speed} = 50\,\text{mph}$$
$$= \frac{(50\,\text{mph} \times 1609\,\text{m/mile})}{3600\,\text{s/hour}}$$
$$= 22.3\,\text{m/s}$$

Step 2: Estimate the reaction time and calculate the distance:

$$\text{reaction time} = 0.2\,\text{s}$$
$$\text{thinking distance} = \text{speed} \times \text{time}$$
$$= 22.3\,\text{m/s} \times 0.2\,\text{s}$$
$$= 4.5\,\text{m (2 significant figures)}$$

B Suggest the relationship between speed and thinking distance.

What factors affect thinking distance?

There are many factors that affect thinking distance because they affect reaction time, such as:

- drinking alcohol
- using drugs, as well as some medicines
- being tired.

Your reaction time also increases as you get older.

Other factors that affect the time it takes a driver to react include whether they are:

- distracted by other people in the car
- eating or drinking
- using a radio or satellite navigation system.

It is illegal to hold a mobile phone while driving, but many people are tempted to speak on the phone (Figure 3), or check messages or social media.

Figure 3 *If you are distracted, the distance that the car travels while you react is longer.*

Calculating reaction time

In Figure 2 the ruler drops a distance of 25 cm while a student reacts. Use the equation

(final velocity (m/s))² − (initial velocity (m/s))²

= 2 × acceleration (m/s²) × distance (m)

to calculate the final velocity and estimate the reaction time.

Step 1: Write down what you know:

distance travelled = 25 cm = 0.25 m

acceleration (due to gravity) = 10 m/s²

initial velocity = 0 m/s

Step 2: Calculate the final velocity:

final velocity = $\sqrt{2 \times 10 \text{ m/s}^2 \times 0.25 \text{ m}}$

= 2.23 m/s

Step 3: Use the speed and distance to estimate the time:

$$\text{time} = \frac{\text{distance}}{\text{speed}}$$

$$= \frac{0.25 \text{ m}}{2.23 \text{ m/s}}$$

= 0.11 s (2 significant figures)

Automatic measurement

Using light gates eliminates problems with reaction time.

1 Describe the link between reaction time and thinking distance. *(1 mark)*

2 **a** Calculate the reaction time of a driver of a car that is travelling at 50 mph (22 m/s) if the thinking distance is 20 m. *(2 marks)*

b Suggest a reason for this reaction time being greater than a typical reaction time of 0.2 s. *(1 mark)*

3 Explain how you can use the dropping the ruler experiment to show different reaction times. *(3 marks)*

4 You stand near the finish line of a 100 m race on school sports day. You press the start button when you hear the gun, and the stop button when you see the winner cross the line. Suggest and explain whether the accurate time is more, less, or the same as, the reading on the stopwatch. *(6 marks)*

Learning outcomes

After studying this lesson you should be able to:

- explain the factors that affect the distance required for road transport vehicles to come to rest in emergencies and the implications for safety
- explain the dangers caused by large negative accelerations.

Specification reference: P6.1e, P6.1f

Figure 1 *Many residential areas have 20 mph speed limits.*

Figure 2 *Braking distances increase if the road is icy.*

Why is 20 mph (Figure 1) so much safer than 30 mph?

What is braking distance?

When the signal from a driver's brain reaches their foot they push on the brake pedal. The car travels a certain distance while the force of the brakes is applied to the car. This is called the **braking distance**. It depends on the brakes, the surface that is being driven on (Figure 2), and the speed – but not on the driver.

A Explain why thinking distance does not depend on road conditions.

What is stopping distance?

The **stopping distance** is the *total* distance that the car travels from the moment the driver sees the problem until the car is stationary.

stopping distance = thinking distance + braking distance

The *Highway Code* for driving in the UK has a chart of approximate stopping distances that you need to know to pass your driving test.

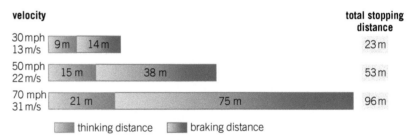

Figure 3 *Stopping distances for different speeds.*

As you can see, the thinking distance for a speed of 50 mph is much further than the thinking distance that you calculated in the example *Calculating thinking distance* in P8.1.2. The *Highway Code* uses a reaction time that is greater than the typical value.

B Calculate the difference between stopping distances for 70 mph and 30 mph.

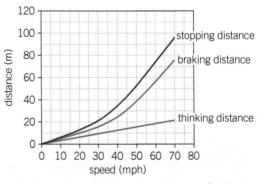

Figure 4 *The graph shows how thinking, braking, and stopping distances vary with speed.*

Why are large negative accelerations dangerous?

If you are sitting in a car that is moving you will be wearing a seatbelt.

If the car slows down suddenly the belt exerts a force on you. Without it you would continue to move with your original speed, and could collide with the dashboard or the seat in front of you, causing injury to yourself or others. Seatbelts have to be replaced after an accident because they stretch.

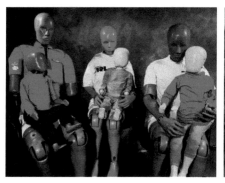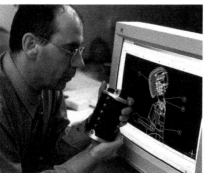

Figure 6 *Engineers have designed a whole family of crash test dummies. They use them to work out how to make cars safer.*

If your deceleration (negative acceleration) is very large the seatbelt can cause compression injuries. Also, you can injure your internal organs because they continue to move inside your body even if your ribs are stopped by the seatbelt.

Figure 7 *You carry out crash tests on cars to see what happens in a crash.*

1 Compare thinking distance and braking distance. (*3 marks*)

2 a Use the graph in Figure 4 to find the stopping distance for 20 mph. (*1 mark*)
 b Suggest why the speed limit in some towns has been reduced to 20 mph. (*2 marks*)

3 If something goes wrong in a fighter plane a pilot can use an ejector seat to send him upwards out of the plane. An ejector seat accelerates a pilot vertically to a speed of 15 m/s in 0.15 seconds. Calculate the acceleration in m/s^2 and compare it with the acceleration due to gravity, *g*. (*4 marks*)

4 a Calculate the speed that a car would need to be travelling at to produce the same acceleration as that of a rollercoaster (5*g*) if the car stops in 2 seconds. (*4 marks*)
 b Comment on your answer. (*1 mark*)

Figure 5 *Cars can check that they have enough distance to brake by staying two chevrons (^) behind the car in front.*

Figure 8 *Since 1967 cars have had to have seatbelts fitted, and it has been compulsory to wear them since 1983.*

Go further

Find out why you should *not* say 'ABS system'.

Summary questions

1 a Select an approximate value for human reaction time.

    20 s   2 s   0.2 s   0.002 s   0.2 ms

b Describe how to measure reaction time.

c Match each distance to its definition. Write the matched letters and numbers to show your answer.

Distance	Definition
A thinking distance	**1** the distance the car travels while the brakes exert a force
B braking distance	**2** thinking distance + braking distance
C stopping distance	**3** the distance the car travels while the driver reacts to the situation

2 a Write down typical speeds for the following in m/s: walking, sound, cycling, wind.

b A runner in a 100 m race reaches a speed of 10 m/s from stationary, over a time of 1.5 seconds. Calculate the acceleration of the runner.

c Suggest how distance and time are measured in the 100 m race.

3 a Sort these factors into those that affect thinking distance, and those that affect braking distance: being tired, condition of the brakes, age, icy road, drinking alcohol, using drugs

b Calculate how an increase of 0.1 s in reaction time affects thinking distance at 30 mph and at 70 mph. (1609 m = 1 mile)

4 a On a motorway there are sometimes marks on the road to try to keep motorists a larger distance apart than they might usually be. Explain why a larger distance between cars reduces the dangers of large accelerations.

b Describe the dangers of large accelerations.

c Suggest and explain two features of a car that are there to reduce the risk of injury.

5 A student is modeling stopping distances with a toy car on a ramp.

She holds one end of the ramp at 10 cm above the floor with a retort stand and clamp, and puts surfaces made of different materials on the floor at the end of the ramp.

She puts the toy car at the top of the ramp, releases it, then measures the distance from the end of the ramp to the point where the car stops.

a Write down two control variables for this experiment.

b Suggest one source of uncertainty in this experiment.

c Write down the name of the force that stops the car.

d Here are her results.

   i Copy and complete Table 1 by calculating the mean stopping distance for each material.

Table 1 *Stopping distances for toy cars on ramps with different surfaces.*

Material	Stopping distance (cm)	Stopping distance (cm)	Stopping distance (cm)	Mean stopping distance (cm)
A	45	48	46	
B	89	102	95	
C	88	74	72	
D	47	53	55	

   ii Write down and explain how many significant figures you used in the answer to your calculations.

   iii Suggest which measurement is an outlier.

   iv Explain how you took account of this outlier when calculating the mean stopping distance.

e Comment on the precision of the measurements.

f Suggest materials that might have been used for the longest and the shortest stopping distances.

g i Suggest and explain how this is a good model for comparing stopping distances in different driving conditions.

   ii Suggest a limitation of this model.

Revision questions

1 a What is the acceleration of a typical car?

    A 0.2 m/s^2

    B 2 m/s^2

    C 20 m/s^2

    D 200 m/s^2 *(1 mark)*

  b What is the typical human reaction time?

    A 0.02 seconds

    B 0.1 seconds

    C 0.2 seconds

    D 0.8 seconds   *(1 mark)*

  c What is the typical speed of a train?

    A 0.3 m/s

    B 3 m/s

    C 30 m/s

    D 300 m/s   *(1 mark)*

2 A group of students are investigating the best way to protect an egg in a crash.

They strap an egg to a trolley and crash it into a wall.

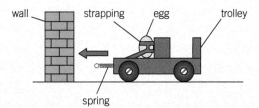

a Explain what they would need to do to find out how effective the spring is at protecting the egg.

                          (2 marks)

b The students then try wrapping the egg in bubble wrap.

Describe how they would need to modify the equipment to investigate the effectiveness of bubble wrap.   *(2 marks)*

3 Two students decide to measure the speed of sound. One student stands 60 m from a reflective surface and claps. The student claps again when an echo is heard. The second student times how long it takes for 30 claps.

  a Explain why this method will give not give an accurate measurement for the speed of sound.

                          (2 marks)

  b How could the students improve their method?

                          (2 marks)

4 a An emergency stop in a car causes people to experience large decelerations.

Explain the dangers of large decelerations and how they can be reduced.   *(3 marks)*

  b Describe what is meant by *stopping distance*.

                          (2 marks)

  c Explain the factors that affect the distance needed for a car to come to a stop.   *(6 marks)*

Learning outcomes

After studying this lesson you should be able to:

- describe the main energy sources available for us to use on Earth
- explain the difference between renewable and non-renewable energy sources
- describe how we use energy resources.

Specification reference: P6.2a

Figure 1 *The Sun and the energy sources on Earth are all we have.*

Figure 2 *A solar cell generates electricity to power a radar gun to show your speed.*

Which two places supply the energy sources that we need (Figure 1)?

What are the main energy sources we use on Earth?

Some of the **energy sources** (Table 1) we use on Earth are **renewable**, so they will *not* run out on a timescale of millions of years. Other sources are **non-renewable** because they take millions of years to form.

Energy sources, unlike energy, are physical things, such as a piece of coal. Sometimes we call them energy resources.

Table 1 *Energy sources.*

		Renewable energy sources	Non-renewable energy sources
fuels		• **biofuels** (that come from living material, such as wood, ethanol from sugar, or methane from sewage)	• **nuclear fuels** (e.g. uranium) • **fossil fuels** (e.g. coal, oil, gas)
other sources		• the Sun (Figure 2) • tides (Figure 3) • wind (Figure 4) • waves • hot rocks beneath the ground (geothermal) • water high up (for example, behind dams) (hydroelectric)	

Nuclear fuels were formed in stars, and fossil fuels were formed from the effects of heating and pressure on the remains of wood and sea creatures over millions of years. When these fuels are used up we will not be able to produce more.

A   Name a renewable fuel.

How do we use the main energy sources?

Table 2 gives the three main uses for energy sources.

Table 2 *Uses for energy sources.*

Heating	Transportation	Generating electricity
• fossil fuels • biofuels • the Sun (solar heating, also called thermal solar) • water pumped into hot rock	• fossil fuels • biofuels (e.g. bioethanol)	• fossil fuels • biofuels (biogas generator) • nuclear fuel • solar power • tidal power • wind power • wave power • geothermal power • hydroelectric power

When renewable sources are used to generate electricity we add the word 'power'.

In the UK we rely on fossil fuels and use them for heating, transport, *and* to generate electricity.

There are alternatives. In terms of heating, you can:

● build houses that maximise the heating by the Sun

● heat water using a solar water heating system that contains water in pipes on your roof, called a solar panel

● heat your house with hot water from beneath the ground (which is possible only in certain areas), but this is expensive to set up.

In term of generating electricity you can use:

● solar cells (photovoltaics), also known as solar panels

● turbines and generators driven by the wind, waves, falling water, steam from hot rocks, or burning biofuels.

B Write down which of the alternative methods of generating electricity produces carbon dioxide when it is operating.

In all cases it is very expensive to build the cells or generator systems, and doing so produces carbon dioxide. This contributes to climate change.

In addition, only some areas are suitable for certain types of generator systems, such as wind power and geothermal power.

C Use Figure 5 to calculate the total percentage of our electricity generated from non-renewable sources.

What is 'renewable'?

Renewable does *not* mean that you can use the energy source again. Explain why.

1 Compare renewable and non-renewable
energy sources. *(5 marks)*

2 Explain why coal is non-renewable, but wood
is renewable. *(2 marks)*

3 a Explain why there are two types of 'solar panel'. *(1 mark)*
  b Suggest and explain why it is difficult to work out whether using photovoltaic cells on your roof does or does not contribute to climate change. *(2 marks)*

4 Suggest why there is a similarity between biofuels and fossil fuels, but not between biofuels and nuclear fuels. *(2 marks)*

Figure 3 *Tidal power generators are expensive to build, install, and maintain.*

Figure 4 *Offshore wind turbines can provide electricity, but only work if the wind blows.*

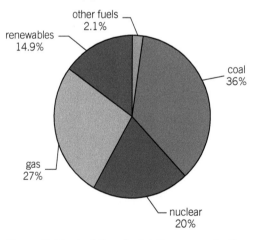

Electricity generation in the UK – 2013

other fuels 2.1%
renewables 14.9%
coal 36%
gas 27%
nuclear 20%

Figure 5 *Most of the electricity we use in the UK is generated from fossil fuels.*

Study tip

You need to distinguish between energy sources (or resources) and energy stores.

Should you be worried that fossil fuels (Figure 1) might run out in your lifetime? And will they?

Figure 1 *Coal, oil, and natural gas were formed over millions of years from trees and sea creatures. We cannot make more when they run out.*

How and why has our use of different energy sources changed over time?

Our use of energy sources has changed because there has been an increase in:

- *population* from about 1 billion people in 1820 to over 7 billion people today
- the *use of devices* that use fuels, such as steam engines, and now cars
- *electricity generation*.

In ancient times, people used wood as a fuel, and wood is still an important fuel in some parts of the world (Figure 2).

A Suggest a reason why people have always used wood as a fuel.

Figure 2 *People have used wood for cooking for thousands of years, and still do.*

Figure 3 *Geysers, like this one in Iceland, can be a sign that you can use hot rocks for geothermal power.*

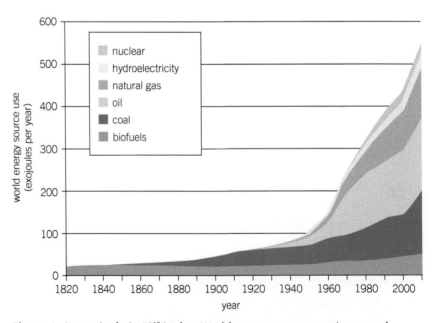

Figure 4 *An exojoule is 10^{18} joules. World energy source use increased enormously between 1820 and 2010, and is still increasing.*

During the Industrial Revolution (between 1790 and 1840) people began to use coal in machines in factories, and for transport. From about 1920 there has been a huge increase in the use of oil, as people use it for cars and planes. Figure 4 shows how world energy source use increased from 1820.

B Name one other use of oil, or its fractions, that you have learned about in chemistry.

Since the first power station (a hydroelectric station) was built in Niagara Falls in 1881, we have built many more. In the UK, most use fossil fuels.

What are the issues with energy supply?

People in countries such as the UK are used to being able to fuel their cars, and to have mains electricity. Demand for electricity will increase as people in developing countries expect similar things.

The supply of fossil fuels is finite and eventually they will run out. There *are* **reserves** of fossil fuels in many parts of the world that are difficult to reach, which makes them expensive to extract. As fossil fuels become scarcer they will become more expensive, so it will make economic sense to extract them from difficult locations (Figure 6).

Burning fossil fuels or biofuels produces carbon dioxide, which contributes to the greenhouse effect and climate change. Climate change is a big threat to the environment. Sea levels are likely to rise, leading to flooding, and there will be more extreme weather events. Climate change threatens food supplies.

When individuals or governments are deciding which energy sources to use they need to consider:

- cost (to set up, and to remove)
- effect on the environment (pollution, how it looks if you live nearby)
- contribution to climate change
- how long the sources will last.

Energy sources and climate change

Providing energy sources and generating electricity without causing climate change is one of the biggest challenges for the world's population in the future.

1 Describe how the use of different energy sources has changed since 1820. *(5 marks)*

2 **a** Explain why the demand for oil has changed in the last 100 years. *(1 mark)*
   b Suggest why very little oil is used to generate electricity. *(1 mark)*

3 Explain why there will always be an uncertainty in the prediction for when fossil fuels will run out. *(2 marks)*

4 Suggest and explain what might happen to the behaviour of individuals and governments as fossil fuels begin to run out. *(6 marks)*

Figure 5 *Modern hydroelectric power stations are expensive to build.*

Figure 6 *Climate scientists extract ice in Antarctica to find out about carbon dioxide levels in the past. There may be oil under the Antarctic ice.*

Go further

In energy source terms there are 'reserves' and 'recoverable reserves'. Find out the latest estimate for the recoverable reserves of coal.

Synoptic link

You can learn more about the greenhouse effect in C6.2.3 *Climate change.*

Learning outcomes

After studying this lesson you should be able to:

- describe the National Grid
- explain why the National Grid is an efficient way of transferring energy
- describe how transformers are used in the National Grid

Specification reference: P6.2c, P6.2d, P6.2e

Figure 1 *Electricity pylons.*

Figure 3 *Many cables of the National Grid are hidden underground.*

Why are electricity pylons (Figure 1) so tall?

What is the National Grid?

You may not live near a power station but you still have electricity supplied to your house. The power stations, transformers, grid network (underground wires, as in Figure 3, and wires on pylons), and transformer sub-stations are all part of the **National Grid** (Figure 2).

How are transformers used in the National Grid?

Transformers (Figure 5) change the potential difference (p.d. or **voltage**) across different parts of the National Grid. The potential difference produced is 25 000 V.

Step-up transformers increase the p.d. to nearly 400 000 V, which is the p.d. across the wires on electricity pylons. This p.d. is far too high for people to use safely. **Step-down transformers** decrease the p.d. to the 230 V needed in homes and offices.

> **A** Suggest something else (apart from the wires) in the National Grid that heats the surroundings.

You can show how energy is transferred in the National Grid using a Sankey diagram (Figure 4).

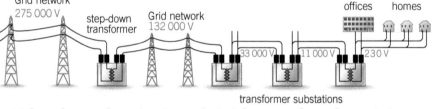

Figure 2 *The National Grid.*

Why does the National Grid transfer electricity at high voltages?

There is a large amount of wire in the grid network, and when a current flows in any wire the wire gets hot. If the current is bigger, the wire gets hotter.

It is important that the wires in the National Grid do not heat the surroundings too much, so transformers are used to reduce the current.

When you use a transformer:

- a high p.d. means a small current flows
- a low p.d. means a large current flows.

If the electricity were transferred at 230 V, a current of over 200 000 A would be needed. Transferring the same power at 400 000 V reduces the current to 125 A. This is still a high current, and the wires do get hot. In the National Grid are very thick so that they do not melt.

Transformers increase the p.d. to reduce the heating effect. This makes the National Grid an efficient way to distribute energy using electricity to factories, homes, and other buildings.

B Describe what 'efficient way to distribute energy' means.

How efficient is the National Grid?

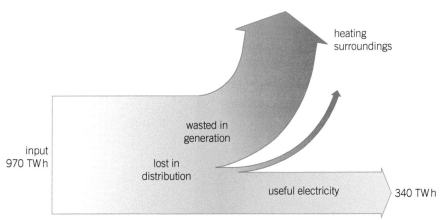

Figure 4 *Most of the wasted energy in the National Grid is wasted at power stations.*

Transformers are very efficient, but some energy is wasted because it contains wires that get hot. The wires are wrapped around a core made of iron. When an alternating current flows in the wires, a p.d. is generated in the core, and this makes a current flow in the core. The core heats up.

However, most of the energy wasted in the National Grid is a result of the way that the electricity is generated.

About a third of our electricity is generated by thermal power stations. Most of these power stations use coal.

A lot of energy is wasted when the fuel is used to produce steam in a thermal power station. The steam drives turbines that also get hot. This means that the energy wasted in the power station is much greater than the energy wasted in transmitting the electricity to homes.

The National Grid does not just use thermal power stations. Electricity is generated by wind, water, and nuclear fuel. If you have solar photovoltaic cells on your roof, you can sell any spare power that is generated back to the National Grid.

Figure 5 *You need a transformer to change the high p.d.s in the grid network to the 230 V supplied to your house.*

Figure 6 *A thermal image shows that both the transformer on the pole and the wires are hot.*

1 a Describe what the 'National Grid' is. *(2 marks)*
   b Explain why the power lines supported by pylons have to be so high off the ground. *(1 mark)*

2 Explain why we need to use transformers in the National Grid. *(4 marks)*

3 Use the definition of efficiency to explain in words why transformers are not 100% efficient. *(3 marks)*

4 The National Grid is 35% efficient and transfers 340 TWh of useful energy electrically. Use the equation for efficiency to calculate the wasted energy in TWh. Give your answer to an appropriate number of significant figures. *(6 marks)*

Study tip

Remember that the potential difference, or voltage, is *across* wires in the National Grid, not along them.

Go further

Transformers are very efficient. Find out how heating losses in the core are minimised.

Learning outcomes

After studying this lesson you should be able to:

- describe the domestic electricity supply in the UK
- explain the difference between direct and alternating voltage
- describe the functions of the wires in a plug, the potential differences between them, and why we have an earth wire
- explain why a live wire may be dangerous even when an appliance is not switched on.

Specification reference: P6.2f, P6.2g, P6.2h, P6.2i

Figure 1 *An electrical wall socket.*

Figure 3 *Electrical fuses contain a piece of thin wire.*

Table 1 *Mains electricity wires.*

If you connected a voltmeter between these wires...	... it would read...
live and neutral	230 V
live and earth	230 V
neutral and earth	0 V

What *is* behind a wall socket (Figure 1)? (Don't look for yourself!)

What is the 'mains'?

When people talk about the 'mains', or **domestic supply**, they usually mean mains voltage, or potential difference, which is 230 V. Generators in power stations produce an alternating voltage (Figure 2**A**) with a frequency of 50 Hz. This is transmitted to your house using the National Grid.

When you use a torch, or any appliance with a battery, then the voltage is a **direct voltage** (Figure 2**B**).

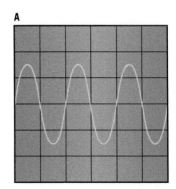 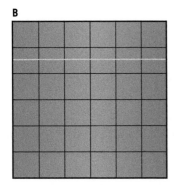

Figure 2 *The voltage from a battery shown on the oscilloscope screen in **2B** does not change, but an alternating voltage, shown in **2A**, does.*

> **A** Describe how you could use a rope model to demonstrate alternating voltage.

How does using a plug connect an appliance to the mains?

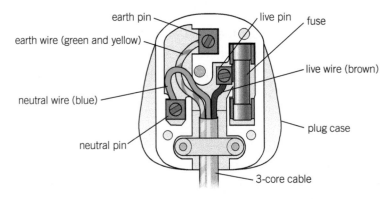

Figure 4 *A UK plug has three pins which are connected to three different wires inside the socket in your wall.*

In a plug (Figure 4), the **live wire** (brown) and the **neutral wire** (blue) are the two wires that make a complete circuit with your appliance (Figure 5). The **earth wire** (green and yellow) is not connected to the mains. It is connected to 'earth', which is usually a large metal pole buried in the ground outside your house.

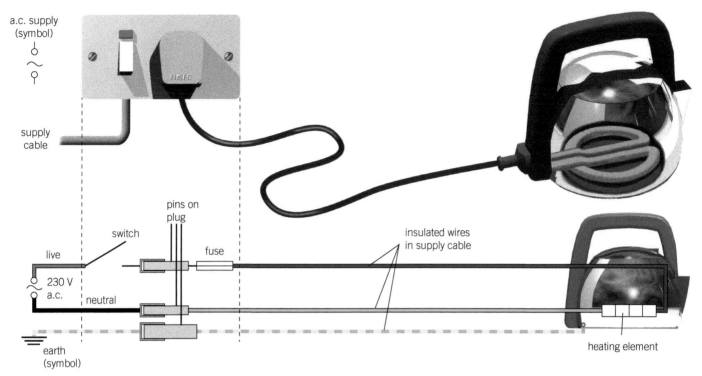

Figure 5 *The live and neutral wires are effectively connected to an alternating generator.*

B State which wires are effectively at 0V.

What safety features are there in plugs and appliances?

If the live wire becomes loose inside an appliance it can touch a metal casing, and we say the casing is live. If you touch the casing there is a potential difference of 230V across you because you are also connected to the earth. A dangerous current could flow through you.

To prevent this happening, the earth wire connects the case to the pole in the ground so that the current flows through the earth wire and not through you (Figure 6). The earth wire has less resistance than you. Also, the wire inside the fuse melts and switches off the circuit (Figure 3).

Alternatively, the case can be made of plastic so no current can flow through the case to you. These appliances are 'double insulated'. Appliances that are double insulated do not need to use the earth pin.

Figure 6 *The Earth pin is longer than the other pins. It opens shutters so that the live and neutral pins can be inserted.*

1 Compare the wires in a plug. (*4 marks*)

2 Suggest why the earth pin of a plug for a hairdryer with a plastic casing is also made of plastic. (*3 marks*)

3 Explain why the potential difference from the National Grid is alternating and not direct. (*3 marks*)

4 On the oscilloscope trace in Figure 2 each square represents a certain number of milliseconds. Use the fact that mains voltage is 50 Hz to calculate the number of milliseconds per square. (*6 marks*)

Figure 7 *Electricians need a good understanding of mains electricity.*

Global challenges

Summary questions

1 a i Copy Table 1 and tick the energy sources that are renewable.

Table 1 *Energy sources.*

Energy source	Renewable?
wind power	
oil	
coal	
hydroelectricity	
gas	
geothermal power	

ii Name a renewable *fuel*.

b In terms of the National Grid, write down which one of these objects is the odd one out:

power lines   transformers   power stations
motors   generators

2 a There are three wires in the cable that connects an appliance to the socket in the wall.
Match the wires to their colours and functions. Write the matched letters and numbers to show your answer.

Wire	Colour	Function
A live	**1** brown	**X** to provide a pathway of low resistance if an appliance becomes live
B neutral	**2** green/yellow	**Y** connected to 230 V, part of the circuit for the appliance
C earth	**3** blue	**Z** connected to 0 V, part of the circuit for the appliance

b Write down what the earth wire is connected to.
c Describe mains voltage.
d A fuse should have a current rating as low as possible, but higher than the normal current flowing. Choose the correct fuse for a plug for a 2 kW kettle from these:

3 A   5 A   13 A

e Describe the type of appliance that does not need an earth wire.

3 a Describe why there is a potential difference between the live and neutral wires in a plug. Start at the power station.

b A power station generates a potential difference of 25 000 V.

i Explain why electricity is not transmitted at this potential difference.

ii When electricity is transmitted some energy is transferred to a less useful thermal store. Suggest one part of the National Grid that gets hot.

iii A transformer at the power station steps up the potential difference to 400 kV. If the current in the grid wires is 125 A calculate the current in the primary coil at the power station.
Use the equation: $V_p \times I_p = V_s \times I_s$

iv State an assumption that you are making.

4 Electricity demand varies during the day.

a i Sketch a graph of how a household's demand for electricity varies over a 24-hour period from midnight to midnight. Assume the maximum demand at any time is about 5 kW h.

ii Explain the shape of the graph.

b Most electricity is generated by fossil fuels and the output of the power station matches the demand as shown on your graph. Suggest which renewable source, or sources, could be used if there was a sudden increase in demand for electricity, such as for a royal wedding or sporting event on television.

5 Electric cars use batteries that are charged by the National Grid at night. They are described as 'clean' or 'green'.

a i Suggest and explain what these terms might mean.

ii Explain whether or not you agree with the statement that they are 'clean' or 'green'.

iii Suggest and explain what might happen in terms of the National Grid if everyone used electric cars.

b Electric cars are just one thing that might change the demand for electricity in the future.
Describe and explain how our future demand for electricity might be met.

Revision questions

1 **a** Which energy source is non-renewable?

   A nuclear fuel

   B wind

   C hydroelectricity

   D solar panels   (*1 mark*)

   b The three wires in a plug are the live, earth, and neutral.

   Which wire is at +230 V?

   A earth wire

   B live wire

   C neutral wire

   D none of them   (*1 mark*)

   c What is the correct sequence for transferring electrical power from a power station to your home?

   A Your home, step-up transformer, grid network, step-down transformer, power station.

   B Power station, grid network, step-up transformer, step-down transformer, your home.

   C Power station, step-down transformer, grid network, step-up transformer, your home.

   D Power station, step-up transformer, grid network, step-down transformer, your home.   (*1 mark*)

2 The pie charts show the sources for electricity generation in the UK in 1980 and 2013.
   Describe how the sources have changed during this period.   (*2 marks*)

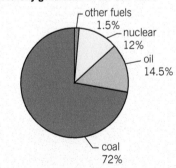

Electricity generation in the UK: 1980

other fuels
1.5%
nuclear
12%
oil
14.5%
coal
72%

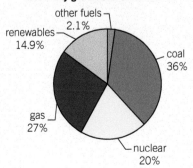

Electricity generation in the UK: 2013

other fuels
2.1%
renewables
14.9%
coal
36%
gas
27%
nuclear
20%

3 **a** Explain the difference between a step-up and a step-down transformer.   (*2 marks*)

   b Explain why electrical power is transferred at high voltages in the National Grid.   (*2 marks*)

4 **a** Explain why a live wire can be dangerous even when a switch in a mains circuit is open. (*2 marks*)

   b Describe how the safety features reduce the risk from a live wire.   (*2 marks*)

5 Here is a model steam engine. It uses methylated spirit as a fuel.

The methylated spirit is burned to heat up water and turn it into steam. The steam then drives a piston, which drives the steam engine.
Describe the energy transfers that take place in the steam engine.   (*6 marks*)

P6 Global challenges: Topic summary

P6.1 Physics on the move

- Describe how to measure speed in everyday situations.
- Write down approximate speeds for everyday objects.
- Estimate the acceleration of everyday objects.
- Describe how to measure reaction time.
- Describe what thinking distance means.
- Describe some factors that affect thinking distance.
- Describe factors that affect braking distance.
- Explain the implications of stopping distance for safety.
- Explain the dangers of large decelerations.

P6.2 Powering Earth

- Describe the main energy sources we use on Earth.
- Explain the difference between renewable and non-renewable energy sources.
- Describe how we use energy resources.
- Describe how our use of energy sources has changed.
- Explain why our use of energy sources has changed.
- Describe some of the issues with the use of energy sources.
- Describe the National Grid.
- Describe how transformers are used in the National Grid.
- Calculate using potential difference and currents for transformers. **H**
- Describe the domestic electricity supply in the UK.
- Explain the difference between direct and alternating voltage.
- Describe the functions of the wires in a plug, the potential differences between them, and why we have an earth wire.
- Explain why an appliance can still be dangerous even when it is switched off.

Motion

How fast?
- running: 10 m/s, car: 22 m/s or 50 mph
- measure distance (trundle wheel, bike wheel diameter)
- measure time (radar pulses, radar gun)

Accelerations and forces
- large accelerations can cause injury
- speed limits reduce risk
- everyday accelerations ~ 1 m/s^2 to 10 m/s^2
- everyday forces (in large accelerations) ~ 100 N

Stopping a car

thinking distance (speed × reaction time) + braking distance (speed × time to brake) = stopping distance (thinking distance + braking distance)

- about 0.2 s
- measured by dropping ruler
- depends on driver

- depends on road conditions
- depends on car

Energy sources

- renewable energy sources will not run out
- non-renewable energy sources took millions of years to form/formed in stars

Energy in the future

- energy needed has increased and will continue to rise
- increased energy requirement predominantly for electricity generation
- solutions: more efficient devices, developing renewables, reducing demand

P6 Global challenges

The National Grid

power station
(boiler → turbine → generator → transformer)

↓

overhead and underground power lines

↓

houses/businesses

- energy transferred as wires get hot/boiler gets hot
- transmitting at higher voltage/p.d. is more efficient (lower current) **H**

Mains electricity

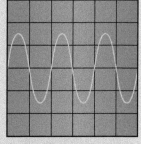

- alternating current changes
- direct current doesn't change

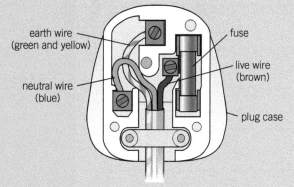

earth wire (green and yellow)

fuse

live wire (brown)

neutral wire (blue)

plug case

- for safety, all current flows to earth wire if there is a fault → fuse melts
- plastic case (double insulation) alternative to earth wire

Learning outcomes

After studying this lesson you should be able to:

- use appropriate apparatus to make and record a range of measurements accurately, including length, mass, and volume
- use these measurements to determine densities of solid and liquid objects.

Specification reference: PAG P1

Figure 1 *Density can help to distinguish real gemstones from fake gemstones, such as quartz (left) from a rough diamond (right).*

Density (Figure 1) is one of the properties of a material that engineers use to choose the right material for a job, such as the material for a tennis racket frame. To calculate density, you need to measure mass and volume.

You need to work carefully to make accurate and precise measurements of mass and volume in order to find an object's density.

How do I measure mass?

You measure mass using a digital balance.

To measure the mass of a solid, place it on the balance and record the reading.

To measure the mass of a liquid:

- place a measuring cylinder on a digital balance
- write down the reading, or zero the balance (if possible for your balance)
- pour in the liquid that you are investigating
- write down the new reading and subtract the mass of the cylinder, or note the mass.

How do I measure volume?

You can measure the volume of a liquid using a measuring cylinder. Pour the liquid into the cylinder and read off the scale.

You can measure the volume of a regular solid, such as a cube or rectangular block, by measuring the width, length, and height. Then multiply the measurements together to find the volume.

For an irregularly shaped solid object, you can use a measuring cylinder to measure the volume.

- Pour water into a cylinder large enough to hold the object, and note the reading.
- Put the object into the water and note the new reading.
- Subtract the initial reading from the final reading to find the volume.

Measuring the density of a piece of rock

1   Use a digital balance to measure the mass of the rock. Repeat your readings and calculate the mean, ignoring outliers if appropriate.
2   Use a measuring cylinder and water to measure the volume of the rock. Repeat your readings and calculate the mean, ignoring outliers if appropriate.
3   Calculate the density using the equation: $\text{density} = \frac{\text{mass}}{\text{volume}}$
4   Include units in all stages of your calculation and answer.

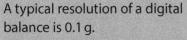

Using a digital balance

A typical resolution of a digital balance is 0.1 g.

Make sure the balance reads 0.0 g before taking a measurement. Press the T (tare) button before each use, and ensure the reading is not fluctuating.

Place your object gently on the balance, and wait for a consistent reading to be displayed before recording your measurement.

Designing your practical

1 List the apparatus you need to measure the density of an object. Justify your choice of apparatus.

2 Write a detailed, step-by-step method for making the measurements.

3 Write a risk assessment for this activity.

4 Draw an appropriate results table, including headings.

Analysing your results

5 Use your measurements and the equation to calculate the density of the object.

Evaluating your practical

6 Evaluate your data:

   a Identify any outliers.

   b Comment on the precision of your measurements. (Hint: look at the spread of your repeat measurements.)

7 Evaluate your method:

   a Describe what you did to obtain accurate measurements.

   b Describe what you did to obtain precise results.

   c Suggest how you could use alternative equipment or methods to obtain more accurate or more precise results.

Table 1 *Measuring the densities of two rocks.*

Object	Mass 1 (g)	Mass 2 (g)	Mass 3 (g)	Mean mass (g)	Volume 1 (cm³)	Volume 2 (cm³)	Volume 3 (cm³)	Mean volume (cm³)
rock 1	12.3	12.2	12.2		25	26	24	
rock 2	17.5	17.3	17.4		56	65	58	

A student has two pieces of rock and has been asked to measure the density of each. Her results are shown in Table 1.

1 State the two pieces of equipment that the student needed to obtain these results. *(2 marks)*

2 Copy and complete Table 1. *(4 marks)*

3 Calculate the density of each rock. *(6 marks)*

4 Evaluate the data in the table in terms of accuracy and precision. *(3 marks)*

5 Suggest a reason for any outliers. *(1 mark)*

Using a measuring cylinder or ruler

When you record the volume in a measuring cylinder, read the scale at eye level, from the bottom of the curved surface (meniscus), as shown in Figure 2. If you look from above or below, your measurement will not be accurate.

When you measure a length using a ruler, look from directly above the ruler, at eye level with the edge of the object, as shown in Figure 3.

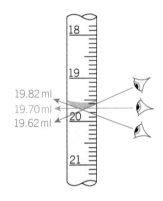

Figure 2 *Reading from above or below the surface of the liquid will give an inaccurate reading.*

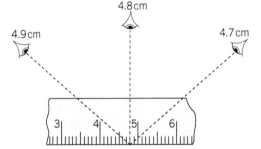

Figure 3 *Your eye should be directly above the scale when you use a ruler.*

Learning outcome

After studying this lesson you should be able to:

● measure and observe the effects of forces, including the extension of springs.

Specification reference: PAG P2

Figure 1 *Springs in a car's suspension ensure a smooth ride.*

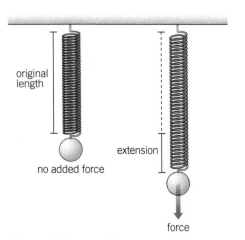

original length

no added force

extension

force

Figure 2 *You need to measure the extension, not the length of the spring.*

The predictable behaviour of springs gives them a wide variety of uses, from newtonmeters to car suspensions (Figure 1). When choosing a type of spring for a particular use, an engineer will consider several factors, including the stiffness required. The spring constant of a spring tells you how far it stretches when you apply a force.

You need to work carefully to make accurate and precise measurements of force and extension in order to investigate the behaviour of a spring.

How do I measure the force and extension of a spring?

To measure the force, you can:

● attach a newtonmeter directly to the spring and read the force from the scale, or

● use the fact that a 100 g mass has a weight of 1 N.

When you measure the extension (Figure 2):

● measure the length of the spring when there is no force on it (the original length)

● measure the length of the spring when there is a force on it

● subtract the original length from the length when there is a force on it to calculate the extension.

Hazard: If the spring breaks, the end of it can fly up and cause injury.

Investigating the behaviour of a spring

1 Take a retort stand, boss, and clamp.

2 Attach the spring to the clamp using one of the loops of the spring.

3 Measure the original length of the spring.

4 Place a 1 N weight on the spring.

5 Measure the length again, then record the extension.

6 Repeat with more weights.

7 Repeat your measurements for each value of the force, and calculate the mean extension.

Using a ruler

When you use a ruler vertically, look from directly in front of the ruler, at eye level with the end of the spring, as shown in Figure 3.

Designing your practical

1   List the apparatus you need to investigate the behaviour of a spring. Justify your choice of apparatus.

2   Write a detailed, step-by-step method for making the measurements.

3   Write a risk assessment for this activity.

4   Draw an appropriate results table, including headings.

Calculating a spring constant

The relationship between force and extension is:

force (N) = spring constant (N/m) × extension (m)

This is also known as Hooke's Law.

You could calculate the spring constant for one set of values of force and extension. However, you will get a more accurate result if you calculate the gradient of a graph of force against extension. You use the initial linear (straight) section of the graph.

Plot the graph using force in newtons, and extension in metres.

Analysing your results

5   Plot extension (*x*-axis) versus force (*y*-axis). (Note: this is not the usual way of plotting results. You would normally plot the force on the *x*-axis, because it is the independent variable.)

6   Calculate the spring constant from the gradient of the graph.

Evaluating your practical

7   Evaluate your data:
   a   Identify any outliers.
   b   Comment on the precision of your measurements. (Hint: look at the spread of your repeat measurements.)

8   Evaluate the method:
   a   Describe what you did to obtain accurate measurements.
   b   Describe what you did to obtain precise results.
   c   Suggest how you could use alternative equipment or methods to obtain more accurate or precise results.

A student measures the extension of a spring as she pulls the spring down. Table 1 shows her results.

1   State the two pieces of equipment that the student needed to obtain these results, apart from the spring. (*2 marks*)

2   Copy and complete Table 1. (*2 marks*)

3   Plot a graph of extension (*x*-axis) versus force (*y*-axis). (*3 marks*)

4   Calculate the spring constant from your graph. (*4 marks*)

5   Identify any outliers and suggest a reason for them. (*2 marks*)

6   Evaluate the data in the table in terms of accuracy and precision. (*2 marks*)

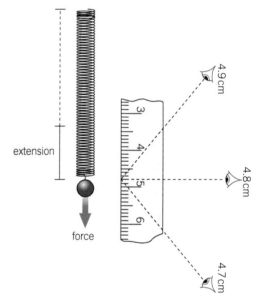

Figure 3 *Your eye should be directly in front of the scale when you use a ruler vertically.*

Table 1 *Results of measuring the extension of a spring as the spring is pulled down.*

Force (N)	Extension 1 (cm)	Extension 2 (cm)	Extension 3 (cm)	Mean extension (cm)
0	0	0	0	
1	2.1	2.2	2.1	
2	4.0	4.6	4.1	
3	6.2	6.0	6.1	
4	8.1	8.3	8.0	
5	10.2	10.1	10.1	
6	14.2	15.2	14.1	

Learning outcome

After studying this lesson you should be able to:

- use appropriate apparatus and techniques for measuring motion, including determination of rate of change of speed.

Specification reference: PAG P3

Figure 1 *The Saturn V rocket provided a huge acceleration to launch the module into space.*

Making a friction-compensated slope

If you want to make measurements to link force and acceleration, you need to compensate for the force of friction on the moving object. Otherwise your measurements of force will not be accurate.

To compensate for friction, raise the ramp until a trolley moves down the ramp at a steady speed, with no acceleration. At this point the component of gravity down the slope cancels out the force of friction.

Acceleration tells you how quickly the speed changes. The *Saturn V* rocket (Figure 1) launched *Apollo 11*, the first spacecraft to land on the Moon. The astronauts in the rocket experienced an acceleration about 5 times that of Earth's gravity, or 5 *g*.

You need to work carefully to make accurate and precise measurements of speed and time.

How do I take measurements to find the acceleration?

To calculate the average acceleration, you need to find the speed at two different times. It is difficult to do this using a stopwatch and a metre ruler. Using light gates connected to a datalogger allows you to make accurate and precise measurements.

An object moving past a light gate reflects the beam of light as it passes in front of it.

To find the speed at two different times (Figure 2):

- fix a piece of card of known width to a trolley or other moving object
- let the object pass in front of the light gates
- read from the datalogger the time it took the card to pass in front of each light gate.

To find the time between the two measurements of speed, read the time from the datalogger.

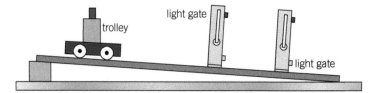

Figure 2 *A trolley with a piece of card attached passes in front of two light gates.*

Investigating acceleration

1. Connect the light gates to a datalogger. Set the datalogger to record the time it takes objects to pass each gate.

2. Fix a card to the top of a trolley. The card should be several centimetres wide, but much smaller than the distance between the light gates. Measure the width of the card with a ruler.

3. Raise a ramp on some books or a block of wood, and place the trolley on the ramp.

4. Let the trolley accelerate down the ramp.

5. Take readings of the time for the card to pass each light gate, and the time that it took the trolley to pass from one light gate to the next.

6. Use the width of the card and the time it took for the card to pass each light gate to calculate two speeds.

7 Use the two speeds and the time between the two measurements to calculate the average acceleration.

Designing your practical

1 List the apparatus you need to make measurements to calculate the acceleration of a falling tennis ball. Justify your choice of apparatus.

2 Write a detailed, step-by-step method for making the measurements.

3 Write a risk assessment for this activity.

4 Draw an appropriate results table, including headings.

Calculating acceleration

You can measure the speed of the ball as it passes each light gate using the equation:

$$\text{speed (m/s)} = \frac{\text{distance (m)}}{\text{time (s)}}$$

where distance = the diameter of the ball.

Then you can calculate the change in speed by subtracting the lower speed from the higher speed.

If you know the time between the measurements of speed, and the change in speed, you can calculate the acceleration:

$$\text{acceleration (m/s}^2) = \frac{\text{change in speed (m/s)}}{\text{time (s)}}$$

Analysing your results

5 Use your measurements and the equation above to calculate the average acceleration.

Evaluating your practical

6 Evaluate your data:
   a Identify any outliers.
   b Comment on the precision of your measurements. (Hint: look at the spread of your repeat measurements.)

7 Evaluate your method:
   a Describe what you did to obtain accurate measurements.
   b Describe what you did to obtain precise results.
   c Suggest how you could use alternative equipment or methods to obtain more accurate or more precise results.

Table 1 *Results of changing the height of the ramp.*

Height of ramp (cm)	Time for card to pass gate 1 (s)	Speed at gate 1 (m/s)	Time for card to pass gate 2 (s)	Speed at gate 2 (m/s)	Time between gates (s)	Acceleration (m/s²)
10	1.020		0.867		0.514	
20	0.887		0.524		0.428	
30	0.591		0.169		0.257	
40	0.201		0.087		0.164	

Using light gates

A light gate measures the time that it takes for an object to interrupt a beam of light. The measurement of time is much more accurate and precise than a measurement you might make with a stopwatch.

You connect a light gate to a datalogger, which records the times. You need to work out which connections on the datalogger are needed to calculate the two times.

The datalogger will record the data, which you can usually see by scrolling through a display. Alternatively, connect the datalogger to a computer to display the data as it is recorded.

A student fixes a piece of card 5 cm wide to a trolley, and puts the trolley on a ramp with two light gates. He changes the height of the ramp. For each height, he records the time it takes for the card to pass each light gate. He also records the time it takes for the card to pass from the first light gate to the second light gate. Table 1 shows the student's resutls.

1 Explain why the student chose to use light gates for this experiment. (*1 mark*)

2 Copy and complete Table 1. (*4 marks*)

3 Suggest why it is unlikely that there will be outliers in these data. (*1 mark*)

4 Suggest why there will still be an uncertainty in the value calculated for the acceleration. (*1 mark*)

P4 Waves

Learning outcomes

After studying this lesson you should be able to:

- make observations of waves in fluids and solids
- identify the suitability of apparatus to measure speed, frequency, and wavelength.

Specification reference: PAG P4

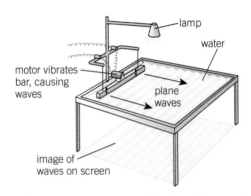

Figure 2 *You can use a ripple tank to make measurements of the properties of waves.*

Measuring frequency

The frequency is the number of waves or oscillations per second. It is difficult to count the number of waves in a time period as short as 1 second.

Instead, you find the number of waves in a much longer time period, such as 10 seconds. Divide the number of waves that you count by 10 to find the frequency.

Earthquakes cause huge amounts of damage (Figure 1). Seismic waves travel through the Earth, and can cause large waves in oceans (tsunamis). Scientists need to know the speed of waves in solids and liquids so that they can warn people of the hazards.

Figure 1 *The movement of the Earth in an earthquake produces waves that can cause a huge amount of damage.*

You need to work carefully to make measurements of the speed, frequency, and wavelength of waves.

How can I measure the wavelength of water waves?

You can use a ripple tank (Figure 2) to investigate the properties of water waves. It is helpful to use a stroboscope to 'freeze' the waves. To measure the wavelength:

- place a ruler in the tank and measure the wavelength, or
- use the stroboscope to 'freeze' the waves on the bench or floor below the ripple tank, and use a ruler to measure the wavelength there.

How can I measure the frequency of water waves?

To find the frequency:

- place a marker in the tank and count the number of waves passing it each second, or
- place a small piece of paper touching the top of the vibrating bar as it vibrates. Make sure the bar can still vibrate. Listen to the bar hitting the paper, and count the vibrations per second.

How can I measure the speed of water waves?

You can use a ripple tank to investigate the properties of water waves.

- Measure the wavelength.
- Measure the frequency.
- Use the wave equation to calculate the speed.

Here is an alternative way to measure the speed of water waves.

- Work with a partner. Place a piece of paper on the bench or floor. The first student should draw a pencil line that follows the peak of one wave as it moves along. The other student should time how long it takes to move a certain distance, and calculate the speed.

There will be large uncertainties in all your measurements.

Measuring the speed of waves in a ripple tank

1 Measure the wavelength of the waves.

2 Measure the frequency of the waves.

3 Use this equation to calculate the speed:

$$speed\ (m/s) = frequency\ (Hz) \times wavelength\ (m)$$

Designing your practical

1 List the apparatus you need to measure the wavelength, frequency, and speed of water waves in a ripple tank. Justify your choice of apparatus.

2 Write a detailed, step-by-step method for making the measurements.

3 Write a risk assessment for this activity.

4 Draw an appropriate results table, including headings.

Analysing your results

5 Use your measurements and the equation to calculate the speed of the water waves.

Evaluating your practical

6 Evaluate your data:

  a Identify any outliers.

  b Comment on the precision of your measurements. (Hint: look at the spread of your repeat measurements.)

7 Evaluate your method:

  a Describe what you did to obtain accurate measurements.

  b Describe what you did to obtain precise results.

  c Suggest how you could use alternative equipment or methods to obtain more accurate or precise results.

Table 1 *Results from a ripple tank.*

Experiment	Wavelength (m)	Number of waves in 10 seconds	Frequency (Hz)	Speed (m/s)
1	0.02	16		
2	0.03	23		
3	0.02	17		

A student uses a vibrating bar to make plane (straight) waves in a ripple tank. Table 1 shows her results.

1 State the equipment that the student needed to obtain these results, apart from the ripple tank. (*3 marks*)

2 Copy and complete Table 1. (*3 marks*)

3 Identify any outliers and suggest a reason for them. (*2 marks*)

4 Suggest why the speed is only an estimate. (*1 mark*)

Using a stroboscope

It is very difficult to measure the wavelength of a wave that is moving.

You can use a stroboscope to make the waves appear stationary, or 'freeze' them.

There are two types of stroboscope. A hand-held stroboscope is a card disc with slits cut into it, which you spin (Figure 3). Alternatively, you can use a flashing light. Adjust the speed of the disc or the number of flashes per second until the waves appear stationary.

Hazard: Some people are sensitive to flashing lights, so always check that using a stroboscope will not cause a problem.

Figure 3 *You spin a hand-held stroboscope to 'freeze' waves, so you can measure the wavelength.*

Learning outcome

After studying this lesson you should be able to:

● safely use appropriate apparatus in a range of contexts to measure energy changes/transfers.

Specification reference: PAG P5

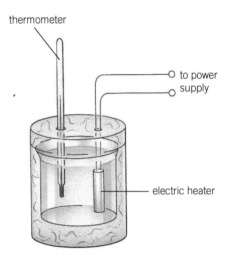

Figure 1 *Equipment to measure the specific heat capacity of water.*

Using a thermometer

Thermometers used in schools usually contain liquid ethanol. When you read the temperature on a thermometer, read it at eye level to the bottom of the curved surface (meniscus). If you read it from above or below this level, your measurement will not be accurate.

When engineers design a device, or even a building, which will change in temperature, the specific heat capacity is an important property of the materials they choose. Water has an unusually high specific heat capacity. This helps to keep the temperature of the Earth in a range that makes life possible.

You need to work carefully to make accurate and precise measurements of mass, energy transferred, and temperature rise in order to measure specific heat capacity. When you are using a power supply, you need to consider the hazards to minimise the risk of injury.

How do I measure mass?

You measure mass using a digital balance.

How can I measure the energy transferred?

If you heat a material using an immersion heater, you can work out the energy transferred to the material by measuring:

● the potential difference across the immersion heater

● the current through the immersion heater

● the time for which the heater is on.

● Then calculate the energy transferred using this equation:

energy transferred (J) = potential difference (V) × current (A) × time (s)

Alternatively, use a joulemeter connected between the immersion heater and the power supply to measure the energy transferred directly.

You need to insulate the material to reduce the transfer of energy from the hot material to the thermal store of the surroundings.

How do I measure temperature difference?

Measure the temperature difference using a thermometer (liquid or digital) or a temperature probe.

Measure the temperature before you turn on the immersion heater, and then the temperature at the end of the heating period. To find the temperature difference, subtract the starting temperature from the final temperature.

You will usually measure temperature in °C. Remember that 1 °C = 1 K.

Measuring specific heat capacity

1 Use a digital balance to measure the mass of the object.

2 Use a voltmeter, ammeter, and stopwatch to measure the energy transferred.

3 Use a thermometer to measure the temperature rise, by reading the scale at eye level.

4 Repeat your readings, and take an average, ignoring outliers.

5   Calculate the specific heat capacity using the equation:

$$\text{specific heat capacity (J/kg K)} = \frac{\text{change in thermal energy (J)}}{\text{mass (kg)} \times \text{change in temperature (K)}}$$

6   Include units in your calculation and answer.

Designing your practical

1   List the apparatus you need to measure the specific heat capacity of the material you have been given. Justify your choice of apparatus.

2   Write a detailed, step-by-step method for making the measurements.

3   Write a risk assessment for this activity.

4   Draw an appropriate results table, including headings.

Analysing your results

5   Use your measurements and the equation to calculate the specific heat capacity of the material.

Evaluating your practical

6   Evaluate your data:

   a   Identify any outliers.

   b   Comment on the precision of your measurements. (Hint: look at the spread of your repeat measurements.)

7   Evaluate your method:

   a   Describe what you did to obtain accurate measurements.

   b   Describe what you did to obtain precise results.

   c   Suggest how you could use alternative equipment or methods to obtain more accurate or more precise results.

Using a voltmeter and ammeter

To measure potential difference, connect the voltmeter across the component. You connect one lead from one side of the component to the voltmeter, and one lead from the voltmeter to the other side of the component.

To measure the current, connect the ammeter in series with the component.

Make sure that you connect meters so that the positive (red or +) terminal leads back to the positive side of the power supply, and the negative (black or –) terminal leads back to the negative side of the power supply. If you connect it the other way round, the meter will show a negative reading. You should swap the leads to avoid damaging the meter.

Always disconnect the power supply before making changes to a circuit.

Table 1 *Results of an experiment to find the specific heat capacity of copper.*

Experiment	Mass (kg)	Potential difference (V)	Current (A)	Time (s)	Energy transferred (J)	Temperature change (K)
1	1.0	12.0	2.5	90		17
2	1.0	11.5	2.4	500		40
3	1.0	11.5	2.5	260		20

A student has been given a cylinder of copper. She makes measurements to find the specific heat capacity. Her results are shown in Table 1.

1   State the equipment that the student needed to obtain these results, apart from the copper.   (2 marks)

2   Copy and complete Table 1.   (3 marks)

3   Calculate the specific heat capacity of copper for each experiment.   (9 marks)

4   The accepted value for the specific heat capacity of copper is 330 J/kg K. Suggest which experiment is the outlier.   (1 mark)

5   Suggest why the values calculated from her results are higher than the accepted value.   (1 mark)

Figure 2 *Energy transferred from the Sun to the Earth's oceans raises the temperature of the water very slowly. The oceans act as a buffer to keep the Earth's temperature steady.*

P6 Circuits

Learning outcomes

After studying this lesson you should be able to:

- use appropriate apparatus to explore the characteristics of a variety of circuit elements
- use circuit diagrams to construct and check series and parallel circuits, including a variety of common circuit elements.

Specification reference: PAG P6

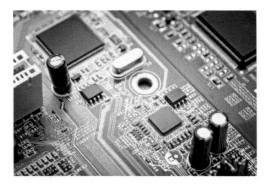

Figure 1 *A circuit board.*

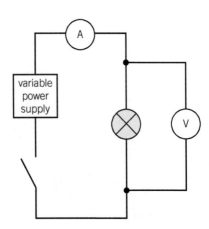

Figure 2 *A circuit diagram for making measurements to plot the characteristic curve of a light bulb. The power supply is variable.*

Circuit boards (Figure 1) contain a wide variety of circuit components. How do you know how each one will behave?

You need to work carefully to make accurate and precise measurements of current and potential difference in order to plot a characteristic curve. A characteristic curve shows how the current through a component changes as you vary the potential difference.

How do I measure potential difference?

Use a voltmeter to measure the potential difference across a component. Connect the voltmeter in parallel with the component (Figure 2).

You need to be able to vary the potential difference across the component. You can do this by:

- adjusting the setting on the power supply (usually by increments of 1 V, between the values 0 V and 12 V) or
- using a variable resistor to change the current in the circuit, which changes the potential difference across the component.

How do I measure current?

Use an ammeter to measure the current through a component. Connect the ammeter in series with your component and the power supply (Figure 2).

When you have taken a set of measurements for the current flowing in one direction, swap the connections to the power supply so that the current flows in the opposite direction. Repeat your measurements. You need to swap the connections to each meter to avoid damage, but remember that you are now reading a negative potential difference, and a negative current.

Drawing a characteristic curve

1 Connect up a circuit with the component that you are investigating.
2 Vary the potential difference across the component, and measure the current through it each time.
3 Use your measurements to plot a graph of current against potential difference, showing current and potential difference in both the positive and negative directions.

Using circuit diagrams to construct series and parallel circuits

When using a circuit diagram to construct a circuit, start by connecting all the components that are in the series part of the circuit that includes the battery or power supply.

Then connect any components (e.g., voltmeters) that are in parallel with components in the series circuit.

194

Designing your practical

1 List the apparatus you need to plot the characteristic curve for the component that you have been given. Justify your choice of apparatus.

2 Write a detailed, step-by-step method for making the measurements.

3 Write a risk assessment for this activity.

4 Draw an appropriate results table, including headings.

Analysing your results

5 Plot potential difference (x-axis) versus current (y-axis) for both the positive and negative potential differences.

6 The ratio of potential difference to current is the resistance. Look at how this changes as you increase the potential difference. Describe the behaviour of the component as you increase the potential difference.

Evaluating your practical

7 Evaluate your data:

  a Identify any outliers.

  b Comment on the precision of your measurements. (Hint: look at the spread of your repeat measurements.)

8 Evaluate your method:

  a Describe what you did to obtain accurate measurements.

  b Describe what you did to obtain precise results.

  c Suggest how you could use alternative equipment or methods to obtain more accurate or precise results.

A student was given a component and asked to plot a characteristic curve for the component. Table 1 shows his measurements.

1 State the two pieces of equipment, apart from the component and connecting wires, that the student needed to obtain these results. (2 marks)

2 Plot a graph of potential difference (x-axis) versus current (y-axis) for both positive and negative values of potential difference. (3 marks)

3 Comment on the shape of the graph. (1 mark)

4 Identify any outliers, and suggest a reason for them. (2 marks)

Study tip

You may find it helpful to connect the series circuit using, say, red wires, and the parallel components using black wires. This helps you check that you have followed the circuit diagram correctly.

Checking series and parallel circuits

When you have connected the series part of your circuit, check that it is working correctly by looking at the reading on the ammeter, or inserting an ammeter temporarily if there is not one in the circuit.

There should be a reading on any voltmeter connected across a component in the circuit. The reading may not equal the potential difference labelled on the power supply, because there will be a small potential difference across the connecting wires and the ammeter, or the power supply output has changed.

Table 1 *Current and potential difference measured in a circuit.*

Potential difference shown on power supply (V)	Current (A)	Potential difference shown on voltmeter (V)
0	0	0
2	0.15	1.8
4	0.31	3.7
6	0.47	5.9
−2	−0.14	−1.7
−4	−0.36	−3.6
−6	−0.48	−5.8

Revision questions

Revision questions for P1–P3

1 A simple circuit contains a piece of *nichrome wire* connected to a battery. The nichrome wire is coiled around the bulb of a thermometer. Nichrome is widely used in heating elements such as those found in toasters and kettles.

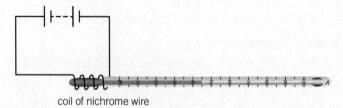

coil of nichrome wire

A student predicts:

The greater the power supplied by the battery, the faster the temperature rise.

Describe how the experiment should be adapted to investigate the student's prediction.

Include:

● the measurements that should be taken

● the calculations that should be made

● how the observations will be presented. *(6 marks)*

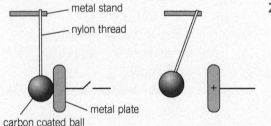

metal stand
nylon thread
metal plate
carbon coated ball

2 An experiment is set up as shown.

The metal plate is part of a circuit containing a switch. When the switch is closed, the metal plate becomes positively charged and the carbon coated ball moves away.

a Explain why the carbon coated ball moves away. *(3 marks)*

b Draw and label a free body diagram to show the forces acting on the ball after the switch has been closed. *(3 marks)*

c When the switch is closed, the ball gains a small amount of gravitational potential energy (g.p.e.).

Describe how the experiment should be improved so that the gain in g.p.e. can be calculated. *(3 marks)*

3 Which of the following descriptions is the correct way to find the power of a lamp?

A measure I across the lamp and V in series with the lamp, then use $V \times I$

B measure V across the lamp and I in series with the lamp, then use $I \div V$

C measure I across the lamp and V in series with the lamp, then use $V \div I$

D measure V across the lamp and I in series with the lamp, then use $V \times I$

(1 mark)

4 A glider of mass 320 kg has a pilot of mass 80 kg and a passenger of mass 70 kg.

   a Calculate the total weight of the glider and its occupants. *(2 marks)*

   b Air flow over the wings of the glider produces a force of lift. The lift accelerates the glider upwards. Copy the diagram and add an arrow to show the force of lift. *(2 marks)*

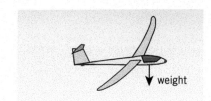

   c A glider has no engine. One way to launch a glider is by using a winch. One end of a long cable is attached the glider and the other end is wound on to a large drum. An engine rotates the drum to wind the cable. This accelerates the glider.

     i It takes 4 seconds for the glider to go from standstill (0 m/s) to a take-off speed of 30 m/s. Calculate the acceleration of the glider. *(2 marks)*

     ii Determine the average force of tension in the cable. *(2 marks)*

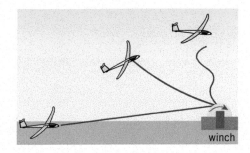
winch

   d The cable is released 45 seconds after take-off at a height of 520 m.

     i Calculate the vertical velocity of the glider. *(2 marks)*

     ii Determine the gravitational potential energy of the glider. *(3 marks)*

   e For a short time after the cable is released, the glider stays at a height of 520 m.

     i Explain why the glider is able to maintain a constant height. *(2 marks)*

     ii Explain how the glider uses forces to decrease its height so that it can land on the ground. *(3 marks)*

5 Hannah has a hot air balloon, a 2000 m length of string wound on to a spool, a marker pen, and a sensitive barometer. The barometer measures atmospheric pressure.

Describe how Hannah should use the apparatus to find out how atmospheric pressure varies with height. Use the data table to predict the atmospheric pressure at intermediate heights. State the assumption that you must make to predict the change in atmospheric pressure.

(6 marks)

Height (m)	Atmospheric pressure (kPa)
0	10.13
2000	9.42

6 The time taken for the temperature of a thermometer to change is measured.

start temperature:

finish temperature:

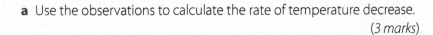

1:22.0
START RESET

   a Use the observations to calculate the rate of temperature decrease. *(3 marks)*

b The liquid inside the thermometer is ethanol. Explain how the density of the ethanol changes as the temperature decreases. *(2 marks)*

c If the thermometer breaks, the ethanol will quickly evaporate. The latent heat of ethanol is 846 kJ/kg.
Use $Q = mL$ to calculate the energy needed to evaporate 1 g of ethanol. (Q is the heat energy needed to evaporate the ethanol, m is the mass of the ethanol, and L is the latent heat of ethanol.) *(2 marks)*

7 A diagram of a circuit containing a variable resistor R_v and a thermistor R_{th} is shown.

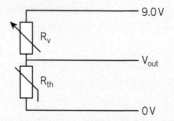

a The variable resistor is adjusted so that its resistance is equal to the resistance of the thermistor.
State the potential difference across **each** resistor. *(1 mark)*

b The relationship between temperature and resistance for a thermistor is shown in the graph.

i The output potential difference, V_{out}, is used to operate a circuit with a buzzer. The buzzer circuit is activated by a potential difference of 6 V.
Use the graph to explain the temperature change that would activate the buzzer circuit. *(3 marks)*

ii When the buzzer circuit is activated the resistance of the variable resistor is 2000 Ω.
Explain why the resistance of the thermistor must be 1000 Ω. *(3 marks)*

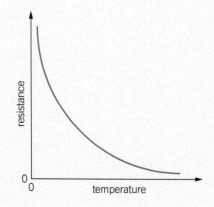

8 A fountain shoots a stream of water vertically at a rate of 1.5 litres of water every second. 【H】
($1.5 \, l = 0.0015 \, m^3$)

a Show that the unit of volume per second (m^3/s) is equal to the units of area (m^2) × velocity (m/s). *(1 mark)*

b i The spout of the water fountain has an area of 0.0002 m^2.
Use the relationship in **a** to show that the velocity of the water is 7.5 m/s. *(1 mark)*

ii The density of water is 1000 kg/m^3. Calculate the mass (in kilograms) of water flowing each second. *(2 marks)*

iii Determine the kinetic energy (in joules) of the water that flows in one second. *(2 marks)*

Assume that all the energy in the kinetic store of the water is transferred to a gravity store as the water moves upwards.

iv Find the height (in metres) that the water will reach. *(3 marks)*

c Two groups of students are discussing the best way to adapt the water fountain so that the height of the water is doubled.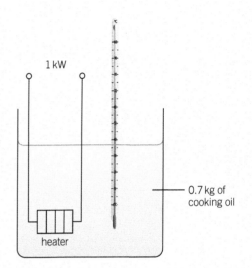
Group A suggests doubling the flow rate.
Group B suggests halving the area of the spout.
Which group, if any, is correct?
Use calculations to justify your answer. *(6 marks)*

9 A heater is connected to a 1 kw (1000 J/s) power supply. The heater is immersed in 0.7 kg of cooking oil. The heater is switched on and 8 kJ of thermal energy is transferred from the heater to the the oil. This causes the level of the liquid in a thermometer to rise by 0.8 cm.
a Calculate the time taken (in seconds) for the level of the liquid in the thermometer to rise 4 cm. *(4 marks)*
b A 4 cm rise in the level of liquid in the thermometer equates to a temperature increase of 29.0 °C.
Calculate the specific heat capacity, *c* (in J/kg °C), of the cooking oil. *(2 marks)*
c At 50 °C, the time taken for a ball to fall 40 cm through a glass cylinder containing the oil is 8 s.
i Describe an experiment to investigate safely the relationship between the temperature of the oil and the time taken by a ball to flow through it. *(2 marks)*
ii Suggest, with an explanation, a possible conclusion for the results of the investigation. *(2 marks)*

1 kW

0.7 kg of cooking oil

heater

10 An iron block of mass 0.15 kg, rests on a wooden surface. An electromagnet exerts a force of attraction on the block. The block does not move.

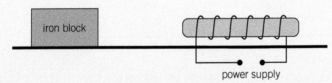

iron block

power supply

a Copy the diagram. Draw and label arrows to represent the forces acting on the block. *(2 marks)*
b Calculate *N* (in newtons), the normal contact force acting on the iron block. *(1 mark)*
c The electromagnet is adapted to increase the force of attraction on the block. The block still does not move.
i Define inertia. *(2 marks)*
ii Describe one adaptation that increases the force of attraction from the electromagnet. *(1 mark)*
iii Explain why there is a force of attraction between the electromagnet and the iron block. *(3 marks)*

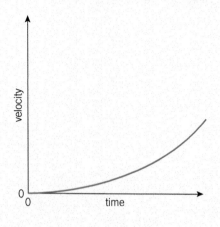

d The block moves towards the magnet with the motion shown in the graph.
  i Describe the motion shown in the graph. *(1 mark)*
  ii Explain why the block moves with the motion shown in the graph. *(2 marks)*
e The resistance of the coil is 8.5 Ω. The potential difference of the power supply is 12.0 V. Calculate the current in the coil (in amperes). *(2 marks)*

11 A snow machine sprays artificial snow at a rate of 4 g/s and a velocity of 6 m/s.
What is the horizontal force exerted by the snow machine on the ground?
  A 0.024 N
  B 1.5 N
  C 24 N
  D 1500 N *(1 mark)*

12 On 29 August, 1831, Michael Faraday wound two long pieces of insulated copper wire around an iron ring. He connected the end of one copper wire to a battery. The other wire was connected to a sensitive meter designed to measure current. He closed and opened the switch and made observations.

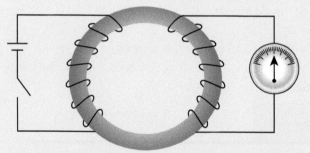

a Describe what Faraday observed on the meter when he opened and closed the switch. Explain these observations. *(5 marks)*
b The electrical power produced by the apparatus is equal to the electrical power supplied by the battery.
Describe how the apparatus should be adapted so that the potential difference across the meter is double the potential difference of the battery. State the effect of this adaptation on the current in the meter. *(2 marks)*

Revision questions for P4–P6

1 a Which formula can be used to calculate the spring constant of a spring?

A $k = $ energy $\times$ (extension)^2

B $k = \dfrac{\text{energy}}{\text{(extension)}^2}$

C $k = \dfrac{2 \times \text{energy}}{\text{(extension)}^2}$

D $k = \dfrac{2 \times \text{energy}}{\text{extension}}$

(1 mark)

b The graph shows braking, thinking, and stopping distances at different speeds.

Which row of the table shows the correct distances at 50 mph?

	Stopping distance / m	Braking distance / m	Thinking distance / m
A	38	53	15
B	73	55	18
C	53	15	38
D	53	38	15

(1 mark)

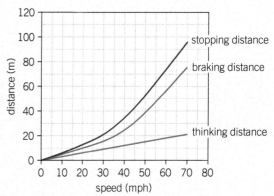

c What measurements are needed to calculate the kinetic energy of a toy car moving at a uniform speed?

A mass of the toy car, distance from A to B, and the time taken to move from A to B

B weight of the toy car, distance from A to B, and the time taken to move from A to B

C mass and acceleration of the toy car

D force needed to move the toy car and the distance from A to B

(1 mark)

d What is the half-life of a radioactive substance? Choose the correct definition.

A the time taken for half the number of atoms in the sample to decay

B the time taken for the activity of the substance to decrease to a safe level

C the time taken for the activity of the substance to decrease by half

D the time taken for the activity of the substance to increase by half

(1 mark)

e The diagram shows a counter being used to measure the activity of a beta source.

beta source

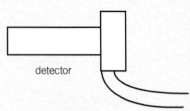

detector

Which action will reduce the activity measured by the counter to almost zero?

A putting a sheet of paper between the source and the detector

B moving the detector about 10 cm further away from the source

C putting a sheet of aluminium foil between the source and the detector

D putting a 4 mm thick sheet of aluminium between the source and the detector   *(1 mark)*

f Uranium-238 is the most abundant form of uranium.
Its nucleus contains 146 neutrons and its nuclear mass is 238.
Which of the following is an isotope of uranium?

A 147 neutrons, nuclear mass 238

B 147 neutrons, nuclear mass 239

C 146 neutrons, nuclear mass 239

D 145 neutrons, nuclear mass 238   *(1 mark)*

g Which row in the table shows increased efficiency of an electric motor?   **H**

	Energy input lower while energy output stays the same	Higher energy losses due to heating	Higher energy transfer to kinetic energy
A	no	yes	no
B	no	no	yes
C	yes	no	yes
D	yes	yes	no

(1 mark)

h The speed of an aeroplane increases from 2 m/s to 80 m/s in 65 seconds.
What is the expression to calculate its acceleration?

A $\dfrac{80 - 2}{65}$

B $\dfrac{80}{65}$

C $\dfrac{80}{65} - 2$

D $\dfrac{65}{80 - 2}$ *(1 mark)*

i The potential difference across the secondary coil of a transformer is 9 V. The current in the secondary coil is 1.5 A.

The potential difference across the primary coil of the transformer is 230 V.

Which expression is used to calculate the current in the primary coil?

A $230 \times \dfrac{1.5}{9}$

B $\dfrac{9 \times 1.5}{230}$

C $\dfrac{230 + 9}{1.5}$

D $\dfrac{230}{9 \times 1.5}$ *(1 mark)*

2 The acceleration of a car is often given as the time taken to accelerate from 0 mph to 60 mph.

A sports car accelerates from 0 mph to 60 mph in 6 seconds.

a Calculate the acceleration of the car in m/s².
Assume that 1 mile = 1.6 km *(3 marks)*

b Calculate the force the engine needs to apply to produce this acceleration.
The mass of the car is 1500 kg. *(2 marks)*

c Calculate the distance the car travels in this time. *(2 marks)*

d Calculate the momentum of the car. *(2 marks)* **H**

3 a $^{241}_{95}$ Am is used in smoke alarms. How many protons and neutrons are in this nucleus? *(2 marks)*

b $^{241}_{95}$ Am decays into neptunium (Np) by emitting an alpha particle.

Write a nuclear equation for this decay. *(2 marks)*

4 Technetium-99m is widely used as a radioactive tracer in medicine. The graph shows the activity of a sample of technetium-99m.

a Work out the half-life of technetium-99m. *(1 mark)*

b You have a sample of techetium-99m with activity 600 counts per second. Work out its activity after 24 hours. *(2 marks)*

c You have a sample of technetium-99m. Calculate the net decline **H** after 36 hours. *(2 marks)*

d You have a sample of technetium-99m with activity 400 counts per second. Explain what its activity will be after one month. *(2 marks)*

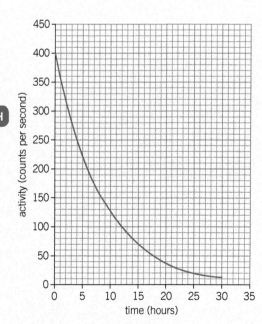

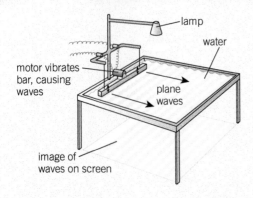

lamp

water

motor vibrates bar, causing waves

plane waves

image of waves on screen

5 The speed of water ripples can be measured using a ripple tank. The wavelength can be measured using a strobe.

   a Define wavelength. *(1 mark)*

   b Explain how you measure the wavelength using the strobe. *(3 marks)*

   c The wavelength was measured as 4 cm and the frequency as 5 Hz. Calculate the wave speed in metres per second. *(2 marks)*

6 **a** Explain the energy transfers taking place in a car engine that uses petrol as a fuel. *(6 marks)*

   b The power output of the engine is 110 kW. The efficiency of the engine is 20%. Work out how much power is wasted. *(2 marks)*

   c 0.8 kg of water is pumped around the engine each second to cool it. Calculate the increase in temperature of the water. The specific heat capacity of water is 4200 J/kg °C. *(3 marks)*

   d Suggest why water is used to cool the engine rather than air. *(1 mark)*

   e Suggest why not all of the energy is transferred to the water. *(1 mark)*

   f Oil is used to lubricate a car engine. Describe how lubrication reduces energy transfers from friction. *(2 marks)*

7 **a** State what the unwanted energy transfers in a house depend on. *(2 marks)*

   b Describe how you can reduce unwanted energy transfers from a house. *(2 marks)*

8 **a** Explain the difference between alternating current and direct current. *(2 marks)*

   b Trains that run between Bedford and Brighton are designed to work with two different power supplies: 750 V d.c. in the southern part and 25 kV a.c. in the northern part. One of the trains used has a power of 1072 kW. Calculate the current required for each power supply. *(3 marks)*

   c With the 750 V d.c. supply, 20% of the energy supplied is transferred by heating to the conducting rails that supply the power. Calculate the resistance of the conductors. *(3 marks)*

   d Calculate how much power is transferred by heating with the 25 kV a.c. supply. Assume the resistance is the same. *(2 marks)*

   e Suggest why 25 kV a.c. is the preferred supply. *(1 mark)* **H**

9 Here is some information about the transfers in a power station while you are using appliances in your home for heating.

- The energy in the chemical store of the coal goes down by 250 MJ.
- The energy is transferred to your appliances electrically by the National Grid to thermal stores in your home.
- The energy transferred to the thermal store of the cooling water in the power station increases by 90 MJ.
- Some energy is transferred to a thermal store of the boiler and the chimney.

a i The power station has an efficiency of 33%. Calculate the energy transferred to the thermal stores in your home. *(2 marks)*

ii Calculate the energy transferred to the thermal store of the boiler and the chimney. *(1 mark)*

Here is some information about a more efficient power station.

- The energy in the chemical store of the coal goes down by 120 MJ
- The energy transferred to your appliances electrically by the National Grid to thermal stores in your home is 42 MJ
- The 48 MJ of energy transferred to the thermal store of the water in the power station is then used to heat local homes and schools
- 30 MJ of energy is transferred to a thermal store of the boiler and the chimney.

b This more efficient power station has an overall efficiency of 0.75 (75%). Use the information above to explain why. *(2 marks)*

c i Nuclear power stations use a nuclear fuel. Describe the process that produces the transfer of energy. *(2 marks)*

ii Describe the changes to the stores of energy before and after the reaction and the energy transfers that take place. *(3 marks)*

iii Explain why the products of the nuclear reaction are dangerous. *(1 mark)*

10 Beta particles are often used in paper mills to check that paper is the correct thickness. The paper passes between a beta particle source and a detector which counts the beta particles getting through the paper. Suggest how this is used to check and control the thickness of the paper. *(4 marks)*

Maths for Physics

How big is a bacterium (Figure 1)? How far away is the Sun (Figure 2)? And what is the size of a red blood cell (Figure 3)?

Scientists use maths all the time – when collecting data, looking for patterns, and making conclusions. This chapter includes all the maths for your GCSE science course. The rest of the book gives you many opportunities to practise using maths in science.

1 Decimal form

There will always be a whole number of people in a school, and a whole number of chairs in each classroom.

When you make measurements in science the quantities may *not* contain whole numbers, but numbers *in between* whole numbers. They will be in **decimal form**, for example 3.2 cm, or 4.5 g.

2 Standard form

Some quantities in science are very large, such as the distance from the Earth to the Sun. Other quantities are very small, such as the size of an atom.

In **standard form** (also called scientific notation) a number has two parts.

- You write a decimal number, with one digit (not zero) in front of the decimal place, for example 3.7.
- You multiply the number by the appropriate power of ten, for example 10^3. The power of ten can be positive or negative.
- For a quantity such as length, you then add the unit, for example m for metres.
- This gives you a quantity in standard form, for example 3.7×10^3 m. This is the length of one of the runways at Heathrow airport.

Table 1 explains how you convert numbers to standard form.

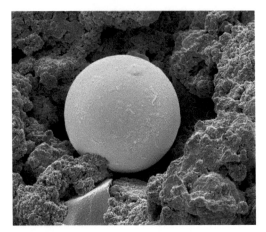

Figure 1 *How big is a bacterium?*

Figure 2 *The Sun is 1.5×10^{11} m from the Earth.*

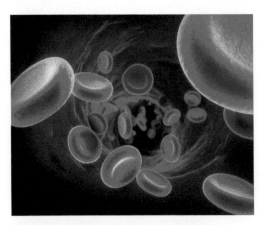

Figure 3 *These red blood cells have a diameter of approximately 7.0×10^{-6} m.*

Table 1 *Standard form.*

The number	The number in standard form	What you did to get to the decimal number	...so the power of ten is...	What the *sign* of the power of ten tells you
1000	1.0×10^3	You moved the decimal point 3 places to the *left* to get the decimal number	+3	The positive power shows the number is *greater* than one.
0.01	1.0×10^{-2}	You moved the decimal point 2 places to the *right* to get the decimal number	−2	The negative power shows the number is *less* than one.

Here are two more examples. Check that you understand the power of ten, and the sign of the power, in each example.

- $20\,000\,Hz = 2.0 \times 10^4\,Hz$
- $0.0005\,kg = 5.0 \times 10^{-4}\,kg$

Note that $1.0 \times 10^3\,m$ is the same as $10^3\,m$.

It is much easier to write some of the very big or very small quantities that you find in real life using standard form. For example:

- The distance from the Earth to the Sun is $150\,000\,000\,000\,m = 1.5 \times 10^{11}\,m$.
- The diameter of an atom is $0.000\,000\,000\,1\,m = 1.0 \times 10^{-10}\,m$.
- The diameter of a red blood cell is around $0.000\,007\,m = 7 \times 10^{-6}\,m$.
- The speed of light is $300\,000\,000\,m/s = 3 \times 10^8\,m/s$.

You need to use a special button on a scientific calculator (Figure 4) when you are calculating with numbers in standard form. You should work out which button you need to use on your own calculator (it could be  **EE** , **EXP** , **10ˣ** , or **×10ˣ**).

2.1 Multiplying numbers in standard form

When you multiply two numbers in standard form you *add* their powers of ten. When you divide two numbers in standard form you *subtract* the power of ten in the denominator (the number below the line) from the power of ten in the numerator (the number above the line). For example:

- $10^2 \times 10^3 = 10^5$ or $100\,000$ (because $2 + 3 = +5$)
- $10^2 \div 10^4 = 10^{-2}$ or 0.01 (because $2 - 4 = -2$)

Pages in a library

A library (Figure 5) contains 200 000 books. Each book has 400 pages. Calculate the total number of pages.

   Step 1: Convert the numbers to standard form.
$$200\,000 = 2 \times 10^5, 400 = 4 \times 10^2$$

   Step 2: Calculate the total number of pages within all the books in the library.

total number of pages = number of books × pages per book
$$= (2 \times 10^5\,books) \times (4 \times 10^2\,pages\ per\ book)$$
$$= (2 \times 4) \times (10^5 \times 10^2)\ pages$$
$$= 8 \times 10^7\ pages$$

Figure 4 *You need a scientific calculator to do calculations involving standard form.*

Figure 5 *You can use standard form to help you work out how many pages are in this library.*

The total length of the shelves in the library is 4 800 m. Calculate the thickness of a page.

Divide the total width of all the books by the total number of pages.

$$\text{width of a single page} = \frac{\text{width of all the books}}{\text{number of pages in all the books}}$$

$$= \frac{4.8 \times 10^3 \, \text{m}}{8 \times 10^7 \, \text{pages}}$$

$$= \frac{4.8}{8} \times \frac{10^3}{10^7} \, \text{m/page}$$

$$= 0.6 \times 10^{-4} \, \text{m}$$

$$= 6 \times 10^{-5} \, \text{m in standard form}$$

3 Ratios, fractions, and percentages

3.1 Ratios

A **ratio** compares two quantities. For example, a ratio of 2 : 4 of ducks to chickens means that for every two ducks, there are four chickens.

You may need to calculate a ratio in which one of the numbers is 1. This is useful if you need to compare two ratios. There are two ways to do this:

1. Divide both numbers by the *first* number (2 : 4 becomes 1 : 2 when you divide by 2). So for every one duck there are two chickens.

2. Divide both numbers by the *second* number (2 : 4 becomes 0.5 : 1 when you divide by 4). For every half a duck there is one chicken.

Notice that there are three ways above to describe the number of ducks in relation to the number of chickens, but they mean the same thing.

Take care if you are asked to use ratios to find a fraction. The ratio of 2 : 4 in the example above does *not* mean that $\frac{2}{4}$ (or half) of the objects are ducks!

Figure 6 *If the ratio of ducks to chickens is 2:4 then $\frac{2}{6}$ or $\frac{1}{3}$ of the animals are ducks.*

Fractions from ratios

The ratio of steel paperclips to plastic paperclips is 2 : 4. What fraction are steel paperclips?

Step 1: Add the numbers in the ratio together.

$$2 + 4 = 6$$

Step 2: Divide the proportion of steel paperclips in the ratio by the total of the numbers in the ratio (which you found in Step 1).

$$\frac{\text{proportion of steel paperclips}}{\text{total paperclips}} = \frac{2}{6} = \frac{1}{3}$$

One third of the paperclips are steel.

You can simplify a ratio so that both numbers are the lowest whole numbers possible.

Simplifying ratios

A student mixed 15 cm³ of acid with 90 cm³ of water. Calculate the simplest ratio of the volume of acid to the volume of water.

Step 1: The ratio of *acid* : *water* is 15 : 90.

Step 2: Both 15 and 90 have a common factor, 5. You can divide both numbers by 5.

$$acid : water = \frac{15}{5} : \frac{90}{5} = 3 : 18$$

Step 3: Both 3 and 18 have a common factor, 3. You can divide both numbers by 3.

$$acid : water = \frac{3}{3} : \frac{18}{3} = 1 : 6$$

Notice that to get the simplest form of the ratio, you have now divided both 15 and 90 by 15 (i.e. 3 × 5), which is the highest common factor of 15 and 90.

3.2 Fractions

The horizontal line in a fraction means 'divide', so $\frac{1}{3}$ means 1 ÷ 3. This is useful to know if you have to convert a fraction into a decimal.

Note that $\frac{1}{3} = 1 ÷ 3 = 0.\dot{3}$ (the dot above the number 3 shows that the number 3 recurs, or repeats over and over again).

Calculating the fraction of a quantity

A student has a 25 g piece of Plasticine. Calculate the mass of $\frac{2}{5}$ of this piece.

Step 1: Divide the total mass of the sample by the denominator (the number on the bottom) in the fraction.

25 g ÷ 5 = 5 g

Step 2: Multiply the answer to Step 1 by the numerator (the number on the top) in the fraction.

5 g × 2 = 10 g

Figure 7 *This slice represents $\frac{1}{8}$ (or 0.125) of a cake.*

The **reciprocal** of a number is 1 ÷ (number). For example, the reciprocal of 4 is 0.25 (which is 1 ÷ 4). The reciprocal of a fraction is the fraction written the other way up. So the reciprocal of $\frac{2}{3}$ is $\frac{3}{2}$.

Nutrition Facts

Serving Size 1 cup (200g)
Servings per Container 4

Amount Per Serving	
Calories 300	Calories from Fat 110

	% Daily Value
Total Fat 12g	20%
Saturated Fat 4g	22%
Cholesterol 0mg	0%
Sodium 70mg	6%
Total Carbohydrate 30g	10%
Dietary Fiber 0g	0%
Sugars 20g	
Protein 5g	

Vitamin A 5%	Vitamin C 0%
Calcium 10%	Iron 0%

* Percent Daily Values are based on a 2,000 calorie diet.

Figure 8 *You see percentages on food labels. They are useful for comparing the masses of different ingredients in foods.*

3.3 Percentages

A **percentage** is a number expressed as a fraction of 100.

Calculating a percentage

Electrical appliances transfer some energy to the stores that you want, and some to stores that you don't want.

Calculate the efficiency of a light bulb that transfers 40 J of lighting for every 200 J of input energy transfer.

$$\text{efficiency} = \frac{\text{useful output energy transfer}}{\text{input energy transfer}} \times 100\%$$
$$\text{(or total energy transferred)}$$

Step 1: Write down what you know.

useful output energy transfer = 40 J

input energy transfer = 200 J

Step 2: Calculate the efficiency

$$\text{efficiency} = \frac{40\,\text{J} \times 100\%}{200\,\text{J}} = 20\%$$

You may need to calculate a percentage of a quantity.

Calculating a percentage of a quantity

A current of 3.2 A flows in an electrical circuit. Calculate 25% of this current.

Step 1: Convert the percentage to a decimal.

$$25\% = \frac{25}{100} = 0.25$$

Step 2: Multiply the answer to Step 1 by the total current.

$$0.25 \times 3.2\,\text{A} = 0.8\,\text{A}$$

You may need to calculate a percentage increase or decrease in a quantity from its original value.

A percentage change

A student heats a 4.75 g sample of copper carbonate and finds its mass decreases to 3.04 g. Calculate the percentage change in mass.

Step 1: Calculate the actual change in mass.

$$4.75\,\text{g} - 3.04\,\text{g} = 1.71\,\text{g}$$

Step 2: Divide the actual change in mass by the original mass.

$$\frac{1.71}{4.75} = 0.36$$

Step 3: Multiply the answer to Step 2 by 100%.

$$0.36 \times 100\% = 36\%$$

Remember that this is a percentage *decrease*.

4 Estimating the result of a calculation

When you use your calculator to work out the answer to a calculation you can sometimes press the wrong button and get the wrong answer. The best way to make sure that your answer is correct is to estimate it in your head first.

Estimating an answer

You want to calculate distance travelled and you need to find 34 m/s × 8 s. Estimate the answer and then calculate it.

Step 1: Round each number up or down to get a whole number multiple of 10.

34 m/s is about 30 m/s

8 s is about 10 s

Step 2: Multiply the numbers in your head.

30 m/s × 10 s = 300 m

Step 3: Do the calculation and check it is close to your estimate.

distance = 34 m/s × 8 s

= 272 m

This is quite close to 300 so it is probably correct.

Notice that you could do other things with the numbers:

34 + 8 = 42

$\frac{34}{8} = 4.3$

34 − 8 = 26

Not one of these numbers is close to 300. If you got any of these numbers you would know that you needed to repeat the calculation.

Figure 9 *Estimating is a useful skill. You can use an estimation to make the answer to a question more accessible. For example, is the mass of a big car, 1000 kg, roughly equal to the mass of students in your classroom?*

Sometimes the calculations involve more complicated equations, or standard form.

5 Significant figures

The following lengths each have 3 **significant figures (sig. fig.).** The significant figures are underlined in each case.

153 m, 0.153 m, 0.00153 m

If you write these lengths using standard form (Table 2), you can see that they are all given to 3 significant figures.

Table 2 *Significant figures and standard form.*

Length	153 m	0.153 m	0.00153 m
Length written in standard form	1.53×10^2 m	1.53×10^{-1} m	1.53×10^{-3} m

Table 3 *Significant figures.*

Number	Number of significant figures
2358 mm	4
7 m/s	1
5.1 nm	2
0.05 s	1

Figure 10 *Birds of prey such as the golden eagle can exceed speeds of 100 mph (45 m/s) as they swoop.*

Figure 11 *At how many kilometres per hour is this snowboarder travelling if his speed is 7700 mm/s?*

Table 3 shows some more examples of measurements given to different numbers of significant figures.

How do you know how many significant figures to give when you answer a question? In general, you should round your answer to the same number of significant figures as you were given in the question. Your answer should never have more significant figures than any of the numbers that were given.

If you are multiplying and dividing two numbers, and each has a different number of significant figures, work out which number has fewer significant figures. When you do your calculation, give your answer to this number of significant figures.

Significant figures are not the same as decimal places. If you are adding and subtracting decimal numbers, work out which number is given to fewer decimal places. When you do your addition or subtraction, give your answer to this number of decimal places.

Significant figures

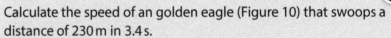

Calculate the speed of an golden eagle (Figure 10) that swoops a distance of 230 m in 3.4 s.

Step 1: Write down what you know.

distance = 230 m (this number has 2 significant figures)

time = 3.4 s (this number also has 2 significant figures)

Step 2: Write down the equation that links the quantities you know and the quantity you want to find.

$$\text{speed (m/s)} = \frac{\text{distance (m)}}{\text{time (s)}}$$

Step 3: Substitute values into the equation and do the calculation.

$$\text{speed} = \frac{230\,\text{m}}{3.4\,\text{s}}$$

= 67.647 058 823 529 m/s (You should not leave your final answer like this as there are too many significant figures.)

= 68 m/s to 2 sig. fig. (Since the question uses 2 significant figures, it is appropriate to give your answer to 2 significant figures.)

6 Bar charts

The word **data** describes observations and measurements which are made during experiments. Data can be:

- qualitative (descriptive, but with no numerical measurements)
- quantitative (including numerical measurements).

Qualitative data includes **categoric variables,** such as the colour of filters. The values of categoric variables are names, not numbers.

Quantitative data includes:

- **continuous variables** – characteristics or quantities that can take any value within certain upper and lower limits, such as length and time
- **discrete variables** – characteristics or quantities which can only take particular values, such as number of paper clips, or shoe size.

You can use a **bar chart** (Figure 12) to display the number or frequency when the independent variable is categoric (for example, type of core in an electromagnet) or has discrete values (for example, number of lamps).

In a bar chart, you plot:

- the dependent variable on the vertical axis
- the independent variable, or class, on the horizontal axis.

You should always leave a gap between the bars.

7 Mean average

To calculate the mean of a series of values:

1   Add together all the values in the series to get a total.

2   Divide the total by the number of values in the data series.

Calculating a mean

A student recorded the time it took her friends to walk around the playground. Her results were as follows:

85 s   63 s   65 s   78 s   72 s   80 s

Calculate the mean time of these values.

Step 1: Add together the recorded values.

85 s + 63 s + 65 s + 78 s + 72 s + 80 s = 443 s

Step 2: Divide by the number of recorded values (in this case, six times were measured).

$$\frac{443\,s}{6} = 74\,s\ (2\ \text{sig. fig.})$$

The **mean** time for the six students was 74 s (2 significant figures).

8 Estimates and order of magnitude

Being able to make a rough estimate is helpful. It can help you to check that a calculation is correct by knowing roughly what you expect the answer to be. A simple estimate is an **order of magnitude** estimate, which is an estimate to the nearest power of ten.

For example, to the nearest power of ten, you are probably 1 m tall and can run 10 m/s.

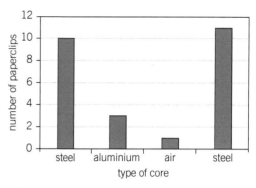

Figure 12 *A bar chart to represent the numbers of paperclips picked up by an electromagnet with different cores. The bars are equal width and separated from one another.*

Table 4 *Frequency table for resting pulse rate in a class of students.*

Pulse rate, r, in beats per minute	Frequency
$60 \leq r < 64$	1
$65 \leq r < 69$	4
$70 \leq r < 74$	12
$75 \leq r < 79$	8
$80 \leq r < 84$	5
$85 \leq r < 90$	1

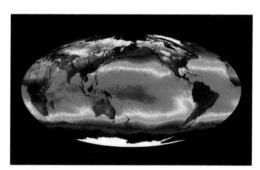

Figure 13 *You may have heard that sea temperatures are increasing because of climate change. Scientists will talk about the mean sea temperature changing over time. The temperature of the ocean varies all over the world.*

You, your desk, and your chair are all of the order of 1 m tall (see also the examples in Figure 14). The diameter of a molecule is of the order of 1×10^{-9} m, or 1 nanometre.

Figure 14 *These are all about 1 m high.*

9 Mathematical symbols

You have used many different symbols in maths, such as +, −, ×, ÷. There are other symbols that you might meet in science, such as those in Table 5.

Table 5 *Mathematical symbols.*

Symbol	Meaning	Example
=	equal to	2 m/s × 2 s = 4 m
<	is less than	the mean height of a child in a family < the mean of an adult in a family
≪	is very much less than	the diameter of an atom ≪ the diameter of an apple
≫	is very much bigger than	the diameter of the Earth ≫ the diameter of a pea
>	is greater than	the pH of an alkali > the pH of an acid
∝	is proportional to	F (force) ∝ x (extension) for a spring
~	is approximately equal to	272 m ~ 300 m (see the example *Estimating an answer* in Section 4)

10 Changing the subject of an equation

An equation shows the relationship between two or more variables. You can change an equation to make *any* of the variables become the subject of the equation.

To change the subject of an equation, you can do an opposite (inverse) operation to both sides of the equation to get the variable that you want on its own. This means that:

● subtracting is the opposite of adding (and adding is the opposite of subtracting)

- dividing is the opposite of multiplying (and multiplying is the opposite of dividing)
- taking the square root is the opposite of squaring (and squaring is the opposite of taking the square root).

You can use these steps to change the subject of an equation, such as the equation for kinetic energy (Figure 15).

Make d the subject

Change the equation $a = b + \frac{c}{d^2}$ to make d the subject.

Step 1: Subtract b to get the term with d on its own. Always do the same on both sides of the equation.

$$a - b = b + \frac{c}{d^2} - b$$

$$a - b = \frac{c}{d^2}$$

Step 2: Multiply by d^2 and divide by $(a - b)$ to get d^2 on its own. Do the same on both sides of the equation.

$$a - b = \frac{c}{d^2}$$

$$(a - b)d^2 = c$$

$$d^2 = \frac{c}{(a - b)}$$

Step 3: Take the square root of both sides.

$$d = \sqrt{\frac{c}{(a - b)}}$$

Figure 15 *If you know the kinetic energy and mass of this roller coaster you can work out the speed.*

Kinetic energy

Change the equation kinetic energy $= \frac{1}{2}mv^2$ to make v the subject.

Step 1: Multiply by 2 and divide by m to get the v^2 on its own. Do the same on both sides of the equation.

$$2 \times \text{kinetic energy} = 2 \times \frac{1}{2}mv^2$$

$$2 \times \text{kinetic energy} = mv^2$$

$$\frac{2 \times \text{kinetic energy}}{m} = \frac{mv^2}{m}$$

$$\frac{2 \times \text{kinetic energy}}{m} = v^2, \quad \text{so} \quad v^2 = \frac{2 \times \text{kinetic energy}}{m}$$

Step 2: Take the square root of both sides.

$$v = \sqrt{\frac{2 \times \text{kinetic energy}}{m}}$$

Figure 16 *Time is measured in seconds.*

Speed = distance/time

A sprinter (Figure 16) can run 100 m in 10 s. Calculate the speed of the sprinter.

Step 1: Write down what you know.

distance = 100 m

time = 10 s

Step 2: Write down the equation you need.

$$\text{speed (m/s)} = \frac{\text{distance (m)}}{\text{time (s)}}$$

Step 3: Do the calculation and include the units.

$$\text{speed} = \frac{100\,\text{m}}{10\,\text{s}}$$

$$= 10\,\text{m/s}$$

m/s is the unit of speed.

11 Quantities and units
11.1 SI units

When you make a measurement in science you need to include a number *and* a unit. This is one of the differences between numbers in maths (which don't need units), and measurements in science (which do).

When you do a calculation your answer should also include both a number *and* a unit. There are some special cases where the units cancel, but usually they do not.

Everyone doing science, including you, needs to use the **SI units**. There are seven **base units**. All other units are derived (worked out) from these base units.

Table 6 gives some of the quantities that you will use, along with their units.

Table 6 *Quantities and units.*

Quantity	Base unit
distance	metre, m
mass	kilogram, kg
time	second, s
current	ampere, A
temperature	kelvin, K
amount of substance	mole, mol

Quantity	Derived unit
frequency	hertz, Hz
force	newton, N
energy	joule, J
power	watt, W
pressure	pascal, Pa
charge	coulomb, C
electric potential difference	volt, V
electric resistance	ohm, Ω

For example, 1.5 N is a *measurement*. The number 1.5 is not a measurement because it does not have a unit.

Some quantities that you *calculate* do not have a unit because they are a ratio – for example, refractive index.

11.2 Using units in equations

When you put quantities into an equation it is best to write the number *and* the unit. This helps you to work out the unit of the quantity that you are calculating.

12 Metric prefixes

You can use **metric prefixes** (Table 7) to show large or small multiples of a particular unit. Adding a prefix to a unit means putting a letter in front of the unit, for example km. It shows that you should multiply the value by a particular power of ten for it to be shown in an SI unit.

For example, 3 millimetres = 3 mm = 3×10^{-3} m.

Most of the prefixes that you will use in science involve multiples of 10^3.

Table 7 *Prefixes.*

Prefix	tera	giga	mega	kilo		deci	centi	milli	micro	nano
Symbol	T	G	M	k		d	c	m	μ	n
Multiplying factor	10^{12}	10^9	10^6	10^3		10^{-1}	10^{-2}	10^{-3}	10^{-6}	10^{-9}

12.1 Converting between units

It is helpful to use standard form when you are converting between units. To do this, consider how many of the 'smaller' units are contained within one of the 'bigger' units. For example:

- There are 1000 mm in 1 m. So $1\,mm = \dfrac{1}{1000}\,m = 10^{-3}\,m$.

- There are 1000 m in 1 km. So $1\,km = 1000\,m = 10^3\,m$.

13 Data and graphs

During your GCSE course you will collect data in different types of experiment or investigation. The data will be either:

- from an experiment where you have changed *one* independent variable (or allowed time to change) and measured the effect on a dependent variable, or

- from an investigation where you have collected data about *two* independent variables to see if they are related.

13.1 Collecting data for two independent variables

You may collect data and plot a graph like those shown in Figure 17, which is called a scatter graph or scatter plot.

You can add a line to show the trend of the data, called a **line of best fit**. The line of best fit is a line that goes through as many points as possible and has the same number of points above and below it.

Figure 18 shows the relationship between body mass and height.

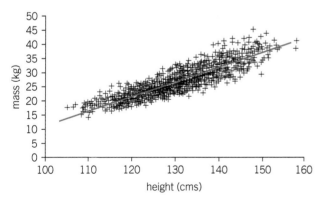

Figure 18 *There is a positive correlation between height and body mass.*

a positive correlation between A and B

a negative correlation between A and B

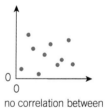

no correlation between A and B

Figure 17 *Scatter graphs can show a relationship between two variables.*

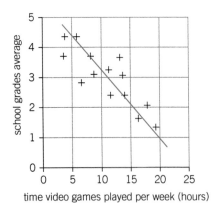

Figure 19 *The line of best fit has a negative gradient. The data for time playing video games and marks gained in school tests shows a negative correlation.*

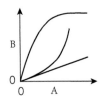

in all these graphs, if A increases then B increases

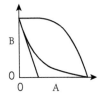

in all these graphs, if A increases then B decreases

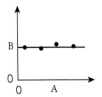

in this graph, if A increases then B does not change

Figure 20 *Different relationships between variables.*

A relationship where there happens to be a link is called a correlational relationship, or **correlation**. This does not mean that A causes B.

Here you can see that being taller does not necessarily mean that your body mass is bigger. Height does not cause mass.

Often there is a third factor that is common to both so it looks as if they are related. You could collect data for shark attacks and ice cream sales. A graph shows a positive correlation, but shark attacks do not make people buy ice cream. Both are more likely to happen in the summer.

Suppose a teacher decided to survey her students to see if there was any correlation between the amount of time spent playing video games and the grades achieved by these students in school. The graph of this data is shown in Figure 19.

The teacher cannot conclude that playing video games *causes* lower scores. There could be another reason.

Sometimes it becomes clear why there is a correlation. For many years you could see a correlation between smoking and lung cancer. Now scientists think that smoking can cause cancer. However, that still does not mean that if you smoke you will get cancer.

13.2 Collecting data by changing a variable

In many practical experiments you change one variable (the independent variable) and measure the effect on another variable (the dependent variable).

You plot the data on a graph, called a line graph. If the gradient of the line of best fit is:

● *positive* it means as the independent variable gets *bigger* the dependent variable gets *bigger*

● *negative* it means as the independent variable gets *bigger* the dependent variable gets *smaller*

● *zero* it means changing the independent variable has no effect on the dependent variable.

We say that the relationship between the variables is positive or negative, or that there is no relationship (Figure 20). We do *not* say that there is a correlation.

For example:

● As you increase the force on a spring, the extension increases.

● As the temperature of water increases, the time it takes sugar to dissolve decreases.

In these cases you can use science to predict or explain *why* changing one variable affects, or does not affect, the other. Changing one variable *causes* the other variable to change. We say there is a **causal relationship**.

Even if there is no relationship there will be a reason why changing the independent variable has no effect on the dependent variable.

14 Graphs and equations

If you are changing one variable and measuring another you are trying to find out about the relationship between them. A straight line graph tells you about the mathematical relationship between variables, but there are other things that you can calculate from a graph.

14.1 Straight line graphs

The equation of a straight line is $y = mx + c$, where m is the **gradient** and c is the point on the y-axis where the graph intercepts, called the y-intercept.

Straight line graphs that go through the origin (0, 0) are special (Figure 21). For these graphs, y is directly proportional to x, and $y = mx$.

When people say 'plot a graph' they usually mean plot the points then draw a line of best fit.

When you describe the relationship between two *physical* quantities, you should think about the reason why the graph might (or might not) go through (0, 0).

14.2 Calculations using straight line graphs

When you draw a graph you choose a scale for each axis.

- The scale on the x-axis should be *the same* all the way along the x-axis, but it can be *different* from the scale on the y-axis.

- Similarly, the scale on the y-axis should be *the same* all the way along the y-axis, but it can be *different* from the scale on the x-axis.

- Each axis should have a label and where appropriate a unit, such as time (s).

You often need to calculate a gradient or an area from a graph. These may represent important physical quantities. Their units can give you a clue as to what they represent.

Hooke's Law

A spring is being stretched by a force, F, and experiences an extension, x.

A line of best fit for a graph of force (y-axis) against extension (x-axis) is a straight line through (0, 0). Explain what the gradient shows in this context, and state why the graph goes through (0, 0).

Step 1: Match the equation to $y = mx$ to work out what the gradient means.

$y = mx$, and Hooke's Law says $F = kx$.

So the gradient shows the value of k, the spring constant.

Step 2: Think about what happens to x when the y quantity is zero.

The line goes through (0, 0) because when the force is zero, there is no extension in the spring.

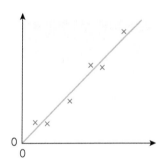

Figure 21 *A line of best fit which passes through the origin.*

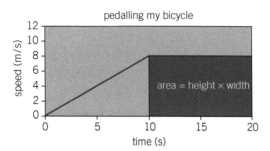

Figure 22 *A bicycle ride.*

Gradients and area

Calculate the gradient of the graph in Figure 22 between 0 s and 10 s, and calculate the area under the graph between 10 s and 20 s.

Step 1: Find the gradient between 0 s and 10 s.

$$\text{gradient} = \frac{\text{change in } y}{\text{change in } x}$$

$$\text{gradient} = \frac{(8\,\text{m/s} - 0\,\text{m/s})}{(10\,\text{s} - 0\,\text{s})} = 0.8\,\text{m/s}^2$$

The unit m/s² is the unit of acceleration. Therefore the gradient of a speed–time graph shows acceleration.

Step 2: Calculate the rectangular area under the graph between 10 s and 20 s.

area = height × width

area = 8 m/s × 10 s = 80 m

The unit m is the units of distance. Therefore the area under a speed–time graph shows the distance travelled.

You can also find the **y-intercept** of a graph. This is the value of the quantity on the *y*-axis when the value of the quantity on the *x*-axis is 0.

For example, if you measure the length of the spring as you change the force on it you get a graph like Figure 23.

If you draw the line back until it hits the *y*-axis you find the value of the length of the spring when the force is zero. It is 4 cm. Here the *y*-intercept is the unstretched length of the spring.

The meaning of the *y*-intercept depends on the quantities that you plot on your graph.

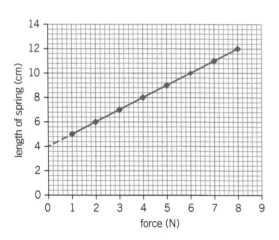

Figure 23 *Graph of length against force for a spring.*

14.3 Graphs with time on the *x*-axis

For all graphs where the quantity on the *x*-axis is time, the gradient will tell you the **rate of change** of the quantity on the *y*-axis with time. For example, in physics the rate of change of distance (*y*-axis) with time (*x*-axis) is speed. In chemistry the rate of change of the volume of a gas (*y*-axis) with time (*x*-axis) can tell you the **reaction rate**.

14.4 Graphs that are *not* a straight line

When you plot a graph of the relationship between certain variables, you may not get a straight line.

However, you may still need to find the area and gradient of the graph.

To find the **area** you can find the value of one square and then count the squares.

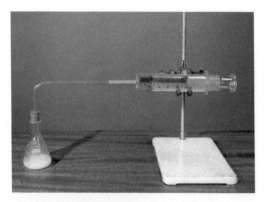

Figure 24 *Measuring the change in the volume of gas in a certain time, usually one second, tells you the reaction rate.*

Finding the distance travelled

The graph in Figure 25 shows a small section of a cyclist's journey.

Use the graph to calculate an estimate of the distance travelled by the cyclist in this section of her journey.

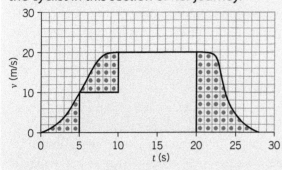

Figure 25 *The cyclist's journey.*

Step 1: Calculate the area of any large squares or rectangles contained under the graph (the pale grey area).

Small shaded square (from $t = 5$ to $t = 10$), distance represented = 10 m/s × 5 s = 50 m

Large shaded square (from $t = 10$ to $t = 20$), distance represented = 20 m/s × 10 s = 200 m

Step 2: Calculate the area of one small square.

The height of each small square is 2 m/s.
The width of each small square is 1 s.

So each small square represents 2 m/s × 1 s = 2 m.

Step 3: Count the remaining small squares under the graph that we didn't include in Step 1. Also add half squares together.

total squares = 64

Step 4: Multiply by the distance represented by each small square.

distance = 64 squares × 2 m/square = 128 m

Step 5: Add together the distances to find the total distance.

total distance = 50 m + 200 m + 128 m = 378 m

15 Angles

You measure angles with a protractor. Angles are measured in degrees (°). The angle shown in Figure 26 is 45°. There are 360° in a circle, 180° in a half circle, and 90° in a quarter of a circle. The angle in the bottom right corner of the triangle is 90°. This is also called a right angle.

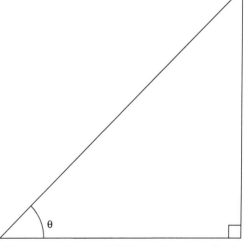

Figure 26 *The symbol for angle is usually θ, the Greek letter theta.*

Glossary

absolute zero The lowest temperature that is theoretically possible, equivalent to −273.14 °C.

absorber A material that absorbs electromagnetic radiation.

absorption spectrum A continuous spectrum with dark lines corresponding to particular frequencies being absorbed by an atom.

acceleration The change in velocity/change in time, measured in m/s².

accurate A measure of how close a result is to the true value. An accurate result is very close.

activity The number of decays per second.

aerial A device for detecting radio waves, usually a piece of metal in which electrons move in the fields of the electromagnetic wave.

alpha (radiation) A particle emitted by an unstable nucleus, a helium nucleus, very ionising but not penetrating.

ammeter A circuit component used to measure current; should be in series with a component.

ampere (A) The unit of current.

amplitude The maximum displacement of a wave.

atom The smallest particle of an element, made of protons, neutrons, and electrons.

atomic number The number of protons in the nucleus.

average speed Total distance/total time, usually measured in m/s.

background radiation Radiation all around from rocks, the Sun, space and artificial sources.

bar chart A way of presenting data when one variable is discrete or categoric and the other is continuous. Numerical values of variables are represented by the heights or lengths of lines or rectangles of equal width.

battery One or more cells.

becquerel (Bq) The unit of activity of a radioactive material, equivalent to one decay per second.

beta (radiation) A particle emitted by an unstable nucleus, a fast electron, not very ionising and quite penetrating.

biofuel A fuel produced from biological matter (e.g. plants or waste).

Bohr model of the atom A model that explains why electrons in orbit do not spiral in to the centre of an atom.

braking distance The distance that a car travels while the driver is braking.

cancer A disease caused by damage to DNA, the uncontrolled dividing of cells.

categoric variable A variable that can take one of a limited, and usually fixed, number of possible values.

causal relationship A relationship in which changing one variable leads to, or causes, a change in another variable.

cell (electricity) A device that produces a potential difference (separation of charge) from chemical reactions; what people normally call a 'battery'.

change of state The process of moving from one physical state to another, for example, melting.

characteristic graph A graph of p.d. on the x-axis, and current on the y-axis for a component.

chemical reaction Process in which substances react to form different substances.

chemical store Energy in a chemical store is associated with rearranging atoms.

closed system A system where there is no energy lost by dissipation due to friction or heating (the term 'closed system' has a different meaning in chemistry).

compass A small magnet that aligns in the Earth's magnetic field to show its direction.

component (of a force) One of two forces that you can use to make up a resultant.

compression A part of a sound wave where the pressure is high.

contact force A force that only acts when objects are in contact.

contamination Having a radioactive material inside the body or on the skin.

continuous variable A variable that has values that can be any number between a maximum and a minimum.

control variable A variable that you have to keep the same in an investigation.

conventional current The model where current flows from positive to negative, opposite to electron flow.

correlation A relationship in which there is a link between two variables.

coulomb (C) The unit of charge.

current (electric) The rate of flow of charged particles (usually electrons), current = charge/time.

data Sets of values for variables.

decimal form Numbers that are between whole numbers can be written in decimal form, for example 5.1 or 6.72.

degree celsius (°C) A unit of temperature.

density Mass/volume, usually measured in kg/m³.

dependent variable A variable that changes when you change the independent variable.

diode A circuit component that has a very low resistance in one direction, but a very large resistance in the reverse direction.

direct voltage (potential difference) A potential difference that does not change direction, e.g. from a battery.

discrete variable A variable that can only have whole number values.

displacement The distance from a point in a particular direction.

dissipation (of energy) The transfer of energy to stores that are not useful (e.g. the thermal store of the surroundings), which cannot be used for working or heating.

domain (model of magnetism) A model of a magnet which says that it is made of small magnetic regions called domains.

domestic supply The electricity supply that we use in homes and businesses, which has a potential difference of 230 V and frequency of 50 Hz.

drag A force that acts opposite to the direction of motion of a body.

earth wire (in a plug) The wire connected to the earth, through which current flows if there is a fault instead of flowing through you.

economic impact The effects of an application of science that are to do with money.

efficiency A percentage that shows how well a device or process transfers energy in the way that you want, calculated with: efficiency = useful output energy transfer/input energy transfer (or total energy transferred) × 100%.

elastic collision A collision in which kinetic energy is conserved.

elastic limit The force beyond which an object, such as a spring, does not return to its original shape when the force is removed.

elastic material A material that returns to its original shape when the force is removed.

elastic store Energy in an elastic store is associated with materials that are deformed; for a spring it can be calculated with $E = \frac{1}{2}kx^2$.

electric charge A property (like mass) of a particle; it can be positive or negative.

electromagnetic spectrum A group of waves (radio, microwave, infrared, visible light, ultraviolet, X-rays, gamma rays) that forms a continuous spectrum.

electromagnetic store Energy in an electromagnetic store is associated with the separation of charges or poles of a magnet or distortion of electric or magnetic fields.

electromagnetic wave A wave that consists of oscillating electric and magnetic fields; one of a spectrum ranging from radio waves to gamma rays.

electron Subatomic particle surrounding the nucleus of an atom. It has a relative charge of −1, and a very small mass.

electron shells The orbits around an atom that are allowed for electrons in the Bohr model.

emission spectrum A set of frequencies of radiation emitted by an atom when excited electrons move to lower energy levels.

energy (in an circuit) This is shifted from a chemical store (for example, a cell) to other stores by electrical working (charges flowing and doing work in components).

energy analysis An analysis where you choose two points and calculate the energy changes to stores between those points using the energy store calculations or the electrical/mechanical working calculations.

energy levels (of an atom) The allowed orbits for electrons at different distances from a nucleus.

energy source Something that you can use for heating, transportation or generating electricity, found on Earth or the Sun.

energy store An energy store is a system (object/objects in a state/position/motion) where you can do a calculation to find the energy associated with it.

environmental Relating to the natural world and the impact of human activity on its condition.

equilibrium An object is in equilibrium if all the forces cancel – the resultant force is zero.

ethical issues Relating to moral principles or the branch of knowledge dealing with these.

fair test An investigation in which all the variables are kept constant except the variable that the investigator changes and the variable that is measured.

Fleming's left-hand rule You use your first finger (field), second finger (current), and thumb (force) to work out the direction of a force on a wire.

force arrow A way to model forces.

fossil fuel Coal, oil, or gas.

free body diagram A diagram that shows the forces acting on a single object.

frequency The number of waves per second (related to the pitch of a sound).

friction A contact force. It occurs because the atoms that make up the surfaces interact when rough surfaces slide over each other.

gamma rays Very high frequency electromagnetic waves, used in medical imaging, sterilising and treating cancer.

gas pressure The pressure exerted by a gas due to the collisions of the particles in the gas with the container.

Geiger counter A device for measuring the activity of a radioactive material.

gradient The degree of steepness of a graph at any point. Also called slope.

gravitational field The region where a mass experiences an attractive force towards another mass.

gravitational field strength, g The force on 1 kg in a gravitational field, also known as the gravity constant.

gravitational potential energy The energy transferred to a gravity store when you lift an object in a gravitational field.

gravitational/gravity store Energy in a gravitational store is associated with separation from the centre of the Earth, calculated with: $E = mgh$.

gravity constant, g The force on 1 kg in a gravitational field, also known as the gravitational field strength.

half-life The time it takes for half the unstable nuclei to decay, or for the activity to halve.

hazard Something that can cause damage or injury.

heating A method of transferring energy by the movement of particles or radiation (by sound, electromagnetic radiation, conduction, convection).

Hooke's Law Below the limit of proportionality, the extension is proportional to the force.

hypothesis An idea that is a way of explaining scientists' observations.

independent variable A variable you change that changes the dependent variable.

induced magnet A magnet that is produced when a magnetic material is placed in a magnetic field, which may or may not stay magnetic when the field is removed.

inelastic collision A collision in which kinetic energy is not conserved.

inertia The measure of how difficult it is to change an object's velocity.

infrared (radiation) Electromagnetic radiation with a longer wavelength than visible light, used in cooking and communication.

insulation A material, such as foam, that reduces energy dissipation by heating.

internal energy The energy of a system because of the arrangement and movement of the particles in it.

ion Charged particle formed when an atom, or group of atoms, loses or gains electrons.

ionising radiation Particles or waves that can completely remove an electron from an atom.

irradiation Being exposed to radiation from an external source.

isotope (of an element) Atoms with the same number of protons and electrons, but different numbers of neutrons, are isotopes of the same element.

joule (J) The unit of energy.

kelvin (K) A unit of temperature.

kilowatt (kW) 1 kW = 1000 W.

kilowatt-hour (kWh) The energy transferred by a 1 kW appliance used for 1 hour, equivalent to 3 600 000 J.

kinetic energy The energy associated with a kinetic store, calculated with $E = \frac{1}{2}mv^2$.

kinetic store Energy in a kinetic store is associated with a moving object, calculated with: $E = \frac{1}{2}mv^2$.

Law of Conservation of Energy Energy cannot be created or destroyed, only transferred between stores.

Law of Conservation of Momentum In any interaction or collision, the momentum before a collision = momentum after.

light-dependent resistor (LDR) A circuit component which has a resistance that depends on light levels, a semiconductor.

limit of proportionality The point (applied force) beyond which extension is no longer proportional to force.

line graph A way of presenting results when there are two numerical values.

line of best fit A smooth line on a graph that travels through or very close to as many of the points plotted as possible.

linear circuit element A circuit component which has a resistance that does not change.

linear relationship A graph of two variables is a straight line through (0, 0) if the relationship is linear.

live wire (in a plug) The wire that is connected to 230 V.

longitudinal A wave whose vibrations are in the same direction as the direction of energy transfer of the wave.

lubrication Using a lubricant (e.g. oil) to reduce energy dissipation by friction.

magnetic field lines Lines that model a magnetic field; denser lines mean a stronger field.

magnetic north pole The place on the surface of the Earth where a compass points, not the same as geographical north.

mass The amount of matter, usually measured in kilograms.

mass number The number of protons and neutrons in the nucleus of an atom.

mechanical waves Waves that require a medium (e.g. air, water) to travel through.

mechanically A method of transferring energy between energy stores using forces, calculated using: work done = force × distance.

megawatt (MW) 1 MW = 1 000 000 W.

metric prefix A symbol used to show multiples of a unit, such as the k in km.

microphone A device that converts a sound wave into an electrical signal.

microwaves Electromagnetic radiation with a longer wavelength than infrared radiation, used for cooking and communication.

milliamp (mA) 1 milliamp = 1/1000 amp.

momentum Mass × velocity.

motor A component that produces rotation from the combination of the fields due to magnets and current-carrying wires.

National Grid The power stations, underground and overland wires, pylons, and transformers that supply electricity to homes and businesses.

net force The force when two or more forces are added together as vectors, also called the resultant force.

net resistance The resistance of a circuit if all the components were replaced by a single resistor.

neutral wire (in a plug) The wire that is connected to 0 V.

neutron Subatomic particle found in the nucleus of an atom. It has no charge and a relative mass of 1.

newton-metre (N m) The unit of work, equivalent to the joule. It is also the unit for a moment.

Newton's First Law The motion (speed and direction) of an object does not change when the resultant force is zero.

Newton's Second Law If the resultant force is not zero the motion of an object (speed or direction) changes.

Newton's Third Law Forces come in pairs: the force of X on Y and the force of Y on X. The forces are equal and opposite.

non-contact force A force produced because an object is in a field; the objects do not need to be in contact for the force to act.

non-linear circuit element A circuit component which has a resistance that does change.

non-linear relationship A graph of two variables is not a straight line through (0, 0) if the relationship is non-linear.

non-renewable source An energy source that will run out (in the next million years or so).

normal A line at 90° to the surface where the wave hits it.

normal contact force A force that is exerted by a solid surface on an object. Solid objects deform slightly when you exert a force on them, and the bonds between the particles are compressed.

normal distribution A function that represents the distribution of many random variables as a symmetrical bell-shaped graph.

nuclear fuels Fuels that heat water by energy transfer from fission, for example, uranium.

nuclear store Energy in a nuclear store is associated with fission or fusion as a result of a change in mass.

nucleus The small centre of an atom made of protons and neutrons.

ohm (Ω) The unit of resistance.

order of magnitude A number to the nearest power of ten.

oscilloscope A device that shows a changing potential difference on a screen.

outlier A result that that is very different from the other measurements in a data set.

parallel circuit A circuit with more than one loop; each loop works independently of the rest.

pascal (Pa) The unit of pressure; 1 Pa is equal to 1 N/m².

peer review Peer review is the checking and evaluation of a scientific paper by other expert scientists in order to help decide whether or not the paper should be published.

penetrating power The ability of radiation to travel through a material (e.g. air, metal), which is linked to ionisation.

percentage A rate, number, or amount in each hundred.

permanent magnet A magnet that stays magnetic when other magnets, or an electric current, is removed.

photon A 'packet' of electromagneic radiation, how radiation is emitted or absorbed.

physical change Change, such as a change of state, that does not result in new substances being made.

plastic material Does not return to its original shape when the force is removed.

plum-pudding model of the atom Outdated model of the atom in which electrons are embedded in a sphere of positive charge.

potential difference (p.d.) A difference in (electrical) potential produced by the separation of charge; a potential difference produces an electric field which produces a force on charged particles in it.

power Rate of transfer of energy, or work done/time.

power rating The rate of transfer of energy by an appliance.

prediction A statement that says what you think will happen.

prefix A letter or symbol in front of a unit that shows that it is a larger or smaller quantity, for example, k in km.

proportional Two quantities are proportional if they change in the same ratio.

proton Subatomic particle found in the nucleus of an atom. It has a relative charge of +1 and a relative mass of 1.

qualitative Data that are descriptive or difficult to measure.

quantitative Data that are obtained by making measurements.

radiation Anything (waves or particles) emitted from a source.

radio waves Electromagnetic radiation with the longest wavelength, used for communication.

radioactive A material containing unstable nuclei that emit radiation.

radiographer a technician responsible for producing medical images (e.g. X-rays, MRI scans) to help diagnose illness in a hospital

random The nature of radioactive decay as each nucleus has a fixed probability of decay.

random error An error that causes there to be a random difference between the measurement and the true value each time you measure it.

rate of change How much one variable changes when

another changes. Usually refers to the change of a variable with time.

ratio The quantitative relation between two amounts showing the number of times one value contains or is contained within the other.

reaction rate The reaction rate for a given chemical reaction is the measure of the change in concentration of the reactants or the change in concentration of the products per unit time.

reaction time The time from seeing (or hearing) an event and starting to brake, or to use a stopwatch.

reciprocal Related to another so that their product is 1.

relationship The way in which two or more people or things are connected.

renewable source An energy source that will not run out (in the next million years or so).

repeatable A measure of how close values are to each other when an experiment is repeated with the same equipment.

reproducible When other people carry out an investigation and get similar results to the original investigation the results are reproducible.

reserves (energy sources) How much energy sources we have left (usually refers to fossil fuels).

resistance A measure of how easy it is for a current to flow, resistance = p.d./current.

resolution A measure of the smallest object which can be seen using an instrument.

resultant force The force when two or more forces are added together as vectors, also called the net force.

risk The chance of damage or injury from a hazard.

Rutherford model of the atom A model with a positively charged nucleus and electrons in orbit around it.

sankey diagram A diagram that shows energy transfer where the width of the arrow on the diagram is proportional to the energy transfer.

scalar A quantity that has a magnitude (size) but no direction.

scientific question A question that can be answered by collecting and considering evidence.

semiconductor A material that contains atoms with loosely bound electrons that can be released if energy is transferred to the material (for example, by heating).

sensing circuit A circuit which contains a component with a resistance that changes with a change in the environment (for example, temperature or light level).

series circuit A circuit with only one loop.

SI unit The Système International d'Unités, or SI units; the agreed set of units that we use in science.

significant figures (sig. fig.) Each of the digits of a number that are used to express it to the required degree of accuracy, starting from the first non-zero digit.

slope Slope measures the steepness of a line on a graph. Also called gradient.

solenoid A coil of wire.

sound wave A wave produced by a vibration that needs a medium to travel through.

source Something that emits electromagnetic radiation.

spark The breakdown of air that discharges a charged object; the heating of the air produces light and sound.

specific heat capacity (J/kg K) The energy required to raise the temperature of 1 kg of a substance by 1 K.

specific latent heat of fusion (or melting) The energy required to fuse or melt 1 kg of a substance.

specific latent heat of vaporisation The energy required to vaporise or condense 1 kg of a substance.

spectrum A continuous range of frequencies, for example, visible light or the electromagnetic spectrum.

split-ring commutator A component of a direct current motor or generator. In a motor it ensures that the coil always spins in the same direction. In a generator it means that a direct potential difference is produced.

spread The difference between the highest and lowest measurements of a set of repeat measurements.

spring constant The ratio of force to extension, a measure of stiffness.

stable (isotope) An isotope that is not radioactive.

standard form A way of writing down very large or very small numbers easily.

static electricity The charge that insulating objects acquire because of the transfer of electrons.

step-down transformer A transformer that decreases the potential difference.

step-up transformer A transformer that increases the potential difference.

stopping distance The total distance that a car travels from the driver seeing the hazard to the car reaching a complete stop; stopping distance = thinking distance + braking distance.

subatomic particles Particles from which atoms are made, including protons, neutrons, and electrons.

systematic error An error that causes there to be the same difference between a measurement and the true value each time you measure it.

technology The application of scientific knowledge for practical purposes, especially in industry.

temperature A measure of the average kinetic energy of the particles in a material. It does not depend on the amount of material that you have.

tension Solid objects deform slightly when you exert a force on them, and the bonds between the particles are stretched.

terminal velocity The velocity that a moving object achieves when the resultant force is zero.

tesla (T) The unit of magnetic field strength, or magnetic flux density.

thermal conductivity (W/m K) A property of a material that measures the rate of energy transfer through a material.

thermal store Energy in a thermal store is associated with a change in temperature, calculated with: $E = mc\Delta T$.

thermistor A circuit component which has a resistance that depends on temperature; a semiconductor.

thinking distance The distance that a car travels while the driver reacts to a hazard.

time period The time for one wave to pass a given point, measured in seconds.

transformer A circuit component that uses two coils and a core (usually iron) which changes a potential difference.

transverse A wave whose vibrations are at right angles to the direction of transfer of energy by the wave.

ultrasound Sound with a frequency higher than human hearing (about 20 kHz), used in medicine, and for finding distances.

ultraviolet (radiation) Electromagnetic radiation with a wavelength shorter than visible light, used for detecting forgeries, bodily fluids, making vitamin D.

uncertainty The doubt in the result because of the way that the measurement is made.

unstable (nucleus) A nucleus that decays by emitting radiation or splitting (fission).

upthrust The force on an object in a fluid due to the difference in pressure in the fluid acting on the area of the object.

vacuum A region with no particles of matter in it.

variable resistor A circuit component which has a resistance that you can vary by changing the amount of wire or other resisting material.

variable A quantity that can change, for example, time, temperature, length, mass.

vector A quantity that has a direction as well as a magnitude (size).

velocity The speed in a particular direction, a vector.

vibrations The backwards and forwards motion of a solid, or particles, displaced from an equilibrium position.

visible light Electromagnetic radiation that we can detect with our eyes, used for seeing and photography.

volt (V) The unit of potential difference.

voltage Another name for potential difference, usually used when you talk about domestic electricity supply.

voltmeter A circuit component used to measure potential difference; it should be connected either side of a component.

volume The amount of space an object takes up, usually measured in m^3.

watt (W) The unit of power.

wave velocity The speed at which the energy or information of a wave is transferred, equal to frequency x wavelength.

wavelength The distance from one point on a wave to the same point on the next wave.

weight The force due to gravity that acts on an object.

work The transfer of energy. Work is commonly done against gravity or friction. It can be calculated by multiplying force and distance.

X-rays Electromagnetic radiation with a short wavelength, used for imaging, security and treating cancer.

y-intercept The y-intercept of a straight line graph is where the line crosses the y-axis.

Index

Reference material

SI base units

Physical quantity	Unit	Unit
length	metre	m
mass	kilogram	kg
time	second	s
temperature	kelvin	K
current	ampere	A
amount of a substance	mole	mol

SI derived units

Physical quantity	Unit(s)	Unit(s)
area	squared metre	m^2
volume	cubic metre; litre; cubic decimetre	m^3; l; dm^3
density	kilogram per cubic metre	kg/m^3
temperature	degree Celsius	°C
pressure	pascal	Pa
specific heat capacity	joule per kilogram per degree Celsius	J/kg/°C
specific latent heat	joule per kilogram	J/kg
speed	metre per second	m/s
force	newton	N
gravitational field strength	newton per kilogram	N/kg
acceleration	metre per squared second	m/s^2
frequency	hertz	Hz
energy	joule	J
power	watt	W
electric charge	coulomb	C
electric potential difference	volt	V
electric resistance	ohm	Ω
magnetic flux density	tesla	T

electrical component	symbol
junction of conductors	
switch	
electric cell	
battery of cells	
power supply	
diode	
light-emitting diode (LED)	
ammeter	
voltmeter	
fixed resistor	
variable resistor	
light-dependent resistor (LDR)	
thermistor	
lamp	

A person	Typical speed (m/s)	Typical speed (mph)
walking	1	2.2
running	5	11
cycling	7	15
cycling (Olympic)	20	45

Object	Typical speed (m/s)	Typical speed (mph)
strong wind	13	30
car	22	50
train	56	125
sound	330	738

Numbers you need to know

Acceleration due to gravity = 10 m/s^2

Gravitational field strength (on Earth) = 10 N/kg

Accelerations are about 5 m/s^2

Forces in large accelerations are about 500 N

Estimate forces involved in situations on the public road are of the order of 100 N–1000 N **H**

Estimates

Estimates speeds: 30 mph = 13 m/s

Reference	Equations to recall and apply	Maths skills
PM1.1i	density (kg/m^3) = mass (kg) / volume (m^3)	M1a, M1b, M1c, M3b, M3c
PM2.1i	distance travelled (m) = speed (m/s) × time (s)	M1a, M2b, M3a, M3b, M3c, M3d, M4a, M4b, M4c, M4d, M4e
PM2.1ii	acceleration (m/s^2) = change in velocity (m/s) / time (s)	M1a, M3a, M3b, M3c, M3d
PM2.1iv	kinetic energy (J) = 0.5 × mass (kg) × (speed (m/s))^2	M1a, M3a, M3b, M3c, M3d
PM2.2i	force (N) = mass (kg) × acceleration (m/s^2)	M1a, M2a, M3a, M3b, M3c, M3d
PM2.2ii	momentum (kgm/s) = mass (kg) × velocity (m/s)	M1a, M2a, M3a, M3b, M3c, M3d **H**
PM2.2iii	work done (J) = force (N) × distance (m) (along the line of action of the force)	M1a, M2a, M3a, M3b, M3c, M3d
PM2.2iv	power (W) = work done (J) / time (s)	M1a, M2a, M3a, M3b, M3c, M3d
PM2.3i	force exerted by a spring (N) = extension (m) × spring constant (N/m)	M1a, M2a, M3a, M3b, M3c, M3d
PM2.3iii	gravity force (N) = mass (kg) × gravitational field strength, g (N/kg)	M1a, M2a, M3a, M3b, M3c, M3d
PM2.3iv	(in a gravity field) potential energy (J) = mass (kg) × height (m) × gravitational field strength, g (N/kg)	M1a, M2a, M3a, M3b, M3c, M3d
PM2.3v	pressure (Pa) = force normal to a surface (N) / area of that surface (m^2)	M1a, M2a, M3a, M3b, M3c, M3d **H**
PM2.3vi	moment of a force (Nm) = force (N) × distance (m) (normal to direction of the force)	M1a, M2a, M3a, M3b, M3c, M3d
PM3.1i	charge flow (C) = current (A) × time (s)	M1a, M3c, M3d
PM3.2i	potential difference (V) = current (A) × resistance (Ω)	M1a, M2a, M3a, M3b, M3c, M3d
PM3.2ii	energy transferred (J) = charge (C) × potential difference (V)	M1a, M2a, M3a, M3b, M3c, M3d
PM3.2iii	power (W) = potential difference (V) × current (A) = (current (A))^2 × resistance (Ω)	M1a, M2a, M3a, M3b, M3c, M3d
PM3.2iv	energy transferred (J, kWh) = power (W, kW) × time (s, h)	M1a, M2a, M3a, M3b, M3c, M3d
PM5.1i	wave speed (m/s) = frequency (Hz) × wavelength (m)	M1a, M1b, M1c, M2a, M3a, M3b, M3c, M3d
PM7.2i	efficiency = useful output energy transfer (J) / input energy transfer (J)	M1a, M1b, M1d, M2a, M3a, M3b, M3c, M3d

Reference	Equations to select and apply	Maths skills
PM1.2i	change in thermal energy (J) = mass (kg) × specific heat capacity (J/kg °C) × change in temperature (°C)	M1a, M3b, M3c, M3d
PM1.2ii	thermal energy for a change in state (J) = mass (kg) × specific latent heat (J/kg)	M1a, M3b, M3c, M3d
PM2.1iii	(final velocity (m/s))^2 – (initial velocity (m/s))^2 = 2 × acceleration (m/s^2) × distance (m)	M1a, M3a, M3b, M3c, M3d
PM2.3ii	energy transferred in stretching (J) = 0.5 × spring constant (N/m) × (extension (m))^2	M1a, M2a, M3a, M3b, M3c, M3d
PM4.2i	force on a conductor (at right angles to a magnetic field) carrying a current (N) = magnetic field strength (T) × current (A) × length (m)	M1a, M1b, M1d, M2a, M3a, M3b, M3c, M3d **H**
PM8.2i	potential difference across primary coil (V) × current in primary coil (A) = potential difference across secondary coil (V) × current in secondary coil (A)	M1a, M1b, M1c, M1d, M2a, M3a, M3b, M3c, M3d

Great Clarendon Street, Oxford, OX2 6DP, United Kingdom

Oxford University Press is a department of the University of Oxford.
It furthers the University's objective of excellence in research,
scholarship, and education by publishing worldwide. Oxford is a
registered trade mark of Oxford University Press in the UK and in
certain other countries

British Library Cataloguing in Publication Data
Data available

978 0 19 835976 0

10 9 8 7

Paper used in the production of this book is a natural, recyclable
product made from wood grown in sustainable forests.
The manufacturing process conforms to the environmental regulations
of the country of origin.

Printed and bound by CPI Group (UK) Ltd, Croydon, CR0 4YY

This resource is endorsed by OCR for use with specification J250 OCR
GCSE (9–1) Gateway Combined Science A (Gateway Science). In order to
gain OCR endorsement, this resource has undergone an independent
quality check. Any references to assessment and/or assessment
preparation are the publisher's interpretation of the specification
requirements and are not endorsed by OCR. OCR recommends that a
range of teaching and learning resources are used in preparing learners
for assessment. OCR has not paid for the production of this resource,
nor does OCR receive any royalties from its sale. For more information
about the endorsement process, please visit the OCR website,
www.ocr.org.uk.

All Revision questions written by Jim Newall and Richard Field.

The authors and series editor would like to thank Sophie Ladden
and Margaret McGuire at OUP for their patience, encouragement,
and attention to all the small – but important – details.

Helen Reynolds would like to thank her friends, Michele, Rob, and
Luke for all their support, encouragement, tea, and reminders to take
time off.

Philippa Gardom Hulme would like to thank Barney, Catherine,
and Sarah for their never-ending support and patience, and for
keeping quietly out of the way in the early mornings. Thanks,
too, to Claire Gordon for her wise counsel over tea and scones,
and for getting us all going in the first place.